# LGBTQ

REVISED & UPDATED THIRD EDITION

## The Survival Guide for Lesbian, Gay, Bisexual, Transgender, and Questioning Teens

KELLY HUEGEL MADRONE

free spirit
PUBLISHING®

**Library of Congress Cataloging-in-Publication Data**

Names: Huegel Madrone, Kelly, 1974– author.

Title: LGBTQ : the survival guide for lesbian, gay, bisexual, transgender, and questioning teens / by Kelly Huegel Madrone.

Other titles: GLBTQ

Description: Revised & updated third edition. | Minneapolis, MN : Free Spirit Publishing, [2018] | Includes bibliographical references and index. | Identifiers: LCCN 2018002137 (print) | LCCN 2018004931 (ebook) | ISBN 9781631983030 (Web PDF) | ISBN 9781631983047 (ePub) | ISBN 9781631983023 (pbk.) | ISBN 1631983024 (pbk.)

Subjects: LCSH: Homosexuality—United States—Juvenile literature. | Coming out (Sexual orientation)—United States—Juvenile literature. | Gay teenagers—United States—Juvenile literature. | Lesbian teenagers—United States—Juvenile literature. | Transgender people—United States—Juvenile literature. | Bisexuals—United States—Juvenile literature.

Classification: LCC HQ76.25 (ebook) | LCC HQ76.25 .H84 2018 (print) | DDC 306.76/60973—dc23

LC record available at https://lccn.loc.gov/2018002137



The names of the teens and young adults quoted throughout this book have been changed to protect their privacy and/or safety.

Edited by Alison Behnke
Cover and interior design by Shannon Pourciau

Printed in China

**Free Spirit Publishing**
An imprint of Teacher Created Materials
9850 51st Avenue, Suite 100
Minneapolis, MN 55442
(612) 338-2068
help4kids@freespirit.com
freespirit.com

FSC
www.fsc.org
MIX
Paper | Supporting responsible forestry
FSC® C144853

# Dedication

For Mala—my partner in all things—who taught me to love outside of labels.

For our daughters: May you grow as big as you want to be in a world that loves you for who you are.

And for queer kids and young adults everywhere: Keep going. Keep being you to your fullest. Keep pushing the world to grow. You have my full love, respect, and support.


# Acknowledgments

Thank you to my family, on whose continued support and encouragement I rely. I'm so grateful to be linked to you by blood.

To my family of choice—my friends. You've not only supported me in my work, you've become crusaders yourselves. A special shout-out to my dear friends Jen Celestin and Lissa Miller for their ongoing (and pretty much daily) support, and to Leo Caldwell and Jillian Weiss for their eagle-eyed reviews of and extremely thoughtful input on chapter 2.

Thanks to Free Spirit for going out on a limb with this book 15 years ago, for still believing in it, and for being a voice for young people on so many issues.

I wish to thank again all those who contributed to the earlier editions of this book, including the national organizations that provided facts, opinions, and expertise on these varied and sometimes complicated issues. I am just the mouthpiece—you are doing the work.

Finally, thank you to the fearless teens and young adults who lent their voices and their personal stories to this book. You are our future, and that future is very bright indeed.

# Contents

# Foreword by Jillian Weiss

LGBTQ+ people have been around pretty much as long as recorded human history. To give you an idea, we're in the Old Testament of the Bible, and that was written about 3,000 years ago. Societies throughout history and around the world have had many different attitudes toward us—some positive, and some negative. In the United States, dominant attitudes toward LGBTQ+ people were very negative in the 1950s, which pushed more activists to work for LGBTQ+ civil rights in the 1960s. That's where I come in. For more than 20 years, I've worked as a lawyer to help LGBTQ people—particularly trans people—overcome discrimination and achieve equality through the use of US law. I'm one of a small group of trans civil rights lawyers, and it makes me so happy every day to work for greater freedom, acceptance, and respect for trans people and our community. Some days are better, and some days are worse. And I'm glad to know that one day, if society continues on its current path, people will understand being LGBTQ+ as just another way of being, like being left-handed or having green eyes. Reading this book is part of that process, so thank you.

You may not know that there was a time not long ago when lots of people thought there were hardly any lesbian, gay, bisexual, transgender, nonbinary, or gender nonconforming people out there. The world was made so hard for us that a lot of us went underground, not telling anyone who we were, like secret agents on a mission. It made me pretty sad when I was young. That's a hard life, and it's not part of any vision of equality that I would like to see. *Everyone* deserves equal protection under the law and equal treatment in the world. That's a vision worth working hard for. It's the work I do as a lawyer for LGBTQ+ people. It's the work *you* are doing right now by reading this book.

In fact, much of the work of equality will be done by people who are young right now, including you. You may be surprised to learn that you are at the forefront of creating change. But young people influence their friends and family just by existing—just by being who they are. Being who you are may not sound like change, but it's more powerful than you might realize. You can see it in history. As more people came out as lesbian, gay, and bisexual in the closing decades of the 20th century, more people started to realize that LGBTQ+ people are human beings, just like them. More people began to see that LGBTQ+ folks deserve to have dignity and civil rights and to be treated as nicely as other folks. That gave even more LGBTQ+ people the courage to say who they were.

Nevertheless, even ten years ago, relatively few people had come out as transgender or nonbinary. Plenty of people didn't know of any trans people except maybe some fictional TV characters, and thought there simply *weren't* many trans-identified people. They didn't know about trans identities such as nonbinary or genderqueer. I myself didn't come out as trans until I was older, because it seemed so incredibly scary to do that. It took me a long time to understand myself, partly because the society around me provided practically no guidance, except to tell me not to be true to myself. Today, people are starting to understand that there are more than just a few of us. For example, there are some well-known celebrities who are trans. Plus, a lot more trans young people are coming out to their parents—and a lot of those parents want to support their trans kids. And this brand-new edition of *LGBTQ* contains a lot more information about being trans than the previous edition did. That's great for lots of reasons, one of which is that it can be hard for young people to find the info they need. I sure wish I'd had this book when I was young. I'm very glad you get to have it.

Still, our work is far from done. Today, most people in the United States say they're just fine with LGBTQ+ people. There are, however, some who don't think that way. They're not bad people, but they have some questionable ideas. Maybe they were raised to believe that being LGBTQ+ is wrong in some way. This is where our work lies. Each of us can work toward helping others understand and accept new ideas—just like you might need someone to help you understand an idea that's new or different, so do they.

It's a beautiful thing to help make the world better. But sometimes it can be difficult, and you might feel like you don't want that responsibility. Some days, it can feel like we'll never be able to finish our work. Just remember: You don't have to finish it. You don't have to convince the whole world—or even your whole family—to see things your way. You can start by just being yourself. That may be all it takes to inspire others to join you in changing the world, little by little.

I wish there were a magic wand to wave to make the world all better right now. But real progress happens one conversation at a time, one person at a time, one idea at a time. I hope that this book will help you understand your world and, in turn, help others understand. That would make me very happy. So thank you, again, for reading. Now let's make the world a better place together.

**Jillian Weiss**
Law Office of Jillian T. Weiss, jtweisslaw.com

# Introduction

Dealing with the realization that you are or might be lesbian, gay, bisexual, transgender, or questioning (LGBTQ) can be a real challenge. And I know just how it feels. By the time I was in high school, I was convinced I was somehow different from everyone else—and not in a good way. But LGBTQ people weren't visible where I came from and it was well before the landmark event of Ellen coming out on her TV show, so the idea that there was an option (or *many* options) other than straight hadn't taken shape for me. I figured I just hadn't met the right guy yet—the one who would make me start daydreaming of a perfect wedding like so many of my friends were doing.

When I got to college, I finally met some people who were LGBTQ and out. Looking at them was like looking in a mirror. My feelings started to make sense, as though I'd finally found the missing piece to a big puzzle. At the same time, the thought that *I* might actually be queer frightened me a lot. What would my family and friends say? How could I live "that kind" of life? I felt hopeless. I was afraid to tell anyone what I was going through. I had other stressors in my life as well, and after years of conflict and suffering, I decided at age 20 that the only way to escape the pain was to end my life.

So one night I took an overdose of prescription pills. Then, as I looked at myself in the mirror, something happened. From somewhere deep inside me, I heard a voice telling me that I had to live. That no matter what happened, no matter how hard my life might be, it was a life worth experiencing. I didn't exactly believe it, but I still decided to listen. I told my boyfriend at the time (who was also an old friend) what I'd done and asked him to take me to the hospital.

That night was one of the hardest I've ever endured, but it was almost like the harder it got, the more I decided to fight—to learn how to stand in myself. It was a while before I was comfortable enough to come out to my friends and family, but eventually I did.

The journey from being confused and scared to the out and proud, fulfilled person I am today was a road traveled mostly by many small steps. One big leap, however, came in 2012 when I fell in love with my best friend Mala—a straight woman. Boy, did that throw me for a loop! Suddenly there were these big feelings between us, but we were also terrified of damaging our friendship. To my amazement, after I told Mala I was willing to give it a shot, she said she was too—even though she'd never been attracted to a woman before.

Two years later, we were married. So much for labels! While Mala no longer assumes a straight identity, she doesn't identify as gay or bisexual either. In fact, she doesn't feel the need to declare herself to be anyone other than "the woman who loves Kelly." Ironically, the intense open-mindedness of a "formerly straight" girl has encouraged me to be more open to who I am. Whereas I used to identify as a lesbian, now I typically don't bother with labels.

**A WORD ABOUT WORDS**

This book often uses the word *queer*. This term was once used as a slur to harass or demean LGBTQ people. While some people still use it this way, *queer* is now a word that many LGBTQ people use in a positive way. This book also uses the acronym LGBTQ, which stands for lesbian, gay, bisexual, transgender, and questioning. There are also many other common acronyms to describe the totality of people who identify as "not straight," "not cis" (*cisgender* or *cis* means having a gender identity that matches the sex you were assigned at birth), or "other." Those acronyms include LGBT+ and LGBTQIA (with the *I* for *intersex* and the *A* for *asexual*). LGBTQ is used in this book as a shorthand to represent all of these. For more information on LGBTQ terminology, see chapter 1 on page 10 and the glossary on page 233.

My relationship with Mala has helped me understand that when we as human beings are at our best, most trusting, and most self-aware, we are also most open to finding love—in whatever form it may take. That isn't to say that we're all going to declare ourselves to be pansexual (potentially attracted to any person) or beyond gender. Rather, it means that there are labels that serve us and labels that don't. After all, what label is big enough to encompass the expansiveness and capacity of the human heart?

My personal journey also illustrates two key ideas: First, your life can go places you never imagined. And second, sexuality and gender are evolving concepts. Where you are now is not necessarily where you will be in the future, and that is a beautiful thing. As I've learned over and over, and in many different ways, life has a lot of incredible learning in store for us if we're open to it.

As for me, life is still challenging at times, but I'm so grateful to have it. When I look at our daughters (yep—Mala and I are moms, another label I never thought I'd have), when my family is laughing together, when I get to experience the exhilaration of helping other people, I think back to that night so many years ago when I wanted to end it all and thank my past self for having faith and holding on.

The more I've come to accept and love myself, the more opportunities I've had to get involved with helping other LGBTQ people and their families learn to love and accept themselves and each other. I've talked to young people terrified about coming out and to parents or other family members who are upset about or frightened for children who have just come out as LGBTQ. It's been amazing to watch these teens and families go from confusion and anger to acceptance and even joy about who they are.

(A quick aside: Without a doubt, households can look many different ways. Young people can be raised by one or more parents, an aunt or uncle, or a grandparent, or they may be in a foster home or some other less traditional situation. In this book, the word *parent* is intended to apply to any caring adult family member or other person who helps raise or otherwise take care of younger folks.)

I've also noticed a shift in the people who reach out to me at book signings and other events, on social media, or through letters or emails. More and more people are realizing at younger ages that they fall into the space of "not straight" or "not cis." Consistently I see young people pushing the boundaries of what we understand about gender, sexuality, and sexual orientation, and that's awesome. Also, more and more parents tell me they're proud of their newly out kids and just want to know how they can be supportive and what they can do in their communities to help make these places safer and more welcoming for LGBTQ young people.

Still, for an LGBTQ teen, life can sometimes feel pretty lonely. Sure, there's a national LGBTQ rights movement and loads of organizations out there that support you, but day to day, it's easy to feel separated from all that. It's easy to think that no one cares about what you're going through. But people *do* care. All over the world, LGBTQ people and their parents, friends, family members, and others are working to promote understanding and acceptance of those who are lesbian, gay, bisexual, and transgender (and everything in between and beyond). A lot of these efforts are focused on helping teens specifically. PFLAG has made school safety one of its primary concerns. (PFLAG originally stood for Parents and Friends of Lesbians and Gays, but the organization has since broadened its mission to include all family members as well as bisexual and transgender people.) GLSEN (the Gay, Lesbian & Straight Education Network) is focused entirely on improving the school environment for LGBTQ students. GLAAD (the Gay & Lesbian Alliance Against Defamation) is fighting for more positive and accurate messages about queer people in the media. Lambda Legal is dedicated to achieving full recognition of LGBTQ people's civil rights. And the list goes on.

Every day, people at other national and local organizations, in conjunction with LGBTQ young people, are making extraordinary progress in fighting for our rights. They're educating school boards, principals, teachers, and other school staff. They're holding in-school workshops and lobbying for better legislation at state capitol buildings and in Washington, D.C. Progress *is* being made—sometimes in small steps, sometimes in leaps and bounds, but always moving forward.

This book's first edition was published in 2003. After the second edition was published in 2011, I figured that might be it as far as big updates went. It seemed possible that we'd simply continue along a positive trajectory of achieving more and more rights for LGBTQ people. Then, in the wake of achievements like marriage equality, the repeal of "Don't Ask, Don't Tell," and presidential support of trans rights, a backlash began. Groups that oppose the recognition of LGBTQ civil rights have started using new legal strategies designed to undermine advances. Anti-LGBTQ hate crimes, especially against trans people, are on the rise. The message is clear: There's still much more work to do.

With all that in mind, this third edition of *LGBTQ: The Survival Guide for Lesbian, Gay, Bisexual, Transgender, and Questioning Teens* has been fully revised to reflect (as much as is possible in a single volume) advances in LGBTQ rights and changes in culture, as well as the latest data on the lives and experiences of queer teens. The sections I was most excited to update, however, are about ideas less tangible than facts and figures. They have to do with the continually evolving attitudes among teens.

Today's queer teens are far more likely to be open-minded and to have a broad view of sexuality and gender expression. Back in my day (I get to say that now that I'm in my 40s), LGBTQ people generally identified as lesbian, gay, bisexual, or trans. Now, our understanding of gender and gender expression, and of sexuality and sexual orientation, has broadened exponentially. Today's teens are less likely to identify as one (or only one) of these labels, instead embracing a smorgasbord of identities from agender, ace, and androgyne to pansexual or skoliosexual. (By the way, for definitions of these words and many more, check out the glossary on page 233.)

Perspectives also have changed among straight and cis teens. Overall, they are more accepting and more aware of the issues their LGBTQ peers face (even though it might not always feel like that). The impact of these attitudes on society is exciting to contemplate. Overall, communities are becoming more accepting of all people—LGBTQ and straight/cis alike—due to this expanded awareness and understanding. For some people, challenging gender norms to greater degrees has created a space to explore their beliefs and, in many cases, reshape their understanding of who they are. Some of these people may not have even thought of themselves as LGBTQ in earlier times. When rigid definitions of "male," "female," "gay," "straight," and so on are lifted, all people get more space to be their phenomenal, unique selves.

**PRO TIP**

Many LGBTQ young people and their allies are coming up with creative ways to introduce queer topics at school and in their communities. Throughout this book, I've sprinkled in some "pro tips" alerting you to topics and activities that could make awesome school projects or GSA (gay-straight alliance) activities.

You might be thinking, "That's great, but what about right now? What about at *my* school, where things aren't so awesome?" It's easy to say that everything will be okay someday or that this is just part of growing up. But those kinds of reassurances only go so far when the harassment or isolation is happening right now.

That's why I originally wrote this book. I remember very clearly what it was like—the worries, insecurities, fears. One moment you might be upset about the grade you got on a quiz; the next you're thinking about big questions like what you want to do with your life. And what if, on top of all that, you suddenly discover you're attracted to someone of the same sex? Or what if you dread changing for gym class because you're in the boys' locker room, but inside you've always felt more like a girl? Or what if you just don't see yourself and how you feel reflected anywhere around you?

Discovering that you might be LGBTQ is a big revelation, and for most, accepting it is a process. One thing that can help in that process is information. This book can't answer all your questions or counter all the misinformation and outright lies you may have heard about being LGBTQ. It does, however, have a lot of facts and advice you might not have found anywhere else yet.

## About This Book

What will you find in *LGBTQ*? For starters, you'll read information from experts in psychology, sociology, and healthcare. These authorities offer a lot of insight on what it means to be queer. You'll also find advice from people who work with national organizations advocating for LGBTQ rights, tips for coming out, ideas for creating a more accepting school environment, and help for a variety of other issues and situations.

This book also features true stories from teens and young adults who've been through situations you might be facing. Some of these stories may be very different from your own; others might seem to come right out of your life. These words from young people can offer support and real-life advice, and so can the loads of books, movies, websites, and other resources suggested throughout the book.

I wrote this book with all LGBTQ teens in mind. It's my hope that you'll find it helpful, whether you're secure with your sexual orientation or gender identity or just starting to explore these ideas. It's important to remember that when it comes to questions about being LGBTQ, there aren't a lot of cut-and-dried answers. Every LGBTQ person is unique, so it's difficult to provide answers that are appropriate for everyone. Even in the LGBTQ community, there isn't always agreement on details surrounding certain issues or even on how we refer to ourselves. This book offers commonly accepted answers as well as suggestions for how you can find answers to your own questions.

This book is meant to be a guide—use it as you need it. You might read the book from cover to cover, or you might use the contents and index to direct you to sections addressing the specific issues you face. The book is a pressure-free zone. Regardless of where you are in your life, you can read the parts you're ready for. The goal isn't to come up with definitive answers, because answers often lead to other questions. And that's great. It's all part of getting to know yourself.

And if you're questioning or curious right now, that's okay too. You never have to pick a label for yourself if you don't want to. Many people choose to identify as queer or "other," or to say, "I don't identify. I just am who I am." The purpose of this book is not to encourage you to choose a label, but to help you get to know yourself and be more comfortable with who you are. That's what really matters. Remember, LGBTQ people come in all shapes, sizes, and colors. We are Black, Latinx, white, Native American, Asian, Arab American, and Indian. We are Catholic, Protestant, atheist, Buddhist, agnostic, Unitarian, Jewish, Hindu, and Muslim. We can be teachers, lawyers, doctors, construction workers, executives, athletes, artists, writers, politicians, or have any other type of job or career imaginable. And we are parents, friends, partners, sons, daughters, sisters, brothers, aunts, uncles, and grandparents. LGBTQ people are everywhere, and we can be anything we want to be.

Since the previous two editions of this book were published, I've heard from readers, young and old, who have in some way been touched by its contents. Whether you have a question for me or a story of your own to share, I welcome and encourage you to contact me—I always love hearing from and connecting with readers. I can be reached via email (help4kids@freespirit.com) or at the following address:

Teacher Created Materials
PO Box 1040
Huntington Beach, CA 92647

May you open to the love that surrounds you.

Lots of love,
**Kelly Huegel Madrone**

P.S. For the latest and greatest on all things LGBTQ, follow me on Twitter @LGBTQguide and on Instagram @lgbtqguide. If you're interested in catching up with me in person (I would love to meet you!), you can track me at kellymadrone.com/events.

**IF YOU NEED HELP . . .**

While daily life is getting better for LGBTQ people, it can still be incredibly challenging. This can be especially true for young people who are realizing that they're queer. If you're feeling depressed or confused, or if you just want to talk to someone, call the Trevor Lifeline at 1-866-4-U-TREVOR (1-866-488-7386). Trained counselors will listen without judgment and provide advice on LGBTQ issues. The call is free, and it won't appear on your phone bill. You can call 24 hours a day, any day of the year. Additionally, there's the Trans Lifeline, which is a hotline staffed by trans people, for trans people. You can reach them at 1-877-565-8860. And if you don't want to (or can't) make a phone call, you can text the Crisis Text Line at 741741 to reach a trained counselor 24-7.

CHAPTER 1

# LGBTQ 101

We are everywhere.

Maybe you've known for years that you're LGBTQ. Or maybe you are only now beginning to question your sexual orientation or gender identity. Regardless of where you're at, you're not alone.

A 2016 study reported that in a survey of members of Generation Z (people born between about 1996 and 2010), only 48 percent identified themselves as "exclusively heterosexual," compared with 56 percent of millennials (people born in the 1980s and 1990s). Additionally, 56 percent of Generation Z responders said that they know someone who uses gender-neutral pronouns.

However, it's difficult to come up with a standard figure for how many people are *really* LGBTQ. In any case, it's fair to say that there are a lot of us out there, and research shows that the numbers are growing. (This could be due to many factors, such as greater visibility for LGBTQ people and issues, more willingness among LGBTQ people to self-identify whereas they may have been afraid to do so in the past, and broader definitions of what it means to be queer.)

Think about these statistics the next time you're at the movies or a football game. Whether you're aware of them or not, it's likely that people at your school, in your neighborhood, and in your family are LGBTQ.

**BY THE NUMBERS**

The 2010 census was the first to count same-sex couples identifying themselves as spouses. In 2014, the Census Bureau started counting same-sex spouses as "married couples," rather than grouping them with "cohabitating partners." This new designation provides more accurate data on same-sex households, which could influence future legislative and funding decisions.

Yet many people are uncomfortable talking about differences in sexuality, and that can result in ignorance. You've probably grown up hearing some rumors and myths about LGBTQ people (I'll discuss some of the common ones in this book). Even the most well-intentioned people, including some LGBTQ people themselves, can be misinformed about what it means to be queer.

The most powerful response to bias and ignorance is knowledge. This chapter covers the fundamentals of being LGBTQ. Some of what follows might seem like very basic information. However, even if you consider yourself knowledgeable about LGBTQ issues, you may be surprised by some of what you read.

## LGBTQ Terminology

One thing that can be confusing about the queer community is its terminology. Sometimes it seems like a whole different language exists. Even among LGBTQ people, there's a lack of consensus about definitions and about which words to use and when. And the language is constantly changing as our understanding of sexual orientation and gender identity evolve. Even the title of this book has changed (from *GLBTQ* to *LGBTQ*) as commonly accepted acronyms have shifted.

A few decades ago, it was common to say simply G&L, meaning gay and lesbian. When the *B* (for *bisexual*) was added, the acronym became GLB or LGB. Then the *T* (for *transgender*) and Q (for *questioning*) joined the party. Now you'll commonly see LGBT or LGBTQ (and sometimes GLBTQ), or even LGBTQIA (*I* for *intersex* and *A* for *asexual*) or LGBT+ (with the + representing all the other identities that are not lesbian, gay, bisexual, or transgender).

**SEXUAL ORIENTATION AND GENDER IDENTITY**

The American Psychological Association, which has an entire office dedicated to sexual orientation and gender diversity, describes sexual orientation as an enduring pattern of emotional, romantic, and/or sexual attraction to men, women, or both sexes (assuming a binary gender system in which all people are *either* male or female). It also refers to a person's sense of identity in relation to who they're attracted to.

According to the Sexuality Information and Education Council of the United States, gender identity is the internal sense that people have of being female, male, some variation of these, beyond gender altogether, and so on. For many people, biological sex—which is based on chromosomes and sexual anatomy—and gender identity are the same. (The term for this is *cisgender*.) For those who are transgender (and for some who are nonbinary, which means having a gender identity outside the binary male/female system), their biological sexes and gender identities are different. Intersex people have sexual and/or chromosomal characteristics that are not limited to a single biological sex.

In this book, you'll see the consistent use of the acronym LGBTQ. When an issue applies specifically to lesbian, gay, bisexual, or transgender people, those specific words will be used. And although you'll read about people being either LGBTQ or straight/cis, remember that not all transgender people are lesbian, gay, or bisexual. In fact, many trans people are heterosexual, and others simply don't identify with any of these labels. Referring to trans people as LGBTQ doesn't imply that they are necessarily lesbian, gay, or bisexual in their sexual orientations. But the full acronym LGBTQ is used throughout the book for consistency.

Another word used often in this book is *queer*. This word was once used negatively to describe LGBTQ people (and still is by some people). Now, many LGBTQ people and our allies (supporters) use it very positively. For example, you can find queer studies and queer theory courses at many colleges. People who are nonbinary sometimes identify as genderqueer. The word *queer* is used in this book in a positive and affirming way. Queer is simply "other than the expected or average," which in our culture right now is straight/cis. Some people believe the labels lesbian, gay, bisexual, or transgender are too limiting, so *queer* is also a great word because it frees you from using a specific label if you don't want to.

## A NOTE ON PRONOUNS

One change throughout this edition of the book is that the pronoun *they* appears instead of *he* or *she*. While use of the singular *they* can set many an English teacher's teeth on edge, it is a more inclusive pronoun than the binary *he* and *she*, and I've used it here for that reason. There's also precedent for its use in classic works including those by Chaucer, Shakespeare, Byron, and Austen and in the King James Bible. And there is grammatical precedent for its use. In fact, in 2015, the American Dialect Society named singular *they* as a gender-neutral pronoun as their Word of the Year.

The glossary (page 233) includes a variety of terms used and identities described in this book, along with related words you might come across elsewhere. For now, let's look at the basics.

**L is for lesbian.** Lesbians are women (cis or trans) who are physically and emotionally attracted to other women, often exclusively. The word *lesbian* has its origins with the Greek poet Sappho, who was born sometime between 630 and 612 BCE. For part of her life, Sappho lived on the island of Lesbos. Many of her poems were about same-sex love between women, and as a result, the island's name became synonymous with homosexual women. That's how the term *lesbian* was born.

**G is for gay.** This term often is used to describe both homosexual men and lesbians. As it refers to men, *gay* describes men (cis or trans) who are physically and emotionally attracted to other men. The word *gay* didn't come into wide use to describe homosexual people in general until around the 1950s.

### GOING WITH THE FLOW

For some, identities such as lesbian or gay are fluid. For example, someone (like me) could identify as mostly lesbian, meaning I'm almost always attracted to women, but not exclusively. Likewise, people can be mostly gay or mostly straight. How does this differ from bisexual? Some might say it's the same thing, but it's really up to the individual to decide what terminology best fits them. So maybe you're attracted exclusively to either girls or guys. Maybe you're usually attracted to boys, but there's something about that girl in your chemistry class that really intrigues you. Maybe who you're attracted to just doesn't seem to correspond to sex or gender in any way, or maybe you feel emotional, but not necessarily physical, attraction toward others. It's all natural!

**B is for bisexual.** Classically, bisexual people are emotionally and physically attracted to people of either sex—male or female. However, this definition links it to the binary gender system. Sometimes people refer to themselves as bisexual as a means of identifying as questioning, or they identify as bisexual first and then later as gay or lesbian. However, many bisexual people are and remain bisexual, period—or they identify as pansexual (potentially attracted to any person, regardless of the person's sex or gender identity).

Unfortunately, people who identify as bisexual (or as any identity that includes attraction to more than one orientation or gender) can face ignorance even from within the gay community. They might be told they "just can't admit they're gay" or "can't make up their minds." These statements are judgments—regardless of whether they're coming from LGBTQ or straight/cis people—and, as such, aren't helpful. Bisexual and pansexual people—like all people—should be accepted for who they are.

**T is for transgender.** Transgender people generally have feelings of being a different gender than their sex assigned at birth. What it means to be trans can be complicated and is often misunderstood. One misconception is that all transgender people want to have surgery or to take hormones to change their bodies. Some do, but others don't. Another misconception is that all trans people are homosexual. Trans people can be straight, but just like any other person, they can also be lesbian, gay, bisexual, or something else.

Some trans people start out identifying as lesbian, gay, or bisexual, and then later realize they are transgender (the reverse can happen as well). Also, some trans people are binary (self-identifying as male or female) while others are not.

Some of the issues and emotions transgender people may face, whether they're straight or queer, are similar to those that lesbian, gay, and bisexual people often experience. Feelings of isolation and the desire to come out, for example, are experiences that all LGBTQ people may have. However, there are other feelings and considerations that can come with identifying as a different gender from the sex you were assigned at birth (or from not identifying as a single gender). Some of these issues are addressed in chapter 2.

**Note:** The words *transgender* and *intersex* are sometimes confused, but they are not the same. *Intersex* is a term for a variety of conditions in which a person is born with reproductive or sexual anatomy that doesn't fit the stereotypical definition of male or female. You can read more about this in chapter 2.

**Q is for questioning.** People who are questioning are uncertain of their sexual orientations or gender identities, or they may just prefer not to label themselves with any particular orientation. Many teens are starting to embrace identifying themselves as questioning. A lot of things are changing during adolescence, and deciding that you're questioning can remove the pressure of choosing an identity like lesbian, gay, bisexual, or straight.

### THE ROOTS OF QUEER LANGUAGE

According to *Hidden from History: Reclaiming the Gay & Lesbian Past*, by the late 1800s, lesbians who dressed and "passed" as men had developed a more positive language to describe themselves. While others derogatorily used labels such as *inverts* and *he-shes* to identify them, these women began to use the word *dike*. At the time, this term referred to a man who was dressed up, or "diked out," for a night on the town. Today, the word *dyke* (now spelled with a *y*) is encountered in mixed contexts. Some use it as a derogatory term, while some lesbians embrace the word and self-identify as dykes. For example, a popular contingent at many Pride parades is Dykes on Bikes—a group of lesbians riding motorcycles.

# A Biology Lesson: The Science of LGBTQ

Why are some people LGBTQ and others aren't? At this point, there isn't a definitive answer, and there may never be one. Scientists, philosophers, psychologists, and a host of other thinkers have offered opinions and theories to answer the question, but for now, there isn't a 100 percent proof-positive reason. There has, however, been a lot of research attempting to determine what makes people LGBTQ, including a search for a "gay gene." Thanks to these efforts, scientists, healthcare professionals, and the general public have access to expanded information on sexual orientation and gender identity.

## The Kinsey Report

In the 1940s, a scientist named Dr. Alfred Kinsey and his team of researchers conducted a study of human sexuality in men. Based on this research, Kinsey determined that most men are neither completely gay nor completely straight. Instead, while some are at either end of the spectrum, most fall somewhere in the middle. He developed a six-point scale—the Kinsey scale—to illustrate this spectrum.

The Kinsey scale was revolutionary not only because it looked at queerness as predetermined, but also because it showed a vast gray area between gay and straight. Before Kinsey, many experts thought human sexuality was black and white—straight people were 100 percent straight and queer people 100 percent queer. Many also thought that straight people were "normal" and "well-adjusted," while queer people were "sick" or "deviant." Kinsey's research helped counter this myth and showed that homosexuality and bisexuality were much more common than previously thought.

**SEXUAL ORIENTATION: THE KINSEY SCALE**

**0** Exclusively heterosexual

**1** Predominantly heterosexual, only incidentally homosexual

**2** Predominantly heterosexual, but more than incidentally homosexual

**3** Equally heterosexual and homosexual

**4** Predominantly homosexual, but more than incidentally heterosexual

**5** Predominantly homosexual, only incidentally heterosexual

**6** Exclusively homosexual

Kinsey was so intrigued by his research on male sexuality that he expanded his later work to include women, too. His best-known publications were the books *Sexual Behavior in the Human Male* (1948) and *Sexual Behavior in the Human Female* (1953).

Though the statistical methods Kinsey used to conduct his studies don't measure up to the standards used for research today, there is still strong evidence that people fall within a spectrum of gender and sexuality.

If you've never thought of sexuality as a spectrum, the idea can be confusing at first. But if you think about all the complex factors that contribute to making a single human being, it can begin to make more sense. Every human characteristic is on a spectrum. Even within a single quality, there can be great variety. Take eye color, for example. A person with blue eyes can have light-blue eyes, deep-blue eyes, blue-gray eyes, and so on. Being human means being varied. So it makes sense that our sexual orientations, gender identities, and combinations of biologically male and female characteristics would vary as well.

### NEWER MODELS FOR GENDER AND SEXUALITY

Today, Kinsey's model of looking at everyone relative to a linear identity of gay or straight seems very limited. In recent years, several new multidimensional models for examining and explaining gender and sexual orientation have become popular. Some of them are cute, some are clever, but all take a more expansive view of sexual orientation than Kinsey's 0 to 6 scale. Two of the most popular multidimensional models are the Gender Unicorn (www.transstudent.org/gender) and the Genderbread Person (www.genderbread.org). Ideas addressed by these models include gender identity, gender expression, sex assigned at birth, and who one is physically and/or emotionally attracted to (if anyone). Some schools have even adopted these tools for use in teaching. One of the most useful things about the Gender Unicorn and the Genderbread Person is that the models acknowledge a full spectrum of being rather than assuming that each person is just *this* or just *that*—just gay or just straight, for example.

**Pro tip:** Examining and presenting different gender and sexuality models could be a really interesting school project or activity for your GSA.

**BEEN THERE**

"For me, there was a lot of uncertainty in high school. I liked half the guys in my senior class, but I also had a crush on two girls on my block. That's very confusing at an age when you are changing physically and mentally." —Enrique, 20

## Why Are People Queer or Straight/Cis?

That's the million-dollar question. Over the course of your life, you'll hear a lot of theories about why some people are LGBTQ and others aren't. There are queer people who believe you can choose to be LGBTQ. There are straight/cis people who believe you can't. Some say it's like putting on a suit that you can take off at any time. Others believe that it's something deep inside you. You might even hear someone talk about how an experience "made" a person gay. Lots of people have their own theories about it, and if you haven't already, you might develop one of your own. You might also decide you don't care why.

While some scientists are working to discover a genetic component that makes people queer, most mental health professionals and LGBTQ advocates believe that being LGBTQ is probably the result of a complex interaction of environmental and biological factors. The American Psychiatric Association and advocacy groups like PFLAG don't believe that being queer is a choice. The American Psychological Association (APA) maintains unequivocally that "human beings cannot choose to be either gay or straight." In the APA pamphlet *Answers to Your Questions for a Better Understanding of Sexual Orientation & Homosexuality*, it states, "[N]o findings have emerged that permit scientists to conclude that sexual orientation is determined by any particular factor or factors. . . . Most people experience little or no sense of choice about their sexual orientation."

**COUNTERPOINT**

In *The Tolerance Trap: How God, Genes, and Good Intentions Are Sabotaging Gay Equality*, author Suzanna Danuta Walters, a sociology professor at Northeastern University and self-identified lesbian, lays out several interesting perspectives on why she believes the argument that being queer is not a choice is actually detrimental to the LGBTQ rights movement. But at the end of the day, writes Walters, everyone deserves equal rights under the Constitution, so it shouldn't matter whether it's a choice or whether some people choose and others don't.

**Pro tip:** Regardless of your conclusions on whether or not a person can choose to be gay, this could make a great topic for a school project or debate.

## Wanting to Change and People Who Want to Change You

Developing or realizing an LGBTQ identity involves many stages. Early in that process, many young people wish they could change. Some ignore how they feel and try to act as if they're straight/cis—going on dates, having romantic relationships, and sometimes even having sex to try to feel "normal."

Many of the people who have gone on to become leaders in the LGBTQ community started out just as confused and scared as you might be. Transgender activist and writer Kate Bornstein, who was born with male anatomy but always felt female, writes in her book *Gender Outlaw: On Men, Women, and the Rest of Us* about her experience of trying to hide her feelings of being a girl. "I knew from age four on that something was wrong with me being a guy, and I spent most of my life avoiding the issue," she writes. "I hid out in textbooks, pulp fiction, and drugs and alcohol. I buried my head in the sands of television, college, a lot of lovers, and three marriages." Bornstein eventually stopped trying to hide and grew to accept and love her true identity.

Similarly, Ellen DeGeneres has spoken openly about her reluctance to come out because of her intense fear of rejection. After her very public coming out in 1997, Ellen's career faltered for a period of time. Now, however, she has risen to become one of the most beloved figures on daytime television. *The Ellen DeGeneres Show* won nearly

30 Daytime Emmy Awards in its first six seasons, and by 2017, Ellen herself had won 76 major awards. Times have changed a lot since Kate Bornstein and Ellen DeGeneres were teens, and now LGBTQ people are far more visible. However, realizing you're queer is still a very deep personal experience that many people struggle with at first.

You might initially feel that something is wrong with you, but—overwhelmingly—mainstream medical and professional organizations maintain that there is nothing "wrong" with being queer and that no one should attempt a "cure." In fact, the American Academy of Pediatrics, the American Counseling Association, the American Psychiatric Association, the National Association of School Psychologists, and the National Association of Social Workers all maintain that queerness is *not* a mental disorder.

In *Answers to Your Questions for a Better Understanding of Sexual Orientation & Homosexuality*, the American Psychological Association states, "Both heterosexual behavior and homosexual behavior are normal aspects of human sexuality. . . . Despite the persistence of stereotypes that portray lesbian, gay, and bisexual people as disturbed, several decades of mental health research and clinical experience have led all mainstream medical and mental health organizations in this country to conclude that these orientations represent normal forms of human experience."

However, some people believe you can change your gender identity or sexual orientation through therapy or other means (which is one of the reasons why so many people underscore the idea that being LGBTQ is not a choice). So-called "conversion therapy," "reparative therapy," or "transformational ministries" try to change or "cure" LGBTQ people. Conversion therapy involves psychotherapy aimed at eliminating feelings of homosexuality. Transformational ministries use religion to try to change people. Groups like Exodus International and Brothers on a Road Less Traveled (formerly known as People Can Change) aim to "free" people from being queer by pointing them toward God, though Exodus International finally ceased operations in 2013. More and more people are becoming aware of the detrimental effects of conversion therapy (which is described as torture by many who have experienced it). Nevertheless, a report from the Williams Institute at UCLA School of Law estimated that 20,000 LGBTQ people ages 13 to 17 will receive this type of intervention from a healthcare professional before they turn 18. Another 57,000 are estimated to receive conversion therapy from a religious or spiritual advisor. (For more information on aspects of religion and homosexuality, see chapter 10.)

Conversion therapy and transformational ministries can be very destructive to queer people's self-esteem because the goal of these therapies is to convince those who are LGBTQ that their thoughts and feelings are wrong and unnatural. If you need help coming to terms with being LGBTQ or just want someone to talk to, seeking therapy or counseling to discuss these issues is a good idea. But talk to someone who won't try to make you feel like it's wrong to be who you are. You don't need to try to fix who you are, because nothing is wrong with you in the first place.

**NOT ONLY DETRIMENTAL, BUT NOW ALSO ILLEGAL**

By mid-2018, 15 states and the District of Columbia had passed legislation to ban conversion therapy for minors, citing it as a method that has been disavowed by medical professionals and can be harmful to those subjected to it. In May 2017, the US Supreme Court refused to overturn California's ban on conversion therapy. Connecticut's legislation refers to it as a "destructive and discredited" practice. By mid-2018, legislation had been introduced in 24 states to ban the practice.

The National LGBTQ Task Force published a report called *Youth in the Crosshairs: The Third Wave of Ex-Gay Activism*. The report details efforts by specific organizations to target LGBTQ teens and concludes, "There is a growing body of evidence that conversion therapy not only does not work, but also can be extremely harmful, resulting in depression, social isolation from family and friends, low self-esteem, internalized homophobia, and even attempted suicide." Further, it states, "Many conversion therapy clients were not informed about alternative treatment options, including therapy that could have helped them accept their sexual orientation." The American Psychiatric Association has condemned reparative therapies, stating that attempts to transform gay or bisexual people into heterosexual people are not only pointless, but often motivated by personal prejudices.

### BEEN THERE

"When I first started to understand myself and tried to accept who I was, I was devastated. I remember a day when I took out my student Bible and searched for hours on homosexuality. When I finally found it, I was sobbing so hard I could barely breathe. There were a couple of passages that I thought were scolding me. They told me I was evil and hateful, that my kind is unforgiven and will forever burn. It was the harshest thing I had ever read. I probably prayed more within that week than I had ever prayed in my life. I begged for God to tell me if I was wrong and evil. I cried to myself, trying to get myself to believe that I'm not what they say I am. It took me a while to pull through that." —Sonia, 19

### GET MORE INFORMATION

**Human Rights Campaign (www.hrc.org).** The Human Rights Campaign (HRC) is an advocacy organization that offers information on many LGBTQ issues, including conversion therapy and transformational ministries. Visit the group's website or call them at 1-800-777-4723.

**Beyond Ex-Gay (beyondexgay.com).** This online community offers many true stories from people who have gone through conversion therapies as well as resources with information about the movement to ban the practice.

Additionally, as you'll see in chapter 10, there are many congregations that include and are very supportive of LGBTQ folks. See pages 206–208 for a list of organizations in specific religions.

## Your Personal Geography: Exploring Who You Are

What it all boils down to is that it doesn't really matter what the experts say. The only person who is a true expert when it comes to you is you, so what matters is what *you* say.

### BEEN THERE

"I think the fact that a lot of people don't take young LGBTQ people seriously is really challenging. Also, as a young person it's hard to balance figuring out your gender identity or sexuality along with school, friends, and other parts of your life. And there definitely is not enough representation in media or TV, which can make young LGBTQ people feel alone or wrong for being themselves." —Jayson, 16

## Yes, No, Maybe So: It's Okay to Be Questioning

Even if few people talk about it, questioning your sexual orientation is more common than you might think. Some people don't like to label themselves as questioning because they feel like it just makes them sound confused. Being questioning simply means that you're open to understanding your sexual orientation or gender identity as it's unfolding—and that's a great thing! (Couldn't the world use more open-minded people?)

### BEEN THERE

"If you are questioning, that doesn't necessarily mean that you're gay. It means exactly what it implies: You are questioning and unsure of yourself or your sexuality. In time, you will understand who you are." —Nolan, 19

## What's the Rush?

According to Caitlin Ryan and Donna Futterman—two of the first researchers to broadly address issues of LGBTQ teens—many lesbian and gay young people begin to self-identify around age 16. Their first awareness of same-sex attraction, though, likely occurred around age 9 for males and age 10 for females (using the gender binary). Children start to become aware of biological differences around age 3. Trans people often report feeling conflict between their physical anatomies and gender identities throughout childhood and adolescence. The point is, for most LGBTQ young people (and even adults), developing an understanding of their sexuality is an ongoing process.

## BEEN THERE

"I realized I was LGBTQ when I was young, like 11 or 12. I always had an interest in the female sex, ever since I can remember. I distinctly remember watching television and 'liking' a pretty woman on the screen and wanting to touch her. I didn't really think anything of it until I was 16 and I finally came out to myself." —Elena, 20

"It's hard to say definitively how I became aware of my gender identity. I think it was really while I was surfing websites and reading stories about transgender people. It was then that I realized not all guys had dreams of suddenly and inexplicably being changed into a girl." —Chris, 19

"I think I've known all my life that I am bisexual, even though I didn't always have a word for it. I can remember playing with another little girl when I was young, seven or eight maybe, and we'd play 'boyfriend' and 'girlfriend.' I have always been attracted to boys and girls, but it wasn't until a friend of mine came out and told me he was gay that I started thinking that I was bisexual." —June, 19

## Common Feelings When You're Awakening

Although everyone reacts differently to the idea that they might be LGBTQ, people usually experience a common progression of stages. Some go through this process more quickly than others, and many people spend more time in one stage than in another. Sociologist Richard Troiden described the process in the *Journal of Homosexuality*:

**Stage One: Sensitization.** Feelings of being different from the majority in a fundamental way can begin well before puberty. This is usually a very challenging time during which people can feel isolated from family and friends.

**Stage Two: Identity confusion.** People start becoming more aware of actual same-sex or differently gendered thoughts and feelings. During this stage, learned negative thoughts about homosexuality and being transgender can cause individuals to feel betrayed by their own thoughts and feelings.

**Stage Three: Identity assumption.** Things get better at this point in the process. It's typically when people begin to find more-positive, accurate information about what it means to be LGBTQ and start to identify that way.

**Stage Four: Commitment.** Historically, people often didn't reach this stage until adulthood. Today, more teens are reaching it at progressively younger ages. This is likely the result of more positive portrayals of LGBTQ people in the media and broader access to accurate information about what it means to be LGBTQ. During this stage, people openly incorporate their LGBTQ identity into their lives. (See chapter 4 for more information on coming out.)

**BEEN THERE**

"I came out to my sister and she was very weird about it, but things are becoming easier as I get older. I'm just becoming more comfortable with being bisexual." —Charlotte, 19

## Myths, Generalizations, and Just Plain Absurd Ideas About LGBTQ People . . . and the Truth

At school, stereotypes abound. Based on how people dress or what they like to do after class, individuals often get pigeonholed into categories such as jock, geek, player, slacker, baller, goody-goody, and so on. You've probably noticed that the problem with these labels is that they're one-dimensional and don't fully describe a person. You could dress like an athlete and have the soul of an artist, and vice versa.

The more you get to know someone, the less appropriate labels seem. For example, try describing your closest friend using a one- or two-word stereotype. You'll probably find that just doesn't do your friend justice.

LGBTQ people are especially susceptible to stereotyping. One reason is that some individuals are afraid to challenge these stereotypes because they fear others might assume they're LGBTQ and start to harass them. Another reason stereotypes are strong is the lack of positive and accurate portrayals of LGBTQ people in the media. Although more exist now, they still aren't abundant.

Also, many LGBTQ people are afraid to come out because they fear rejection or even physical harm. The lack of an accepting environment keeps some individuals in hiding, which allows misinformation to thrive.

Fortunately, things are improving. Activists have helped change how LGBTQ people are viewed in society. And the media is showing more LGBTQ teens as everyday people, including in TV shows.

Still, ignorance persists. For example, take the following LGBTQ stereotypes. You might have heard some of these misguided ideas or statements before. And don't think it's just straight/cis people who say these things. Unfortunately, stereotyping exists within the LGBTQ community, too.

## 12 Absolutely Ridiculous Queer Stereotypes (and the Truth)

**Myth #1: LGBTQ people are unhappy being who they are.**
***The truth:*** For a long time, society painted a picture of LGBTQ people as living secretive or tormented lives. But many (perhaps even most) queer people live open and happy lives with loving families, just like anyone else. The reality is that LGBTQ people can encounter difficulties for being what many in society view as "different." This is not related to what it means to be queer. Rather, a lack of understanding among others can cause challenges for LGBTQ people. And being straight/cis doesn't guarantee a life free of difficulties, either. For both LGBTQ and straight/cis people, how we deal with life's challenges helps determine our happiness and success.

**Myth #2: Gay men are attracted to all men, lesbians are attracted to all women, and bisexuals are attracted to just plain everyone.**
***The truth:*** Just like straight/cis people, queer people have personal tastes in what they like—whether it's food, cars, or people they're attracted to. Because the stereotype is so common, some people may be uncomfortable when they first meet an LGBTQ person. ("Oh, he's

gay. . . . He must be checking me out.") Bisexual and pansexual people deal with this perhaps more than any other group—people assume that because they can be attracted to people of both or all genders or no gender, they're attracted to *everyone*. That's simply not true. Look at it this way: Some people like apple pie and only apple pie. Others like pies, cookies, cakes, and so on. But that doesn't mean they're happy with just any pie, cookie, or cake. You can be open to a broad range of desserts (or people) and still be discerning about which you'd choose. Fortunately, the more people actually get to know others who are queer, the more they come to understand that.

**Myth #3: Gay men want to be women and lesbians want to be men.**
***The truth:*** Being transgender and being gay or lesbian are very different things. Some people have such a hard time understanding same-sex attractions that they assume that gay men and women actually want to be a different physical sex. This stereotype also has roots in how some gay men and lesbians challenge gender norms when expressing themselves (also called being gender nonconforming, which straight/cis people can be, as well). Gay men who are seen as more *femme* (a term used to describe people of any gender who act and dress in stereotypically feminine ways) and lesbians who are seen as more *butch* (a term used to describe people of any gender who act and dress in stereotypically masculine ways) are sometimes assumed to be trans, but this may or may not be true. A related myth is that butch lesbians and femme gay men just want to draw attention to themselves. The reality is that the way femme guys and butch girls present themselves is simply a form of expression in the same way that anyone's—queer or straight/cis—personality or style of dressing is a representation of who that person is. When we start criticizing anyone's right to dress or be who they want to be, we start suppressing all people's rights to do so.

**Myth #4: Gay men hate women and lesbians hate men.**
***The truth:*** Being gay or lesbian means you are physically and emotionally attracted to people of the same gender as you. It has nothing to do with a hatred for people of different sexes or genders. For example, women aren't lesbians because they hate men. Lesbians want to form physical and/or love relationships with women because of a deep desire to be with women, and gay men want to form physical and/or love relationships with men because of a deep

desire to be with men. (However, some people do claim that being queer is a choice. For more on this idea, see pages 17–18.)

**Myth #5: Queer people "flaunt it."**
***The truth:*** LGBTQ people who have bumper stickers on their cars, get involved in the queer civil rights movement, wear cause-oriented clothing or buttons, or hold hands in public are sometimes accused of "flaunting it." Some straight/cis people wonder why queer people don't just keep it to themselves. However, in a society where the assumption is that people are straight/cis, LGBTQ people often feel the need to challenge that assumption or self-identify to let other LGBTQ people know they're not alone. Sometimes people make their orientations known as a means of standing up for themselves or simply as a gesture to increase visibility by reminding others that not everyone is straight/cis.

Additionally, straight/cis people who hold hands in public are rarely accused of flaunting being straight/cis. Most LGBTQ people simply desire the same freedom to express their love for their partners, significant others, or spouses. Often they're not trying to make any political or social statement. They're just being themselves.

**Myth #6: Transgender people are all drag queens and drag kings.**
***The truth:*** Drag queens are typically men who dress as gender-conforming women and perform for entertainment, and drag kings are typically women who dress as gender-conforming men and perform for entertainment. Transgender people have a deep, personal identification with a gender that is different from their sex assigned at birth. Transgender people don't dress or act certain ways to get attention or for entertainment, but instead to reflect who they are inside. Some trans people are also drag queens or drag kings, but most are not.

**Myth #7: LGBTQ people are all into partying and drugs.**
***The truth:*** For a long time, some of the only safe places for LGBTQ people to get together were in queer or queer-friendly bars and clubs. They became not only places to socialize, but also, in some cases, places to organize civil rights efforts. The club and bar scenes are still popular today, but LGBTQ people socialize in loads of other places as well. Nevertheless, many media portrayals of LGBTQ people are limited to sensational and racy depictions of the queer

## QUEERS IN THE MILITARY

LGBTQ people are highly decorated soldiers, sailors, Air Force members, and Marines, who can now serve openly. (While there has been some debate over whether trans people will continue to be allowed to serve in the military, thousands of trans people do and have done so proudly.) The federal "Don't Ask, Don't Tell" (DADT) policy—which had forbidden openly gay people from serving in the US military—was officially repealed by President Barack Obama on December 22, 2010. In the months and weeks preceding DADT's repeal, the debate over the policy had grown in intensity as conflicts in Iraq and Afghanistan continued.

In 2009, President Obama pledged to end DADT. In 2010, Defense Secretary Robert Gates severely limited how it could be enforced. Most senior military leaders, including the highest ranking military officer in the nation at the time—Admiral Mike Mullen, the chairman of the Joint Chiefs of Staff—voiced support for DADT's repeal. However, strong opposition to the repeal remained among some members of the Senate and the military. As a result, the military conducted one of the largest surveys in the history of the armed forces, asking service members and their families their feelings about the potential repeal of the policy. The committee's report, issued November 30, 2010, stated, "The results . . . reveal a widespread attitude among a solid majority of service members that repeal of 'Don't Ask, Don't Tell' will not have a negative impact on their ability to conduct their military mission."

After an intense series of debates, the Senate and House voted to overturn the policy. The repeal of DADT was a huge step forward in the LGBTQ civil rights movement and a landmark in American history. However, in 2017, President Donald Trump announced that his administration would seek a ban on trans people serving in the military. Several groups filed suit opposing the ban and federal courts issued temporary injunctions against the policy, but the White House declared it would continue to push for the policy. The ban was widely criticized by politicians from both major parties and by military leaders, including the top officers of the four main branches of the US military (the Army, Navy, Marine Corps, and Air Force). In addition, Commandant Admiral Paul Zukunft, head of the US Coast Guard, stated in

2018 that the Coast Guard was "committed to [transgender members'] continued service in the Coast Guard." And Admiral Mike Mullen declared, "Thousands of transgender Americans are currently serving in uniform and there is no reason to single out these brave men and women and deny them the medical care that they require."

It's not as if LGBTQ members of the military are a new concept. Historically, countless queer people have served their countries. For example, Friedrich Wilhelm von Steuben (also known as Baron von Steuben) was a Prussian and American military officer who played a key role in the Continental Army's victory in the American Revolutionary War by teaching the rag-tag soldiers military drills and tactics. Oliver Sipple was a highly decorated Marine and Vietnam War veteran who once saved President Ford's life during an assassination attempt. And Kristin Beck is a trans woman who distinguished herself as a hero while serving as part of the Navy's elite SEAL Team 6 (and later coauthored the book *Warrior Princess: A U.S. Navy SEAL's Journey to Coming Out Transgender*). These and many other queer people have proudly defended their countries around the world and through the years.

party scene. Even worse, those are the only images some straight/cis people have been exposed to. Just like everyone else, though, queer people have interests that go well beyond partying. And plenty of queer people don't "do the scene" at all.

**Myth #8: Queer people recruit.**

***The truth:*** This myth is rooted in the idea that LGBTQ people choose to be who they are, and therefore can talk or turn someone else into being queer. An especially vicious aspect of this myth is the accusation that LGBTQ people "recruit" others. In fact, this book has been banned from a few libraries because some people allege that the information in it is designed to "turn" young people LGBTQ. Being queer isn't like buying a car—a skilled salesperson can't just talk you into it. Personal identity and attraction are highly individual and can't be dictated by someone else.

What is true is that after seeing or spending time with LGBTQ people, a person might realize that they have similar personal feelings or characteristics. Many queer people recall understanding themselves better after meeting, reading about, or listening to others who are LGBTQ.

**BEEN THERE**

"In college, I started spending a lot of time with a friend who was a lesbian. I didn't understand why, but I felt really compelled to hang out with her almost all the time. When I came out, my mom accused my friend of turning me gay. But it wasn't that. It was that spending time with her and having her put words to what I had been feeling for years helped me realize I was like her all along." —Jasmine, 22

**Myth #9: Queer people can't be parents.**
***The truth:*** Many queer people (including me!) have children, and same-sex parenting is becoming more common. Some LGBTQ people adopt, while others have children from previous straight relationships. Still others undergo artificial insemination or use a surrogate mother. It used to be that a "normal" family was nuclear—a mom, a dad, and two kids. Today, there might be two moms, two dads, a mom and two dads, or simply "parents" (acknowledging folks who are nonbinary or simply don't use the labels mom or dad). More states allow second-parent adoption in same-sex households and permit same-sex couples to be foster parents. Also, many states now allow same-sex spouses to be listed as the second parent on birth certificates. In the generations to come, more people will have queer parents, which will contribute to an even broader understanding and acceptance of LGBTQ people.

**Myth #10: LGBTQ people only live in urban areas.**
***The truth:*** There's a bumper sticker that reads, "We're everywhere." That's no joke. Being queer isn't dictated by where you live or how you grow up. It's likely that LGBTQ people are more visible in urban areas because there is, generally speaking, greater acceptance of differences in these places (although some rural areas are very

accepting). It's easy to feel alone when you first realize you're queer, but you aren't.

**FIND SUPPORT**

**Advocates for Youth (advocatesforyouth.org).** This website provides information about issues young people face, including issues related to LGBTQ health and rights. It features information on advocacy efforts you can join.

**ACLU Youth & Schools (www.aclu.org).** The American Civil Liberties Union (ACLU) advocates for equality for all people. Visit this site for tools that can be helpful for promoting tolerance in schools, including those in rural areas.

**Myth #11: LGBTQ people are "immoral."**
***The truth:*** Some misinformed people view LGBTQ people as immoral or deviant. Being queer relates to one's personal sexual orientation; being immoral is a subjective assessment or judgment based on how someone views another person's behavior. Everyone has a different view of what is moral or immoral, and a lot goes into making up these personal opinions. What's important is that LGBTQ teens understand that someone's personal judgment is not fact.

**Myth #12: LGBTQ people are not religious or spiritual.**
***The truth:*** This myth is closely related to Myth #11. Many queer people participate in organized religion or abide by a set of personally held spiritual beliefs. Some are even religious officials. And many churches, temples, and other places of worship welcome and accept LGBTQ people. Some churches—the Metropolitan Community Church being one of the best known—take a strong stand on human rights, including LGBTQ civil rights.

Many congregations welcome LGBTQ people. (See pages 204–205 for a profile of a gay priest in a Lutheran church.) For more information on LGBTQ people and issues of religion and spirituality, including examples from other religions and denominations, see chapter 10.

## Your Own Beliefs About LGBTQ People

Some of the most difficult LGBTQ stereotypes to conquer can be the ones you hold yourself. You might not realize it, but even you could believe some inaccurate information about LGBTQ people. By adolescence, most teens have internalized at least some negative messages they've received.

Stereotypes about LGBTQ people can also make it tough to know that you're queer. Some people say they had trouble figuring out that they are LGBTQ because they didn't seem to fit the "definition" of what that meant. But it turns out that definition was based on stereotypes, and what it means to be LGBTQ is different for each person.

Some LGBTQ people adhere to some of the same stereotypes about queer people that many straight/cis people do. Maybe you think that because you're LGBTQ, you won't be able to pursue your chosen profession or have children. Maybe you think it means you'll have to dress or act a certain way. But that's not true. Contrary to popular belief, there isn't a "queer lifestyle." Whatever it means to be LGBTQ is really about what it means to you, not to anyone else. The LGBTQ community is as rich and diverse as the straight/cis community, and there's plenty of room for you just as you are.

## Check Your Head

It can be difficult to face negative stereotypes, especially when you apply them to yourself. Here are some affirmations to help you unlearn some of the misinformation that could be affecting how you feel about yourself. If you're struggling, repeat them to yourself. The more you do, the more you can start to believe them.

1. I am my own person.
2. I love who I am.
3. When I embrace my identity, I make space for others to do the same.

CHAPTER 2

# Transgender and Nonbinary Teens

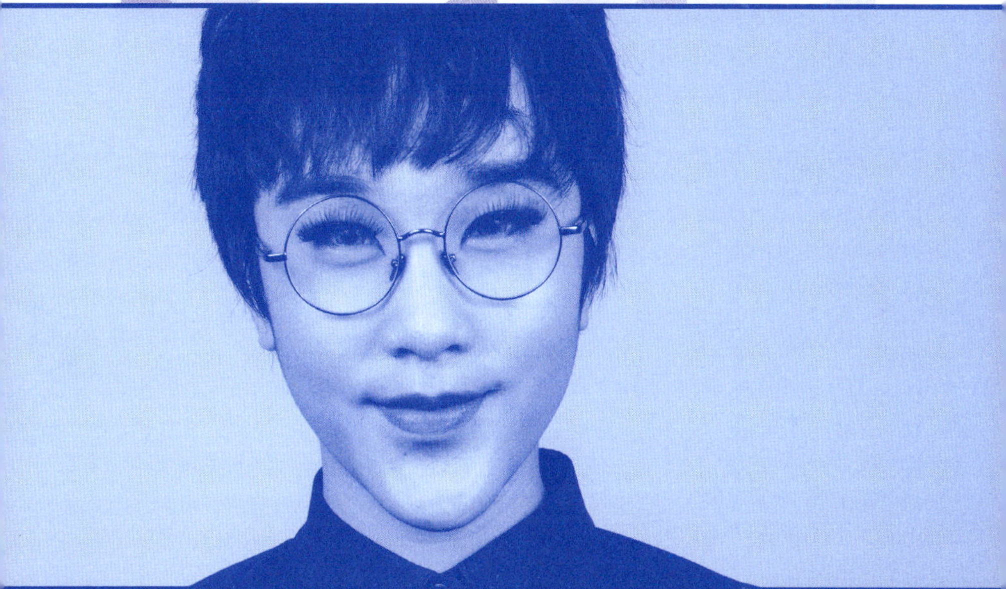

Gender is a galaxy.

In the last few years, the issue of gender has become a hot topic like never before. In January 2017, *National Geographic Magazine* ran a special issue on gender that featured a trans teen on the cover. Trans issues, such as the right to use restroom facilities matching one's gender identity, have been a subject of debate not only in schools, but at state and federal legal and legislative levels in the United States.

Trans and nonbinary celebrities, from actors Laverne Cox and Amandla Stenberg to YouTube star Jazz Jennings and model Casey Legler, have cast a spotlight on trans and nonbinary people. In 2018, the movie *A Fantastic Woman* won an Academy Award for best foreign film. It was the first movie with a transgender storyline featuring an openly trans actor—Daniela Vega—ever to win an Oscar. In addition, Facebook now allows people to specify a custom gender and select the pronoun *them*.

## BEEN THERE

"When I was little I would always lie awake at night and wonder how much better my life would be if I had been born a girl. Then I would think, 'Oh great, the one thing I really want, I can't have.'"
—Alexandra, 14

But even with increased visibility, transgender and nonbinary teens typically face a greater struggle for acceptance and understanding than other queer teens do. Comparatively little is understood about how ideas and feelings of gender are formed, so trans and nonbinary teens can feel even more isolation and loneliness than their gay, lesbian, and bisexual peers. However, this continues to change.

According to the Human Rights Campaign, knowledge of what the term *transgender* means, as well as familiarity with transgender public policy issues, is growing dramatically across the United States. This represents an important stride toward a more understanding society. More work definitely must be done to educate the public about the experiences of being a trans person, but acceptance *is* growing.

### HOW MANY PEOPLE ARE TRANS?

Historically, valid estimates of how many people are trans have been hard to come by. However, in 2017, researchers from the Williams Institute at the UCLA School of Law published a report estimating that in the US, roughly 150,000 people ages 13 to 17 identify as trans, along with an estimated 1.4 million adults.

Unfortunately, many people are still ignorant of the feelings and experiences of trans and nonbinary people. But counseling support and accurate information about being transgender and nonbinary *are* out there. In fact, gender therapists and gender counselors are more widely available than ever before.

If you're transgender or think you might be, it's important to reach out and seek help. Not because something is wrong with you, but because addressing trans issues is much easier if you have support and access to resources. People who identify as nonbinary may also benefit from counseling support.

## What Does It Mean to Be Transgender or Nonbinary?

When you're transgender, you have a gender identity or expression that is different from your sex assigned at birth. A few definitions might be helpful here. A binary gender identity is your internal sense of being male or female. A nonbinary gender identity means you do not identify as male or female, or you may identify as both. Your gender expression is how you express your gender identity and includes the clothes you wear, your hairstyle, and your body language (how you walk, your posture, your gestures). In society, people often assume a person's anatomical sex or gender identity based on the person's gender expression.

### BEEN THERE

"From a very early age I knew I was different. I always preferred dressing up as a princess rather than a police officer or fireman. This carried on through my childhood and into my teenage years, when I became increasingly frustrated about not being able to be the girl I wanted to be. When I came out to my parents, I explained that I never felt right as a male and that I always wanted to be a girl." —Alycia, 19

In recent decades, we've tended to describe trans people as those who have a gender identity that doesn't match their anatomical sex. This is actually a simplistic and not altogether accurate description of what it means to be trans. Talk to people who identify as trans or nonbinary and you'll quickly learn that there simply isn't one easy way to describe the experience for everyone. Even many members of the LGBTQ community have been slow to realize that it's best to let trans and nonbinary people define for themselves the vast range of their experiences. (For example, many trans and nonbinary people say that their experience of gender is limitless.) That said, this chapter aims to provide definitions and information to help give context to these ideas, while at the same time acknowledging the limitations of language and the many different experiences that exist.

What it feels like to be trans is different for every person. Some have described it as feeling "trapped in the wrong body" (though as society grows more aware and accepting of trans experiences, this description is becoming less common). Others describe it more as having an internal sense of self that isn't reflected on the outside by their bodies. And still others describe it as an expansive, evolved feeling of not being limited to one gender. Many people report that the experience of being trans or nonbinary can be incredibly liberating, freeing them from stereotypes about how gender is defined, expressed, and felt.

### GENDER RESOURCES

An excellent resource addressing a full range of topics within the huge category of gender is Sam Killermann's *A Guide to Gender: The Social Justice Advocate's Handbook*. Killermann's illustrations of the Genderbread Person have helped popularize it as a way to explain the continuum of gender and sexuality. Check out the book (and learn more about Sam) at www.guidetogender.com. You can also check out his TED Talk, "Understanding the Complexities of Gender," on YouTube. Another excellent TED Talk is "Hey Doc, Some Boys Are Born Girls," in which Decker Moss talks about his experiences as a trans person.

## Trans Q&A

You might have a lot of questions about what it means to be transgender. If you do, you're not alone. While the LGBTQ community as a whole is working for greater visibility and more rights, lesbian, gay, and bisexual people still tend to receive more recognition and acceptance than those who are trans. As a result, it's still common for people to be uninformed about trans issues. This sometimes is true even within the queer community.

Here are some common questions and answers about being transgender or nonbinary:

**Q: Why are people transgender or nonbinary?**
**A:** According to PFLAG, many in the scientific community believe that being transgender is the result of complicated biological factors that are determined by the time someone is born. Others describe gender as a "performance." This view holds that gender isn't truly rooted in biology. Instead, we're socialized to believe that there are only two genders and that each of us must be one or the other of these.

**Q: Is being transgender a mental disorder?**
**A:** Being transgender is not a mental disorder. The mental health community labels one aspect of the trans experience as *gender dysphoria*—a term for the pain, anxiety, and confusion that can result when a person's gender identity and the sex assigned to them at birth don't match. The pressure to conform to accepted gender roles and expression and a general lack of acceptance from society also can contribute to gender dysphoria.

Mental health professionals used to diagnose trans people with gender identity disorder (GID), a diagnosis that helped people access mental and physical treatment, which was especially helpful for those trying to physically transition their genders. However, many trans people struggled with the stigma of being diagnosed with something termed to be a disorder. In addition, another criticism of GID was that it reinforced the gender binary.

In the most recent version of the *Diagnostic and Statistical Manual of Mental Disorders (DSM-5),* GID was reclassified as gender dysphoria. While gender dysphoria is a mental health diagnosis, it doesn't mean there's something "wrong" with a person who receives this diagnosis. In fact, naming the experience can often help people access the support and care they need.

**BEEN THERE**

"Dealing with dysphoria is awful, along with having to hear the wrong pronouns or name sometimes. But even though being trans is not fun or easy, I'm proud of how far I've come and will continue to go. I also really enjoy educating others in the LGBTQ community." —Jayson, 16

It's also important to know that these definitions and diagnoses are in flux. For example, in 2018 the World Health Organization changed its *International Classification of Diseases,* moving gender diagnoses out of the mental disorders section and into a new chapter called "Conditions Related to Sexual Health." The new diagnosis—gender incongruence—is not considered a mental disorder.

**Q: Do all trans people want to have surgery to change their anatomies?**

**A:** No. Many people do, but others do not. According to the American Society of Plastic Surgeons, in 2016, more than 3,200 people in the US had gender confirmation surgery (also referred to as gender reassignment surgery or gender affirmation surgery). This number was up 20 percent from 2015, likely due to increased access to comprehensive healthcare for trans people.

Many trans people go through a period of gender transition. During this time, they begin to change their appearances, and often their bodies, to match their gender identities. This might mean that they start wearing different clothing and changing their hairstyles to reflect their true genders. People may also change how they walk or move and adjust the sound of their voices. Many take hormones and undergo minor cosmetic procedures like electrolysis (permanent body hair removal).

Gender transition doesn't necessarily mean surgery. It is a misconception that all trans people want to change their anatomies through surgeries that modify primary sex characteristics (the genitals) and secondary sex characteristics (such as breasts or the Adam's apple). People who don't identify with the sex they were assigned at birth might change their bodies to reconcile their gender identities with their anatomies, but not all do.

**Q: What does intersex mean?**

**A:** *Intersex* is a broad term that describes a variety of conditions that result in people having physical characteristics or reproductive organs that do not fit historic definitions of male or female. Examples include a person who appears to have external female anatomy but whose internal reproductive organs are male and a person who has some cells with XX (female) chromosomes and some with XY (male) chromosomes. It's possible for a person not to know they are intersex until puberty, or even to never know.

**A VICTORY FOR TRANS PEOPLE**

On February 2, 2010, the US Tax Court ruled that Rhiannon O'Donnabhain, a trans woman, should be allowed to deduct the cost of her gender confirmation surgery (about $25,000). O'Donnabhain had deducted the expenses when filing her taxes, but the IRS rejected the deduction on the grounds that the surgery was not medically necessary. In its decision, the US Tax Court stated that the IRS's position was "at best a superficial characterization of the circumstances" that is "thoroughly rebutted by the medical evidence." The legal group GLBTQ Legal Advocates & Defenders represented O'Donnabhain.

Some intersex people have surgeries, often in infancy and throughout childhood, to definitively assign them one anatomical sex. Unfortunately, these surgeries are done without children's consent and don't always result in a physical sex assignment that matches the person's gender identity. As a result, some intersex people grow up with gender identity challenges that mirror those experienced by transgender people. In a 2017 report, the organizations Human Rights Watch and interACT (an intersex youth advocacy organization) stated that such procedures should not be performed on intersex children until and unless the child is able to play an active role in the decision.

Some intersex people opt not to have surgery and instead accept and embrace themselves as being on a physical spectrum that is not limited to traditional ideas of male and female.

**GENDER X**

In 2017, Canada introduced the gender-neutral option *X* (instead of *M* or *F*) for their passports. Australia, Denmark, Germany, Malta, New Zealand, and Pakistan already included the *X* option, and still other countries (India, Ireland, and Nepal) allow some other third-gender designation. In the US, Washington, D.C., and Oregon approved the *X* designation for their driver's licenses in 2017. Also in 2017, as part of a bill dubbed the Gender Recognition Act, California lawmakers decided to allow *nonbinary* as a third gender option on official state identification documents.

## BEEN THERE

"I never felt female, but I was often told to act more ladylike. I wasn't sure what that meant. Eventually, I grew into my own skin, started testosterone, and became simply me—neither male nor female. I think it's confusing for people to understand that in my case, I'd be viewed as a straight trans man. It means I was female assigned at birth and now I appear masculine and date women. However, I self-identify as queer." —Leo, 35

**Q: Are trans people also lesbian, gay, or bisexual?**
**A:** It's a common misconception that transgender people are all lesbian, gay, or bisexual. Some trans and nonbinary people identify as straight and others do not. This is another area in which LGBTQ people have long been asked to define themselves, their gender, and their sexual orientation relative to a mainstream culture that considers straight and cis people the norm. In reality, trans people (like all people) can have a wide range of sexual identities that might not easily be labeled as gay, lesbian, sexual, or straight.

## BEEN THERE

"I spent a period of my life going out with other girls, as lesbians. But something didn't quite feel right. I've always wanted to be a guy, physically." —Kevin, 18

**Q: If being trans is about gender identity instead of sexual orientation, why are trans people usually lumped together with lesbian, gay, and bisexual people?**
**A:** Trans and nonbinary people share much of the same struggle for acceptance, recognition, and civil rights as lesbian, gay, and bisexual people. The issues of gender expression and sexual orientation often overlap. Frequently, anti-queer bias and behavior have a lot to do with gender expression (rather than sexual orientation).

For example, a person who identifies as female who wears her hair cut close and prefers to wear what's perceived as traditionally male clothing might be harassed or called a lesbian because she's stepping outside old-fashioned gender roles. In this case, people aren't really reacting to her sexual orientation; they're responding to her gender expression. Some people feel threatened or afraid and might discriminate or get angry when they see people expressing gender in nontraditional ways. (Some of this hostility may arise from a deep-seated fear of change or from not understanding how society is evolving.) Lesbian, gay, bisexual, and trans people often face this same discrimination when they don't conform to other people's ideas of gender. It's also possible for straight/cis people to face this form of discrimination.

**ENBY ON TV**

In 2017, the show *Billions* featured television's first openly nonbinary (enby) character, played by enby actor Asia Kate Dillon. When Taylor (the name of the character) first appears, they say, "Hello, sir. My name is Taylor. My pronouns are *they*, *theirs*, and *them*."

Trans people, at times, even face discrimination from the lesbian, gay, and bisexual communities, even though trans activists including Sylvia Rivera and Marsha P. Johnson—subject of the 2017 documentary *The Life and Death of Marsha P. Johnson*—played major roles in the Stonewall riots (see page 83) and the subsequent LGBTQ rights movement. Historically, this discrimination was largely due to a lack of understanding about trans issues and an unwillingness to work together for greater acceptance of all LGBTQ people. Fortunately, today's LGBTQ community continues to grow more inclusive overall of different gender identities and sexual orientations.

**GENDER IN NATIVE CULTURES**

In North America, many Native American groups have special words, and even hold reverence, for people who today might be characterized as gender-diverse. Many Native American Tribes traditionally referred to these people as "Two Spirits." According to Kelley Blair—CEO and executive director of the Diversity Center of Oklahoma, Native Gender Therapist, and Two-Spirit person—many Tribes believed in poly-gendered systems with three to five different gender roles (though this definition varies somewhat across cultures). Two-Spirit people were often revered as healers, peacemakers, and shamans. Traditionally, a Two-Spirit identity was tied only to gender and had no correlation to sexual orientation. Over the course of history, due to colonization and genocide, many Native traditions—including a belief in the Two-Spirit idea—were lost as Native people adopted European concepts. Today, some Native trans and nonbinary people proudly claim a Two-Spirit identity. Depending on their geographic location and tribal affirmation, these people may include sexual orientation as part of their identity.

The *mahu* are a third gender in Hawaii and include people who exhibit both feminine and masculine traits. Historically, the mahu were guardians of important information, including knowledge of healing plants.

South Asia's *hijras* are called "the third caste" and have a history dating back some 4,000 years. Classically, hijras were respected as spiritual figures. Of those who comprise the hijras, some are trans, some are intersex, and some are eunuchs (men who have been castrated). In 2014, India's Supreme Court declared that hijras would be recognized on official documents under a third gender category. There is similar legislation in Nepal, Pakistan, and Bangladesh.

## Describing Your Gender Identity

Because *transgender* is a blanket term that covers several distinct but related groups of people, self-description can be important to many trans people. People who are transgender may use a variety of different terms to describe themselves.

**BEEN THERE**

"I identify as a transgender guy. I use *he/him* pronouns, but I also believe that gender isn't really a thing. Basically, I want to be perceived and treated as you would any cisgender man, but I also have strong feelings of being gender neutral. Sexuality wise, I really dig the words *queer* and *demisexual* as I feel like they most accurately describe me." —Jayson, 16

In the end, how a person identifies is a very personal decision. No one but the individual can choose what label to use. People choose to identify in many different ways: transgender, female-to-male (FTM), male-to-female (MTF), genderqueer, gender-neutral, multi-gender, trans man, and many others. How you identify (if you choose to identify at all) should be, first and foremost, comfortable and meaningful for you.

## How Do You Know? Figuring Out If You're Trans or Nonbinary

As with figuring out if you're lesbian, gay, or bisexual, self-discovery around gender identity is a process. Maybe you've felt like someone of a different sex or gender for as long as you can remember. Maybe you don't feel like you identify strongly with being male or female—or you identify as both. You might arrive at the conclusion that you're trans or nonbinary relatively easily. Or, it could take months or even years before it's clear, and that's okay.

There isn't a checklist that can clearly indicate whether you're trans, but trans people do tend to share certain common experiences. Perhaps some of these are familiar to you.

**Have you ever felt like you don't fit the typical "boy/girl" experience of gender?** People have sometimes described the experience of being trans as feeling like their body doesn't match with what they feel inside, or feeling that they're in the "wrong body." This is problematic, however, because it's based on the idea that the gender binary is the norm. The reality is that we can all have experiences of gender and sexual orientation that don't have to relate to cultural norms. Today's young people, because of increased openness toward exploring a variety of gender roles and ways of expressing gender identity, more often describe being trans or nonbinary as feeling gender neutral, gender fluid, or simply "other."

### BEEN THERE

"I came out to my family at the age of 15 as a lesbian. At the same time, I was questioning whether I was really a boy or girl. Many times I would let the issue go and then come back to it. Finally, at 25, I was ready to really try to figure it out." —Lee, 26

**Pro tip:** Explore culture's influence on life experiences. One question to consider is this: Do you think trans people would describe conflicted feelings about their identities if social and cultural ideas of gender were more open and expansive? Identify some other common societal standards (norms for styles of dress and language, for instance) and discuss how some people challenge those standards, along with how those folks are viewed or treated.

Part of being a teen is evolving into a stronger sense of yourself. If you're lucky, that evolution continues for years, or even an entire lifetime as you keep growing, learning, and experiencing new things. What matters most is that you understand that whoever you are is okay—better than okay, even!—at *any* stage of your life.

### BEEN THERE

"When I was a kid, everyone else seemed to know they were boys or girls or men or women. That's something I have never known; not then, not today. As a kid, I just figured I was the crazy one; I was the one who really had some serious defect." —Kate Bornstein, writer and performer, from *Gender Outlaw: On Men, Women, and the Rest of Us*

### TRANS AND NONBINARY HISTORICAL FIGURES

They may not show up in your school textbooks, but history is packed with well-known gender benders, some of whom may have been trans or nonbinary. Queen Hatshesut, a pharaoh from Egypt's 18th dynasty, frequently presented as a man. Some statuary shows her as a male with distinctly female breasts. Joan of Arc—who has been canonized as a saint in the Roman Catholic Church—dressed in traditionally masculine clothes. King Henry III of France often cross-dressed and was referred to as "Her Majesty" when dressed as a woman. In the early 1800s, Bíawacheeitchish, the Native American Crow nation's "Woman Chief," dressed as a woman, but took on what were considered male pursuits. She led war parties and was renowned for her fighting skills.

**Do you have thoughts of wanting to be a different physical sex?** It's one thing to occasionally have a thought like, "Life would be easier if I were a guy," or, "I wonder what it would be like to be a girl?" It's another to have a persistent desire to change your name, your pronouns, or your body to better match how you feel inside.

### BEEN THERE

"I've always been fascinated with the idea of being a girl, I guess. I used to watch this show about a boy who suddenly acquires the ability to become a girl when he comes into contact with hot water. I could never really understand, though, why he was so very distressed about being a girl." —Chris, 19

**Do you identify strongly with experiences of people who are transgender or nonbinary?** One way to explore your gender identity is to find out more about trans and nonbinary people. It can be helpful to read about their experiences or talk with someone who identifies as trans or nonbinary. You could find that, while people have different experiences of being trans, what they're talking about really resonates with you and is something you can identify with.

### DIRT DIVA

Professional mountain bike racer Michelle Dumaresq is a trans woman who entered her sport in 2001, six years after completing gender confirmation surgery. She appeared in *Dirt Divas*, a film about female mountain bikers, and is the subject and star of the documentary *100% Woman*. Dumaresq's participation in female competitions has not been without controversy, as some believe she has an unfair advantage since she was born male. Dumaresq has commented, "I never set out to change the world or anything. I just want to race a bike." The topic of trans people competing in sports continues to grow in visibility with stories about athletes such as runner Caster Semenya, who was pressured to take a gender test to prove she could compete with other female runners.

**Pro tip:** The subject of trans and nonbinary athletes would make a great topic for a class project or debate.

## Now What? Options for Trans and Nonbinary Teens

If you do realize you're trans or nonbinary, what then? This is a complex question with many possible answers. You could wait and think about things, taking more time before you decide on any course of action. You could come out as transgender or nonbinary. You could decide to change your name or to start dressing differently. Or, you could decide that you need your body to reflect your identity and start looking into puberty blockers or hormones.

### DELAYING PUBERTY

Some teens who identify as trans wish to delay the onset of puberty, which is when the body releases sex hormones responsible for the formation of secondary sex characteristics, such as body hair or breasts, a changed voice, and menstruation. Puberty blockers (also called puberty suppressors or puberty inhibitors) are a group of medications that inhibit the onset of puberty. Some young trans people opt to take the drugs to allow them time to further explore their identities before developing these sex characteristics and to decrease gender dysphoria. However, some people in the medical community consider it controversial to give young people medications to slow their development. While some argue that the effects of the blockers are completely reversible, others are concerned that there is not enough data on side effects and long-term outcomes to be sure. One thing *is* for certain: Puberty blockers should only be used under the supervision of a qualified and trusted medical professional.

But the first thing you'll need to do is accept yourself. Try to resist any urges you might have to label yourself as odd or abnormal. This can be difficult for some people, but being a trans person definitely does not mean something is wrong with you. In fact, by being who they are, trans and nonbinary people are making the world more open and inclusive for all people—both LGBTQ and straight/cis. Still, it might take time to come to terms with being trans, and you might need help to work through what being trans means for your future.

## Coping with Negative Emotions

Even if you've realized and accepted that you're trans or nonbinary, your process probably isn't over. A disparity between your gender

### TRANS ORGANIZATIONS

All the major LGBTQ organizations (including the Human Rights Campaign, GLSEN, GLAAD, and Lambda Legal) include specific information and resources for trans and nonbinary people. Following are some trans-specific organizations.

**Gender Spectrum (www.genderspectrum.org).** This website provides practical information to help teens and their families understand the concepts of gender identity and expression. It includes a wealth of resources, links, and other media (including materials in Spanish).

**National Center for Transgender Equality (transequality.org).** This social justice advocacy organization for trans people works for policy change to support trans people and their families. It offers a variety of services, including legal assistance and opportunities for trans people to tell their stories.

**Transgender Law Center (transgenderlawcenter.org).** This organization operates litigation, policy, and educational efforts in support of trans and nonbinary people. They have specific programs for young people, including a national trans and gender nonconforming storytelling program called TRUTH.

**Transgender Legal Defense & Education Fund (transgenderlegal.org).** TLDEF works to end discrimination and achieve equality for trans people. Among their programs is the Name Change Project, which helps low-income trans people in certain cities legally change their names.

**Trans Youth Equality Foundation (www.transyouthequality.org).** TYEF provides education, advocacy, and support for trans teens and their families, including a School Action Center.

**World Professional Association for Transgender Health (www.wpath.org).** WPATH publishes the standards of care for trans and gender nonconforming people, which include clinical guidance for health professionals.

identity and your physical self can create challenges since it's not something that simply goes away once you accept yourself. Because you're working through identity issues that can be very complicated and intense, it's important to get help. Here are some ways to do that.

### LOVING YOUR BODY

Most of us struggle with loving our bodies at some point (or many points) in our lives, but if you feel that your physical body doesn't represent who you are inside, the struggle can take on a different dimension. Taking part in body-positive activities like therapeutic yoga, dance, or getting massages or other body-work from an open-minded, skilled, and licensed professional can go a long way toward boosting your body love. There are even some businesses designed especially for this purpose, such as Freed Bodyworks in Washington, D.C., which specializes in massage therapy "for all bodies." Founder and owner Frances Reed identifies as genderqueer, and many of the other therapists on staff also have queer or nonbinary identities.

**Find support.** You might reach out to family members, friends, adults at school, or others you trust. It's important to find support from others who are nonjudgmental. The people you talk to should listen to you and your feelings with your best interests in mind, not push their own agendas onto you. Talk with people who will take time with you and who won't discount your feelings as a phase. Even if you have support from family and friends, it's a good idea to talk with a trained professional at some point—preferably someone knowledgeable about transgender issues. Being transgender can evoke a lot of complex feelings, and it's helpful to talk to someone who understands that.

### BEEN THERE

"I get support from my closest friends or sometimes my parents, mostly my dad. I also have ways to contact my therapist, who is amazing and does everything he can to help me." —Jayson, 16

If you don't feel comfortable talking with someone you know, don't give up. A lot of resources are available to you. In addition to national organizations, many local groups support young people who are trans and nonbinary. A variety of websites have bulletin boards, forums, or chats where you can communicate with other trans people. See page 47 for some resources.

**Seek counseling.** Researcher and trans activist Jessica Xavier advises trans people to seek counseling, not because something is wrong with them that needs to be changed, but because it's a way to get needed support. This therapy should focus on helping you understand, accept, and feel good about your identity. According to a 2014 study by the Williams Institute at the UCLA School of Law, 41 percent of trans and gender nonconforming individuals attempt suicide at some point in their lives, compared with 4.6 percent of the general population. It's not only okay, but *critical* to know when you need support. *We don't want to lose you.*

It's common for people to feel uncomfortable about gender issues and to internalize fears about trans people. A skilled counselor can address these issues and help you understand that absolutely nothing is wrong with who you are. You might start your search for a counselor by contacting a local or national LGBTQ or trans organization. And it's cool to talk to several counselors before deciding who's right for you. It's important to choose someone you feel truly comfortable with.

### CAMP ARANU'TIQ

Ever wish you could be around others who understand what it's like to be trans? Camp Aranu'tiq is a weeklong, tuition-free, overnight summer camp held in Southern New England for transgender and gender variant young people ages 8 to 15. *Aranu'tiq* is a Chugach (an indigenous people of Alaska) word for a person thought to embody both the male and female spirit. Such people were revered because of their abilities to transcend traditional gender norms. For more information, visit www.camparanutiq.org.

But wait, there's more! There are a variety of other camps for trans and gender nonconforming young people. Check out www.transstudent.org/camps for a full list.

## Coming Out

After you realize you're trans, you might decide to come out. It could be to only a few close friends or family members, or it could be to many people. Coming out is particularly important if you want to start living in a way that better reflects your gender identity. Transgender people who wish to transition their genders usually have to come out because changes will be obvious to others.

Coming out as trans—whatever the circumstances are—can be stressful for everyone involved. And similar to when someone comes out as lesbian, gay, or bisexual, the people you're coming out to might react in many different ways. Some may be accepting, while others might be confused, sad, or angry. (See chapter 4 for advice on coming out.) The people you're coming out to also might be confused if you've previously come out to them as lesbian, gay, or bisexual.

Parents especially might have serious difficulties dealing with their children coming out as transgender. Some believe they're losing a son or daughter. When a teen says that they want to live as someone of a different gender (or no gender or multiple genders), family adults might experience feelings of grief similar to those a person feels when a loved one dies. It might feel like the daughter or son they raised has suddenly been taken from them.

The people you come out to might not understand what it means to be transgender and may have a lot of questions for you. It can be hard for your parents and other people who care about you to learn that you've been struggling with such difficult issues. They might worry about you and your future. They might also want to help and support you.

When you come out, it's important to let your family and loved ones know that resources are available to help them, too. One book that can help parents or guardians understand what you're experiencing is *Helping Your Transgender Teen: A Guide for Parents* by Irwin Krieger, a clinical social worker who works with trans teens and their families.

Many national transgender organizations will help you find local support via websites or phone referrals. Your local phone directory might list additional resources. PFLAG also offers resources for trans people and their families and friends, including two excellent brochures: *Welcoming Our Trans Family and Friends* and *Our Trans Loved Ones: Questions and Answers for Parents, Families, and Friends of People Who Are Transgender and Gender Expansive.* (See page 47 for a list of trans and nonbinary resources.)

## BEEN THERE

"Coming out trans was the most nerve-racking thing I have ever done. I had my doubts about it, but I had made up my mind that it had to be done. My parents were shocked, as I expected, but they seemed to be happy that I'd told them. We talked about the possibilities for me for hours. They said as long as I'm happy, they'd support me in whatever I wanted to do." —Alycia, 19

"It was clear to me as a teenager that my parents wouldn't accept me being queer or trans. At first, I was terrified, but then I found adults that supported me, such as teachers and coworkers. Still, even today, I struggle with the idea that I'll never make my parents proud." —Leo, 35

"My dad discovered I was trans when he saw some sites I'd been looking at online. He eventually just said, 'So, let's talk about what you look at on the internet.' This was my cue to explain to him everything. He asked a lot of questions. He was very curious about me. He had done an amazing amount of research on the internet himself. He looked up gender confirmation surgery doctors, including how much the procedure would cost. He found out all he could on hormones, and he even contacted a male-to-female trans person for information that might help me out. It did. It helped me immensely just to know that there is someone who cares about me." —Amanda, 18

## Changing Names

Many trans people change their names to better reflect their gender identities. As a teen, you can't legally change your name without a parent's consent (unless you've been emancipated—freed from legal control by your parents or guardians). But many teens change their names in practice, asking families and friends to use their preferred names.

Changing your name to one that reflects who you are can be a positive way to assert your true identity. It can sometimes be difficult to get people to take your name change seriously or to accept it. Some family members, friends, and school officials will be very supportive and accepting. Others will reject the idea completely.

If you're certain that you are transgender or nonbinary and you're thinking about changing your name, here are some things to consider:

**Come out first.** Telling your family and friends that you're trans or nonbinary and, in the same breath, asking them to call you by a different name can be a lot for people to process. It's likely that they'll have a lot of questions about what it means to be trans. If you can help them understand that, they may be in a better place to understand why you want to change your name. However, if they seem fairly receptive to your coming out, you might want to discuss your name of choice right away. It's up to you, but it can be helpful to take it one step at a time and allow your family and friends to do the same.

**Try to be patient.** Some people will be respectful of your request that they use your new name. Others will not. Even those who are respectful may need time to get used to the change.

According to clinical psychologist Dr. Sandra Loiterstein, a name change can be very difficult for parents to accept. They may see it as a rejection of something very personal they gave their child. Changing names can also deepen the grieving process many parents of trans people go through because it can emphasize the feeling of loss.

If your parents are struggling, it can be helpful for you and your parents to go together to see a therapist who is knowledgeable about gender issues. If your parents agree to this, counseling can help your family understand what you're facing and adjust to your trans identity.

**Choose your name carefully.** Put some thought into your new name. Choose one that's representative of your personality or meaningful for you in some way. Some trans people choose names that are traditionally feminine or masculine versions of their birth names. So Bill becomes Belinda, and Charlotte becomes Charles. Others choose gender-neutral names, such as Alex or Chris. Some people might choose another name entirely. The most important thing is that you pick a name that feels like you.

**If you want to change the name you use at school, get your parents' support.** It can be difficult to get teachers and staff at school to use your new name, but having a parent or guardian backing you up can help. They can be sources of support as you're talking with your principal, school counselor, or teachers. Sometimes changing your name at school is easier if you're starting classes in a different building or a new grade. People might have less to associate with your previous name.

Some trans teens choose to use their birth names at school (or have to if their school refuses to use their new names) and their chosen names at other times, depending on who they're with and where they are. And some trans teens decide to wait until they're older to change their names, either legally or in everyday life. In most cases, your parent or guardian also will have to be on board if you want to have the school change your name and gender on your official school records.

**BEING MISGENDERED**

When someone accidentally or even purposefully uses your birth name or misgenders you (by using the wrong pronouns, for example), try to remember this: It's not personal. Even when intentional, others' actions are reflections of *them*. It can still be super upsetting when people behave this way. But in the end, it just shows you where they are on their paths, and you can let them own that instead of letting it derail you. (We all need a little compassion now and again!) The coming chapters will provide you with some constructive ways to deal with these kinds of situations.

## Gender Transitioning

Gender transitioning is a complex, multistep process of starting to live full-time as a person of a different gender. Transitioning doesn't, by definition, include surgery, hormones, or other physical changes. However, for some people, some or all of those elements are part of their transition. Transitioning primarily involves factors that affect how you relate to others and how they relate to you. It might include changing your name, dressing differently, and altering other aspects of your appearance (like your hair or makeup). It can also mean changing your mannerisms, voice, and how you move.

A physical transition might include taking hormones, puberty blockers, or other medications under the supervision of a medical professional. For some, transitioning may also include surgery. This is an option sometimes reserved for adults, though this isn't always the case. As a trans teen, you may be less likely to have access to gender confirmation surgery, but you could work with an endocrinologist who can assist you with hormone treatments or puberty blockers.

**BEEN THERE**

"Perhaps it all began when I was a child, maybe six years old, watching Saturday morning cartoons—specifically Bugs Bunny donning a dress and wig. I was enthralled at the transformation. This, I decided, was what I would aspire to. That's as far back as I can recall about my 'difference.'" —Zelia, 15

## Physical Transitioning

Undergoing a physical gender transition can be a long and complex process. For some trans people who wish to undergo a surgical change, it can be a vital and rewarding process. But gender confirmation surgeries also are expensive, and many people save for a long time to afford them (though more insurance policies are starting to cover a broad range of care for trans people).

The physical transitioning process takes a long time for many reasons. Some physical changes take months or even years to complete. Medical professionals generally supervise the physical transitioning process, and they can help you explore feelings and decisions along the way.

If you want to transition physically, especially if you want to pursue surgery, you'll want to know about Standards of Care (SOC), which are clinical guidelines for treating trans patients who wish to undergo pharmaceutical or surgical transition.

The most commonly used SOC in the US are from the World Professional Association for Transgender Health (or WPATH, see page 47). They call for a period of psychotherapy (to confirm that physically transitioning is a positive and appropriate step), the beginning of hormone therapy (which is a lifelong process), the administration of the Real-Life Experience (living full-time as a person of your true gender identity for a period of time), and finally, if desired, gender confirmation surgery.

The therapy and assessment period can last for three months or longer, depending on the mental health professional and the person receiving treatment. During this time, a person might feel like the validity of their trans identity is being questioned. It can be frustrating to feel like others are second-guessing something you're very certain about. Try to release those feelings in a positive way, perhaps by writing about them in a journal. (See chapter 9 for more ideas for dealing with difficult feelings.) However, a good and experienced counselor can help you deal with any fears and frustrations around the SOC or otherwise.

### BEEN THERE

"I think the most difficult part of being transgender is the way my gender identity and my body just don't match. It's a constant source of frustration and annoyance for me. I'm not currently on hormones because I have not had enough counseling yet. One of the things that annoys me most is others having the attitude that they have to protect a young trans person from herself."
—Rylan, 19

The Real-Life Experience (RLE) is a period of time during which a transitioning person lives and works full time as someone of their true gender identity. For example, a female-to-male person would live as a man. According to WPATH's standards of care, the purpose of the RLE is "to allow you to overcome awkwardness, establish new behavior patterns, and approach unfamiliar situations with an unforced inner confidence." The experience is designed to confirm for the person that they truly want to make the physical transition and are mentally and emotionally prepared to handle it.

However, while the Real-Life Experience is the SOC guideline, not all therapists require it. In fact, more and more medical professionals are embracing a model of "informed consent." This means that physicians and therapists provide trans people with lots of facts and information about transitioning and what it may mean for their lives—physically, mentally, and emotionally—and then allow them to make their own decisions about hormone replacement therapy or gender confirmation surgery.

Gender confirmation surgery involves the permanent refashioning of a person's sexual anatomy. Beyond genital surgery, many trans people undergo additional procedures. Male-to-female trans people might have facial and body hair removed, an operation to reduce the size of the Adam's apple, and various other cosmetic surgeries to achieve a more classically feminine-looking face and body. Some might also have breast augmentation surgery, though many just rely on their hormone treatments (which cause the body to develop breasts) and/or surgery on their genitalia. Female-to-male trans people might have their breasts removed (often called "top surgery").

Some teens get impatient with the transitioning process or find it difficult to obtain hormones or puberty blockers from a doctor or clinic, so they buy the drugs on the street or online. This could have serious negative physical and legal consequences. As with other drugs, hormones and puberty blockers bought outside official medical channels could contain anything. Also, their strength and dosage are unknown. These drugs should be taken only under the supervision of a doctor, preferably an endocrinologist, and at the proper dosage (which varies from person to person). Even if you're understandably frustrated or impatient with your situation, it isn't worth risking your health.

## Facing Discrimination

Social pressures to conform to gender stereotypes can be extreme. Because gender expression is so visible and obvious, it's easy to find yourself facing unwanted attention or harassment if you've embraced a nontraditional mode of gender expression. Trans people can be especially vulnerable to harassment and physical abuse. According to GLSEN, trans students and others who challenge traditional gender roles in obvious ways often endure the greatest harassment and the worst physical attacks. While safety is a big concern for lesbian, gay, and bisexual students, it is a huge concern for many trans and nonbinary students.

Just as with lesbian, gay, and bisexual people, discrimination against and abuse of trans people is *never* okay, and it is *never* justifiable. If you have been attacked, report the attack to the police. If the police refuse to recognize your claim or file a report, a national organization such as Lambda Legal (www.lambdalegal.org), the National LGBTQ Task Force (www.thetaskforce.org), or the American Civil Liberties Union (www.aclu.org) might be able to help. Many transgender groups can also help (see page 47). These organizations advocate for trans people and lobby for their legal rights. You do not have to suffer alone or in silence.

In spite of the harsh discrimination many trans people face, increasing numbers of people are coming out as transgender. This increased visibility will help educate others about what it means to be trans. Transgender people can face difficult issues, but many live very meaningful, fulfilled, and happy lives. The most important thing you can do is accept yourself for the wonderful person you are.

**GENDER: A MOVING TARGET**

What is gender? According to sex educator and anthropologist Mala Madrone, the answer to that question depends not only on who you ask, but when you ask. Madrone says one of the reasons gender is so hard to define is that due to its many social components, it's not a static concept. She says, "Culture is a living, growing organism. Like an ecosystem, it's constantly changing. And it's interdependent—as we shift some notions and views, others shift as well. So any definition of gender is really just a snapshot of where a culture is at that moment."

CHAPTER 3

# Homophobia and Transphobia

**Hate is not a family value.**

Even though we know there have been LGBTQ people since the beginning of time, many history books largely ignore queer folks. When LGBTQ people are acknowledged, they are sometimes portrayed as immoral or unnatural. This combination of invisibility and misinformation has contributed to widespread ignorance regarding LGBTQ people. That ignorance often reveals itself as homophobia or transphobia.

Homophobia or transphobia can put a lot of pressure on you, especially at school. You may be comfortable with being LGBTQ, but classmates, teachers, and even friends might be pretty *un*comfortable with it. Some people may even be hateful or violent.

**KNOW YOUR ROOTS**

Whether it's because you're doing a project for your history class or you just want to know more about what life was like for the LGBTQ people who came before you, *Gay & Lesbian History for Kids: The Century-Long Struggle for LGBT Rights* by Jerome Pohlen is a great resource packed with fascinating and sometimes little-known information about queer people.

Homophobia and transphobia can make you feel terrible—all you want to do is be yourself, but it seems like no one wants to let you. They can also inspire you to try changing the world. Either way, the absolute most important thing to remember is that *these phobias are not about you.* They're about other people and their ignorance. They're not based on who you really are, but on misconceptions and untruths about what it means to be LGBTQ. Homophobia or transphobia might cause you problems in life, but it's not *your* problem. You didn't do anything to bring it on or to deserve it. Increased awareness and visibility help, but if you're not straight or cis (or even if you're simply perceived not to be), it's likely you'll experience some form of subtle or overt homophobia or transphobia in your life. It's helpful to educate yourself on where homophobia and transphobia come from and how to deal with them.

So where *do* these phobias come from and, if there's nothing wrong with LGBTQ people, why don't they just go away?

**BEEN THERE**

"I'm like everyone else. I'm still human and I still have feelings. The hard part is when ignorant people say you choose to be this way and that it's your fault and it's wrong. It makes you feel like a target." —Shannon, 20

## The 411 on Hate: The Roots of Homophobia and Transphobia

Homophobia and transphobia are emotions like fear, anger, or suspicion—or a combination of these—toward someone because the person is LGBTQ (or is perceived to be). These feelings are rooted in ignorance about LGBTQ people.

## From Uncomfortable to Hateful: Shades of Homophobia and Transphobia

Homophobia and transphobia have degrees ranging from mild to severe (none of which are okay). They can be overt, like someone shouting "dyke!" or "fag!" in the hall, calling you a "trannie" or a "he/she," or using the expression, "That's so gay!" They can also be subtle, like a teammate quietly avoiding being near you in the locker room.

But people who are ignorant about what it means to be LGBTQ *can* change their negative ideas when they learn more about what it actually means to be queer. Many who are homophobic or transphobic change their views after a friend or loved one comes out and they see that, in most ways, LGBTQ people are just like everyone else. It can help them begin to understand that we're all human beings and that drawing arbitrary distinctions among us based on who we are attracted to or love, how we dress, or what pronouns we use is just silly.

### SPOTLIGHT ON CYBERBULLYING

In 2010, 18-year-old Rutgers University student Tyler Clementi jumped to his death from the George Washington Bridge after his roommate used a webcam to film Clementi kissing another man and then posted the video on Twitter. The roommate was federally indicted and ended up pleading guilty to a count of invasion of privacy. Clementi's death brought national attention to the issue of LGBTQ young people and cyberbullying.

For others, homophobia and transphobia are more deeply rooted and manifest as hatred of LGBTQ people. These individuals may act out in ways that range from lobbying for anti-queer legislation to bullying and physically hurting LGBTQ people. While many homophobic and transphobic people would never dream of physically hurting another human being, heartbreaking incidents like Matthew Shepard's brutal murder in 1998 in Laramie, Wyoming; the 2016 mass shooting at Pulse Nightclub in Orlando, Florida; the tragic murders of Brandi Seals in 2017 and countless other trans women of color throughout the years; and widespread occurrences of queer young people committing suicide because of anti-LGBTQ bullying show that a lot of hatred still exists in this world. Such incidents mean that queer people need to think seriously about their safety.

**PREVENTING AND PUNISHING HATE CRIMES**

On October 28, 2009, President Barack Obama signed into federal law an expanded hate crimes bill that includes sexual orientation and gender identity. Known as the Matthew Shepard and James Byrd Jr. Hate Crimes Prevention Act, the legislation was a major step forward for LGBTQ people in the United States. An FBI report from 2015 showed that nearly 18 percent of reported hate crimes were based on sexual orientation, and nearly 2 percent on gender identity or expression.

## Why Are People Homophobic or Transphobic?

The dictionary defines a phobia as an irrational fear. So, by definition, homophobia and transphobia are not based on reason.

According to clinical psychologist Dr. Sandra Loiterstein, who has worked as a support group coordinator for the Washington, D.C., chapter of PFLAG, homophobia can have a variety of sources. One of them, she said in an interview, "is an inability to see LGBTQ people as individuals. Instead, they're seen through stereotypes. Ancient fears of differentness, probably the major source of homophobia, have been perpetuated by religious and other institutions, including mental health organizations."

In some cases, the historic roots of anti-LGBTQ attitudes don't have much to do with homosexuality. In some cultures, any sexual contact between two people that could not result in the conception of a child (such as oral sex) was considered sinful or morally wrong regardless of whether it was between people of different sexes or not. In some cases, it was the act rather than the biological sex of the people engaged in it that was frowned upon. According to *Hidden from History: Reclaiming the Gay & Lesbian Past*, some historians believe that in certain cultures and religions the roots of homophobia and transphobia extend back to such beliefs.

For more information on common fears and myths about LGBTQ people, see pages 25–31 in chapter 1.

## Queer People Can Be Homophobic and Transphobic, Too

Another kind of homophobia or transphobia is called internalized homophobia/transphobia. People with these internalized phobias have difficulty accepting that they are LGBTQ themselves. They feel guilty about who they are or believe that being queer means something is wrong with them. Just like homophobia and transphobia from others, internalized phobias can be overt—from trying to deny feelings of being LGBTQ to trying to "convert" to being straight/cis—or more subtle, such as trying to hide things about yourself that you worry might make it obvious to others that you're queer.

George Weinberg, the psychologist and LGBTQ rights activist who coined the terms *homophobia* and *internalized homophobia*, stated in a 2002 interview in the magazine *Gay Today* that internalized phobias are based on "the dread of being different, of being singled out, punished, or laughed at." Weinberg explained that internalized phobias decrease as people are able to accept themselves for who they are, regardless of what others might think.

### NEGATIVE IMAGES OF LGBTQ PEOPLE IN MOVIES

Hollywood has long been famous for playing off people's fears of LGBTQ people. In *The Celluloid Closet: Homosexuality in the Movies,* Vito Russo explores the history of LGBTQ people in film. He discusses how the portrayal of LGBTQ people in Hollywood movies has run the gamut from invisibility (nope, no queers here) to homophobic and transphobic stereotypes (queer people are silly or scary). From sissies to psychotic killers, you may be surprised at how long certain negative stereotypes about queer people that appear in films today have been around.

## Invisibility as Homophobia and Transphobia

When you're LGBTQ, sometimes you wish people would just stop acting like it's a huge deal. Conversely, there are times when queer people might seem nonexistent. For example, if you identify as a gay male, it can be frustrating, embarrassing, or nerve-racking when relatives or others continually ask, "Do you have a girlfriend yet?"

instead of asking something that makes fewer assumptions, like, "Are you dating anyone special?"

Questions that assume you're straight are classic examples of heteronormativity (also called heterosexism). Heteronormativity is the idea that heterosexual people are the norm and that LGBTQ people are somehow abnormal or inferior. This assumption contributes to homophobia. Cisnormativity (or cissexism) is the idea that cis people are "normal" and that trans folks are somehow abnormal or inferior to cis people. Cisnormativity contributes to transphobia.

**MARRIAGE EQUALITY**

In 2015, the US Supreme Court ruled that marriage between two consenting adults is a basic civil right that should be extended to same-sex couples. The limited marriage rights that existed for same-sex couples before that were an example of heteronormativity.

## The Big Bad World: Homophobia and Transphobia in Society and at School

Have you ever heard of mob mentality? It's when an individual might not normally do something on their own, but because they see a group of other people doing it, they think it must be okay or feel pressure to join in.

One reason homophobia and transphobia are so common is mob mentality. Mob mentality often plays a role when people gang up on LGBTQ teens and bully them in person or online. When a handful of people speak out strongly against LGBTQ people and their ideas go unchallenged, ignorance and hatred can persist and even intensify.

LGBTQ activists all over the world are working to end homophobia and transphobia. In the US, GLAAD (the Gay & Lesbian Alliance Against Defamation) is working to encourage positive, informed portrayals of LGBTQ people in the media. The Human Rights Campaign (HRC) and the National LGBTQ Task Force are working to enact social change by getting legislation passed that protects LGBTQ people and their civil rights. Lambda Legal is working to achieve full recognition of the civil rights of LGBTQ people through work with the legal system and public policy. Internationally, PFLAG is working to increase understanding of and support for

LGBTQ people by changing people's attitudes about queer folks. These are just some of the many groups working to make the world a better place for queer people.

### MARRIAGE RIGHTS AROUND THE WORLD

On July 20, 2005, Canada became the first country in the Americas to recognize same-sex marriage. Other countries with same-sex marriage rights include Argentina, Australia, Belgium, Brazil, Colombia, Croatia, the Czech Republic, Denmark, England, Finland, France, Germany, Greenland, Iceland, Ireland, Luxembourg, Malta, Mexico (in some areas), the Netherlands, New Zealand, Norway, Portugal, Scotland, South Africa, Spain, Sweden, the United States, Uruguay, and Wales. Still other countries, such as Switzerland, allow for same-sex civil unions or registered partnerships.

Every day, people are lobbying legislators to pass queer-friendly laws, such as federal legislation that would prohibit workplace discrimination based on sexual orientation or gender identity. California's Student Safety and Violence Prevention Act states that all California schools have a duty to protect students from discrimination and harassment on the basis of sexual orientation or gender identity. In 2002, student George Loomis, along with a coalition of local groups, PFLAG, the American Civil Liberties Union (ACLU), and the Gay-Straight Alliance Network (GSA Network) used this law as a basis for a successful suit against Loomis's school district for failing to take actions to protect him from harassment.

In 2009, 14-year-old Jacob Sullivan, with the help of the New York Civil Liberties Union, filed suit against the Mohawk Central School District on the grounds that the school district allegedly failed to protect Jacob from ongoing and relentless harassment, physical abuse, and threats of violence based on Jacob's sexual orientation and nonconformity with masculine stereotypes. "People always make fun of what they don't understand, but the school has a responsibility to protect people," Jacob is quoted as saying in an interview. On March 29, 2010, the case was settled and Jacob was awarded $50,000 from the school district.

The Safe Schools Improvement Act (SSIA), which was introduced in the US House of Representatives in 2017, would amend the Elementary and Secondary Education Act (ESEA) to require schools and districts in states receiving ESEA funds to adopt codes of conduct that specifically prohibit bullying and harassment, including bullying and harassment on the basis of sexual orientation or gender identity. SSIA would also require states to report data on bullying and harassment to the Department of Education.

**CANADIAN PRIDE**

Every jurisdiction in Canada (including the Canadian federal government) has a human rights law that explicitly mentions protections based on sexual orientation. Some provincial and territorial human rights laws also mention gender identity and/or expression. In other provinces and territories, gender identity and/or expression are understood to be included in the law.

According to the Canadian Civil Liberties Association, some school boards have adopted specific policies that recognize the unique challenges faced by LGBTQ students, staff, and family members. For example, the Yukon Territory requires all high schools to implement proactive strategies to welcome and include LGBTQ community members and their families. Edmonton Public Schools has a comprehensive policy which stipulates (among other things) that school officials must ensure that staff members appropriately address any sexist, homophobic, or transphobic comments or behaviors. The school board even participates in the Edmonton Pride Festival every year.

## Homophobia and Transphobia in the Hallways: Bullying and Harassment at School

If you've ever been singled out verbally or physically because you're LGBTQ (or perceived to be), you're not alone. According to the *2015 National School Climate Survey* conducted by GLSEN, nearly 60 percent of LGBTQ students reported feeling unsafe at school because of their sexual orientation, and more than 40 percent felt unsafe because of their gender identity or gender expression. More than 70 percent said they avoid school functions because they feel unsafe there, and 65 percent said they don't go to extracurricular activities because of worries about safety. In addition, 27 percent of LGBTQ students surveyed reported experiencing physical harassment (such as being blocked from walking down the hall) based on their sexual orientation, and 20 percent based on their gender expression. Meanwhile, 13 percent reported being physically assaulted (punched, kicked, or otherwise physically hurt) at school in the last year because of their sexual orientation, and 9 percent because of their gender expression.

### LEGISLATIVE UPDATES

**Human Rights Campaign (www.hrc.org).** For updates on the status of bills currently under debate and more information about LGBTQ-related legislation, visit the HRC website. You'll discover that the legislation discussed in this book is just the tip of the iceberg. Many more LGBTQ rights bills are being considered at the state and federal levels.

### BEEN THERE

"When I was in the 11th grade and being harassed constantly in one class, the teacher did nothing. I think that she should have."
—Brian, 19

Legislators, parents, educators, and various activists continue to debate about whether to provide young people in school settings access to information about LGBTQ people. Advocates say that giving students positive and accurate information about LGBTQ issues will reduce bullying and harassment of those who are LGBTQ or are perceived to be. Opponents claim that these efforts encourage and promote queerness. This latter belief hearkens back to one of the commonly held myths about LGBTQ people—that queer people "recruit." (See pages 25–31 for a list of myths—and the truth—about LGBTQ people.)

Many groups including GLSEN, PFLAG, and the HRC have "safe schools" movements where adults and teens work together to make school environments safer for young people who are LGBTQ or are perceived to be. Often these groups work to institute anti-bullying policies that include harassment based on sexual orientation, gender identity, and gender expression. According to GLSEN's 2015 report *From Teasing to Torment: School Climate Revisited*, 87 percent of students surveyed had a general anti-bullying policy in place in their schools. Nearly 55 percent said their school's anti-bullying policy included specific prohibitions against bullying based on sexual orientation or gender identity or expression.

**A MORE INCLUSIVE PRIDE CELEBRATION**

In 1999, President Bill Clinton proclaimed June to be Gay and Lesbian Pride month in the United States. In 2009, President Barack Obama proclaimed June to be National LGBT Pride month, expanding recognition beyond gay people only.

Some schools sponsor assemblies to educate students about LGBTQ people, while others now allow Pride month displays. Some students form gay-straight alliance clubs (GSAs), also called genders and sexualities alliances, to educate others in their schools and work for change. (For more on GSAs and other school issues, see chapter 5 on page 104.)

The safe schools movement is making strides in shining a spotlight on bullying and is helping LGBTQ students feel more welcome and secure at school. However, if you're being bullied or otherwise discriminated against now, it might feel like it will be forever until things change at your school. What can you do to advocate for yourself?

## Responding to Homophobia and Transphobia

Understanding homophobia and transphobia and where they come from is one thing; figuring out what you're going to do about bullying or harassment is another.

Prejudice can show itself in many ways. An LGBTQ teen might be cut from a sports team or dubbed a "troublemaker" by coaches. An administrator could turn a blind eye to bullying or tell a student that they brought it on themselves. A teacher could refuse to use a student's preferred name or pronouns. Whatever the situation, there are a number of possible ways to react to such incidents, ranging from ignoring them to confronting the people involved.

## How Bullying and Harassment Can Make You Feel

Dealing with ongoing harassment and ignorance can make you feel scared, isolated, depressed, angry, or just plain worn out. Sometimes it may feel like fighting homophobia and transphobia is an uphill battle, like things will never get better. Even if you feel comfortable with being LGBTQ and good about yourself overall, facing regular harassment can be extremely difficult and demoralizing.

### BEEN THERE

"Daily, more and more people would use those words—*fag, homo, queer, sissy*. Eventually things moved from not only words, but also to violence and pranks. The word *faggot* was written on the locker next to mine because someone made a mistake about my locker number. People put gum in my hair, stuck papers on my back, and threw things at me. There was physical violence and death threats. The school did 'the best they could do,' as they put it. In my mind, little was done." —Robert, 15

As you'll see in the sections that follow, you can address homophobia and transphobia in many ways. Regardless of how you decide to handle a situation, it's important to remember that you're not to blame for the bad treatment you're receiving, and you're not alone in experiencing homophobia or transphobia. *Remember: These phobias are not about you as an individual—they're about other people and their views.*

Of course, even if you understand that homophobia or transphobia isn't your fault, it can still hurt to be treated that way. It's important to engage in activities that make you feel good about yourself. Writing, drawing, dancing, working out, hanging out with friends . . . the list goes on. Take time to check in with yourself every so often to make sure that others' phobias aren't hurting your self-esteem. For more information on ways to feel healthy and good about who you are, see chapter 9.

In addressing homophobia and transphobia, it's important to understand that you can't control the words and actions of other people. So focus on what you *can* control, which is your response to those words and actions. When determining how best to respond, consider several issues.

## Assessing the Situation

Safety must be your number one concern. Before you decide how to react to homophobia or transphobia, assess the situation:

1. Is the person merely being ignorant? Or do they mean to harm you in some way? Sometimes it's hard to tell, and sometimes it's fairly apparent.
2. Is the person aggressive with their words or body language? Are they threatening you, using an aggressive tone, or moving closer to you? Don't discount your gut instinct—it's usually your best indicator. If you feel even the least bit afraid for your safety, proceed with caution.
3. Has this person harassed you before? If so, has there been an escalation in the harassment? (Perhaps a taunt in the hallway has turned into shoving or worse.)
4. Are you alone, or do you have friends with you? Is there an adult nearby who could help?
5. Where are you? Can you get away? It's important to always know where your exits are.

Homophobia and transphobia stir up a lot of emotions. Even so, it's important to look at the full situation rather than react based on your immediate feelings. Maybe that person in your class wasn't trying to be mean when they made that comment. Maybe they just didn't realize how it sounded or how limited their own experiences are. But the person who bullies you by throwing stuff at you might become increasingly violent in the future.

### BEEN THERE

"My parents signed me up for karate a couple of years ago because I was getting harassed at school. It was scary at first because I didn't know much about it, but now I love it. It's made me more fit and more confident. It's also helped me be a better judge of when a situation might be dangerous so I can either avoid it entirely or get to safety." —Carlos, 16

## Options for Responding

The first option is to turn the other cheek. That's hard to do, because encountering homophobia and transphobia can be so frustrating. Often what you really want to do is lash out, but try to consider the safest, most productive, and most effective ways to respond.

Some people use humor to help them defuse the situation. For example, Nicky, who is gender nonconforming, was at his locker when a passing student observed Nicky's dress and lipstick and shouted, "Dude, *what are you*?" Nicky looked at the student and smiled. "Late for class!" he shouted back, then turned and jogged away.

You can also ignore homophobia or transphobia completely by acting like you didn't hear the remark or by not reacting to the sign stuck on your backpack. Instead, just throw it away. But ignoring or forgiving these actions can be extremely difficult, and it's rarely an option if you're placed in a dangerous situation. And while some choose to respond with humor or turn the other cheek, homophobia is serious business, and you shouldn't feel like you have to laugh it off or ignore it.

### BEEN THERE

"I was just doing my thing at my locker when a group of girls came up to me and one said, 'You're a dyke.' I looked back at her and smiled and said, 'You say that like it's a bad thing.' She was stunned. She just looked at me for a minute, then turned and walked away." —Anna, 17

## Speaking Up

Speaking up is another option. Again, consider the situation—engaging with the person or people should be limited to situations when it would be, or at least could be, productive. (Sometimes productive simply means that it makes *you* feel better.) If you keep your wits about you, you can sometimes turn a negative situation into a more positive one by speaking up when someone demonstrates their phobias.

If you decide to respond to someone who's being homophobic or transphobic, here are a few ground rules that can help achieve a positive result:

1. Don't match insult for insult. Typically, that will only escalate the situation.
2. Try to get the person to acknowledge or name their behavior by asking in a nonconfrontational tone (if you can manage it), "Why would you say something like that?" or, "Are you aware that sounds homophobic/transphobic?" or something similar.
3. State how the comments or actions make you feel instead of saying something negative about the person who said them. Instead of, "You're only saying that because you're ignorant," try, "There are a lot of misconceptions about queer people. We're all human beings, and it really hurts to hear those kinds of things." Or, "It sounds like you have some misinformation about what it means to be trans. If you'd like to have a conversation about it, I can share more accurate information with you."
4. If a person becomes (or already is) threatening or aggressive, get yourself out of the situation as quickly and calmly as possible.

There may be times when it's appropriate just to turn around and say, "I don't appreciate that comment." However, if you're going to respond to homophobia or transphobia, it's ideal if you can

**"LET YOUR SOUL STAND COOL AND COMPOSED"**

In 2009, several schools in Maryland were the targets of protests by a religious group from Kansas. At Walt Whitman High School in Bethesda, Maryland, a group of seven congregants from Topeka, Kansas, protested because the school was named after a gay poet. Students and community members mobilized to counter the protests. At the 2:10 dismissal, 500 students lined up facing the group of seven from Kansas and chanted the name of their high school and "Go home!" Some students wore T-shirts with Walt Whitman's famous words, "Let your soul stand cool and composed."

The protesters later went to Montgomery Blair High School in Silver Spring, Maryland, to demonstrate against the school's GSA. A local open congregation (a religious group that welcomes LGBTQ members) launched a fundraiser in response, encouraging churchgoers to donate money for every minute the Kansas group protested the school. The church donated the money to a local LGBTQ rights organization.

include something constructive in your response. Tell the person why you don't appreciate their comments or how their words or actions make you feel. But again, keep your cool while you're doing it. Homophobia and transphobia are issues that are easy to get upset about. A comment you intended to be constructive could escalate into a fight. In the heat of the moment, it can be tough to think of something to do beyond using four-letter words or colorful gestures.

Following are some common homophobic and transphobic remarks, along with possible responses. Some of the replies are humorous and some are not, but all are designed to encourage people to think about what they said. In each case, you can customize responses based on whether someone is addressing your sexual orientation or gender identity.

**When someone tells a homophobic or transphobic joke.**
***Possible response:*** "When you tell jokes like that, you give the impression that it's okay to make fun of LGBTQ people—that we're less than human. Is that what you really believe?"

**"He's such a fag," or, "You look like a dyke."**
***Possible response:*** "How would you feel if I called you a 'breeder' or a 'hetero'?" or, "What's with the hate?"

**"You're going by Bethanny now? No way—I'm still calling you Bruce."**
***Possible response:*** "How is using my preferred name any different from calling one of your other friends by their middle name or a nickname if that's what they want?"

**"Ugh, that's so gay. Oh, you know, I don't mean it that way. It's just an expression."**
***Possible response:*** "It's still hurtful to hear," or, "I understand what you're saying, but if you don't mean it that way, maybe another expression that doesn't insult people would be more appropriate." Or even, "Maybe you don't mean it that way, but that's how a lot of people hear it. Are you okay with people thinking you're homophobic?"

**"What do queer people do in bed?"**
***Possible response:*** "Sleep. Sometimes we watch TV or read."

**"You don't *look* gay."**
***Possible response:*** "That's because I'm one of our secret agents. It's such a relief to know the disguise is working!" or, "What does gay look like to you?"

**"Men are men and women are women. You can't change your gender."**
***Possible response:*** "When I was born, people decided I was female based on my anatomy. Science shows that gender is a lot more complex than that, and it isn't something a doctor or anyone else can declare for you. I'm not trying to *change* my gender, but to have other people recognize what has always been my true gender."

**To a girl: "You just haven't met the right guy yet."**
***Possible response to another girl:*** "Maybe you just haven't met the right girl yet."

**"You're just going through a phase."**
***Possible response:*** "Is my entire life a phase?" or, "I know I'm queer in the same way you know you're straight." Or even, "It's a common misconception that queer kids are too young to know our own hearts and minds. But by that logic, since we're the same age, I could just as easily say that you don't know your heart and mind and could someday realize you're gay."

**"Why do people like you have to flaunt who they are?"**
***Possible response:*** "Refusing to hide is not flaunting," or, "I'm just being me," or even, "Honey, there are *no* other people like me (snap/mic drop optional)."

**"People like you are disgusting."**
***Possible response:*** "Ignorance and hatred are disgusting," or, "That comment shows me you don't know much about 'people like me.'" Another option when you hear a transphobic (or homophobic) remark or question is to name it. Say, "That comment is transphobic," or even ask, "What is it about trans people that makes you so afraid?"

## Try to Educate Others

Although it can be satisfying to give a cutting reply, it's probably not going to inspire a change in a person's behavior. Another option, which goes hand-in-hand with speaking up, is trying to turn the incident into an educational opportunity. You can address the roots of homophobia and transphobia by asking something like, "What ideas do you have about LGBTQ people that make you say that? Let's talk about them."

Realistically, this approach will be more effective with friends and acquaintances than with someone who is threatening to hurt you. Also, people are more likely to engage in a conversation when they're not surrounded by a group of their friends who might be egging them on (remember mob mentality—people are often more rational on their own than in groups). Use your judgment. Not everyone will be receptive, but even if someone doesn't react positively right away, down the road they might think about what you said—and it might have a lasting and positive effect. (I've had people tell me that something I said years earlier really made them think. You just never know.)

Some people don't even realize that things they say are offensive. It can be particularly painful when a friend or family member makes negative comments or jokes about LGBTQ people. Some people ask personal questions they wouldn't ask their straight or cis friends, and that can be offensive, too. So sometimes it's good to engage with people about their comments instead of zinging them and walking away. They could learn something.

## A BETTER WAY TO COMMUNICATE

Nonviolent Communication (NVC), a method created by Marshall B. Rosenberg, is designed to turn even the most challenging and divisive situations into opportunities for growth and greater understanding. NVC is based on the idea that underlying everyone's words and actions—even the most hateful and aggressive—is a need that the person is trying to meet. For example, a student who calls another student a "fag" in front of a crowd might be trying to meet the need of being accepted by or fitting in with their peer group. A student who files a lawsuit against a school district's policy allowing students to use the bathrooms corresponding to their gender identities may be doing so at the urging of parents and, therefore, the student is trying to meet the need to make their parents proud or not to go against the views of their social or religious group. Of course, that doesn't make the behavior okay. But understanding where people are coming from is the basis of compassion and the beginning of engaging them productively.

NVC is about learning how to listen, communicate your needs, and resolve conflict. It's a powerful tool for anyone, but especially for people in marginalized groups. To learn more about NVC, visit the website for the Center for Nonviolent Communication at www.cnvc.org or check out one of Dr. Rosenberg's books, such as *Speak Peace in a World of Conflict*.

**Pro tip:** Researching NVC or having an NVC expert come to your group to talk about the method could be a great school project or GSA activity.

## Fighting Homophobia and Transphobia Through Activism

Like George Loomis, Jacob Sullivan, and other teens who have taken formal action to end harassment and educate others, young people everywhere are working to create change. For instance, Steven Cozza, an Eagle Scout and professional cyclist, took on the entire Boy Scouts of America when he was just 12 years old. Steven's willingness to speak out against homophobia in Scouting ignited a national movement. Cozza worked with the group Scouting for All to advocate for gay Scouts. Later, several other Eagle Scouts, led by Zach Wahls and Jonathan Hillis, got together and formed Scouts for Equality. In 2013 the Boy Scouts of America dropped their ban on gay Scouts; in 2015 they dropped their ban on gay Scout leaders; and in 2017 they dropped their ban on transgender Scouts.

Other teens choose to focus their activism on issues beyond LBGTQ rights, while drawing on their queer identities for courage and motivation. For example, high school student Emma González became famous in 2018 for her speech on behalf of fellow students and victims of the shooting at the Marjory Stoneman Douglas High School in Parkland, Florida. That same year, she helped organize the March for Our Lives in Washington, D.C.—a massive gun control assembly that became the largest single-day student protest in US history. González identifies as bisexual, and has said that being out as queer has helped empower her as an activist, commenting, "If I wasn't so open about who I was, I never would've been able to do this." She'd also served as president of her school's GSA—a leadership experience that she said was valuable when it came to organizing March for Our Lives.

You can make a difference in a lot of ways. Maybe you'll decide to join or start a GSA or another LGBTQ group at school. Or you might get involved with a local or national organization. Groups like GLSEN, GLAAD, and the Human Rights Campaign, to name a few, are always happy for more volunteers. They also can provide you with ideas for things you can do to make your own area or school a friendlier place for queer people.

## BEEN THERE

"One year we organized a National Coming Out Day event, which consisted of putting up posters and handing out rainbow stickers. It was great. There were rainbows all over the school, including on many people's backpacks who I'd never even met! But best of all, people stopped using *gay* as an all-purpose insult. When people started to realize that they knew gay people and that gay people were being affected by slurs, a lot of people stopped using them." —Jan, 19

"I got involved with a group called Lambda . . . which had a speakers' bureau. We would go to high schools and middle schools and talk to students and teachers about our experiences coming out and answer questions that they had." —Nancy, 19

Getting involved and working for change can make your school or community a more open and accepting place. It may also help you feel better about yourself and be better equipped to handle the homophobia or transphobia you might be facing. Dealing with ignorance again and again can be depressing, frustrating, and isolating. At times, you might even feel helpless against it, like things will never change. Getting involved in LGBTQ causes can empower you to change your world. It's also a great way to gain support and meet other LGBTQ people and individuals who are open-minded and are also working for change.

Being an activist can be a very consuming experience. Be sure to make time for yourself, your schoolwork, your job, your friends, and other positive things you already have in your life.

**BEEN THERE**

"If we are not visible, we will always be in the shadows. People won't notice our needs and the prejudice we still face. A bit of participation in a few events will show the world we are not afraid, even if we are." —Isaac, 20

## When Homophobia and Transphobia = Ongoing Harassment

Sometimes homophobia and transphobia reveal themselves in harassment, which can take the form of bullying, either in person, online (cyberbullying), or a combination of the two—not just a remark here or there (although those remarks can hurt), but constant badgering, escalating teasing, or physical threats. Bullying and harassment are not okay, and you don't have to live with them.

GLSEN advises students to document incidents of bullying (preferably right away while the memory is clear and fresh). Write down who did or said what, when, and where. Note anyone who was there and witnessed the incident. And keep it all together in a file or notebook. That way when you report it, you have a written record of exactly what happened. Also keep a written record of who you report the harassment to, what you said, where you talked, when the meeting happened, and what the person who you reported it to said back to you. This information especially comes in handy if there is no follow-through (or inadcquate follow-through) from the person or people you tell.

So, who do you tell about bullying? Reporting it to an approachable teacher, counselor, or administrator are all options. Maybe one of your teachers or a school staff member witnessed the bullying and will support you if you go to the administration.

It can be daunting to approach an administrator. Not only are you upset about the incident or incidents, you might also be worried about the administrator's reaction. It's even tougher if you aren't comfortable being LGBTQ or talking about it. For that reason, it's a good idea to get a parent or another adult to go with you. This person can support you, and their presence can help show the administrator that bullying is a serious matter and won't be tolerated.

## BEEN THERE

"The majority of my attackers were never punished. On one occasion, three boys were suspended for three days. The principal told me they were suspended for the verbal attacks and not the physical one, as the physical one could not be proven. I had several witnesses report it to him, but he just didn't want to do much about it. Later, I was attacked in the hallway. I do not remember much of it, as my head was hit on the locker several times and I must have blacked out or something. After that, I got a lawyer through the ACLU and a couple of national organizations helped me by talking with school officials. The school has been very supportive recently. Maybe that was because of my influence and pressure on them." —Randy, 15

Here are some tips for approaching a school official or other adult:

1. Stay calm. If you present your case in a rational way, it will be harder for the adult to dismiss you as overreacting or being too emotional.
2. Provide an exact account, as detailed as you can, about what happened. It's also helpful if you have witnesses who can back up your story.
3. Explain that your safety is in jeopardy as long as the issue continues unaddressed.

Some school officials will be outraged by the harassment. Others will be reluctant to take action. Some might imply or say outright that LGBTQ students, or those who are perceived to be LGBTQ, invite harassment by being who they are. If you are assaulted (the legal definition is a threat of harm) or battered (physically attacked), you can file a police report. If no one will help you, you can reach out to a national organization such as GLSEN, Lambda Legal, the National LGBTQ Task Force, or the American Civil Liberties Union

(ACLU). There also might be a local group in your area that can help you. Either way, you don't have to accept harassment, and you don't have to confront it alone.

## The Cyberbullying Epidemic

It has come to light that many teens who were LGBTQ or were perceived to be and who committed suicide in recent years were victims of cyberbullying (using an electronic medium such as a mobile phone to threaten or harm others). The popularity of social media sites and use of text messaging has resulted in an increase of cyberbullying. According to GLSEN's *2015 National School Climate Survey*, nearly half of all LGBTQ students surveyed reported having been victims of cyberbullying in the past year, with 15 percent saying they experienced it often or frequently.

Cyberbullying can take place via a variety of means and forums, such as email, chat rooms, social media pages, instant messaging, text messaging, photos, and blogs. Cyberbullying may include:

- sending mean, vulgar, or threatening messages or images
- posting sensitive, private information or lies about another person
- pretending to be someone else in order to make another person look bad
- intentionally excluding someone from an online group

This form of harassment can be particularly tough to deal with because messages communicated electronically often can be quickly and broadly distributed and it's not always easy to tell who is sending them. Cyberbullying can feel particularly inescapable since texting and social media are everywhere we turn.

Putting an end to cyberbullying involves many of the same steps as stopping in-person harassment. The National Crime Prevention Council (NCPC) advises young people to tell a trusted adult about the harassment so that this person can help you get the proper authorities involved. In the case of online harassment, the NCPC also encourages you to report the abuse to site administrators and to use online tools to block hurtful messages. In severe cases, changing your email address or phone number is suggested.

If it becomes necessary to involve law enforcement or other officials, you will want a record of the bullying. As much as you might want to delete the offensive messages, it's a good idea to keep them as a way of documenting and proving what's happened. Also, if you're not sure who is harassing you, electronic messages often can be traced back to their source. (For more information, go to the NCPC's website at www.ncpc.org.)

## The Good News

Although a lot of negativity still exists toward LGBTQ people, the world continues to change for the better. Not all (or even most) straight/cis people are anti-LGBTQ. Young people—both queer people and straight/cis allies—are helping make the biggest difference when it comes to promoting positive attitudes about queer people. A Gallup poll conducted in May of each year asks Americans about their attitudes toward a variety of things, including homosexuality. In 2015, 63 percent of all Americans surveyed said they found homosexuality acceptable, compared with only 38 percent in 2002.

While it's still likely you'll encounter homophobia or transphobia at some point in your life, you will also—and hopefully far more often—encounter acceptance.

### HELP FOR HARASSMENT

**GLSEN**
(212) 727-0135 • www.glsen.org
GLSEN works to create safe schools for all LGBTQ people, but especially students. The organization's website offers a variety of resources and information on safe schools efforts, including gay-straight alliances (GSAs) and anti-discrimination legislation. It also includes information specific to stopping anti-LGBTQ bullying.

**Human Rights Campaign (HRC)**
1-800-777-4723 • www.hrc.org
The HRC works to protect the rights of LGBTQ people and improve their quality of life. The group is a resource for the latest information on LGBTQ legislative issues and campaigns such as National Coming Out Day.

**Lambda Legal**
(212) 809-8585 • www.lambdalegal.org
Lambda Legal is a national legal organization that works for full recognition of the civil rights of LGBTQ people and those living

with HIV through litigation, education, and public policy work. Lambda Legal has been involved in many cases involving harassment of or discrimination against LGBTQ young people.

**National LGBTQ Task Force**
(202) 393-5177 • www.thetaskforce.org
This task force works at the local, state, and national levels to fight prejudice and violence against queer people. The organization provides many services, including legal assistance and referrals to other professionals.

**American Civil Liberties Union (ACLU)**
(212) 549-2500 • www.aclu.org
The ACLU works in the courts to defend civil liberties for all people, including those who are LGBTQ. It has an extensive track record of advocating for LGBTQ rights.

**PFLAG**
(202) 467-8180 • www.pflag.org
PFLAG provides materials and support services for queer people and their families.

**It Gets Better Project**
itgetsbetter.org
Does it ever seem like bullying and harassment will never end? It's natural to have this fear, but life does get better. If you'd like some proof, check out this website to watch videos from LGBTQ people and allies offering perspective and encouragement.

**Stopbullying.gov**
www.stopbullying.gov
A project of the US Department of Health and Human Services, Stopbullying.gov is a resource designed to help young people end bullying. The site includes tips, video features, and specific information on cyberbullying.

# CHAPTER 4
# Coming Out

**We're here. We're queer. Get used to it.**

Throughout history, LGBTQ people have often felt the need to hide who they are to avoid harassment and discrimination. However, a gradual shift in society's attitudes toward LGBTQ people has been occurring. This shift, combined with massive turning-point events like the Stonewall riots, the repeal of "Don't Ask, Don't Tell," and the nationwide legalization of same-sex marriage, has helped create an atmosphere where more people feel comfortable coming out. Today, more and more LGBTQ people are open about who they are.

On one level, coming out is easy. It just means being open with family, friends, and others about identifying as LGBTQ. On another level, coming out isn't so simple. It can expose you to everything from awkward social situations—such as someone trying to fix you up with the only other queer person they know—to prejudice and harassment.

**STONEWALL**

In June of 1969, a group of LGBTQ people took a stand at the Stonewall Inn in New York City against ongoing police harassment. This event is widely viewed as the start of an organized queer rights movement in the United States. Commemorations of the Stonewall riots eventually turned into the LGBTQ Pride celebrations that take place across the country every June. The event has also been memorialized in books and movies.

According to a 2013 study by Pew Research Center, 92 percent of LGBTQ adults surveyed said they felt society has become more accepting of queer people in the last decade. However, 39 percent said that at some point in their lives, they were rejected by a close friend or family member for being LGBTQ.

The decision to come out is a significant one. This is especially true when you're young, because you still depend largely on others for basic needs like food and shelter and because your legal rights are limited. Some teens who come out are harassed, and they experience violence at home or at school. Some teens are kicked out of the house or run away. These things don't happen to everyone, but it's important to seriously consider your safety and well-being before coming out.

But coming out also has many positive aspects. You can live your life openly and meet other LGBTQ people. Many LGBTQ teens say being out feels liberating. It can be very empowering to be honest about who you are.

**BEEN THERE**

"As a freshman in college I came out to a friend of mine. At first, I thought it might be a big mistake because she was the most popular freshman on campus. But I thought that since she trusted me with her deepest secrets, then I could trust her with mine. When I told her she said, 'Wow, that's cool. You know, I didn't want to ask but . . .' That was the beginning of our friendship on a whole new level." —Sasha, 20

The purpose of this chapter is not to tell you whether or not you should come out—it's to help you decide what's right for you. Even if you don't feel like you have a lot of control over your life, *you* are the only person who can ultimately decide how to live it. That includes making decisions about how out you want to be. If you do decide to come out, this chapter will give you some advice on how to do it.

## What Is Coming Out All About?

As you learn more about the LGBTQ community, you'll find that coming out is a very meaningful issue. Some people will ask you if you're out or who you're out to. They might want to share their coming-out stories. Sometimes it seems like everyone who is queer is obsessed with the idea of being out. A popular LGBTQ magazine is called *Out*, and there's even a National Coming Out Day.

Coming out is the process of telling others that you're queer. The phrase "coming out" comes from the metaphor that you're "coming out of the closet." Conversely, people who are not out often are referred to as being "closeted," meaning they've chosen not to tell others of their LGBTQ identities.

There's a whole range of being out. People can be completely out, meaning they're open with everyone about being LGBTQ. Some are partially out, meaning they're out to some people but not everyone. Others might only be out to one very close person in their lives. Some people aren't out at all.

Coming out has its pluses and minuses. It can open up your social life to other LGBTQ teens and allow you to live freely without having to hide who you are. But it can also cause stress in your family and put a strain on some of your friendships. For most LGBTQ people, coming out is a major milestone and a life-changing experience. It's like taking off a mask and letting people see who you really are. Some people decide to come out because they're tired of hiding who they are. These people are willing to risk telling others in exchange for the freedom of living openly.

### Feeling Pressure to Come Out

This emphasis on coming out can put a lot of pressure on you to come out, but there's no rush. People can be ready to come out at different times. Some come out at 14, others at 40. Coming out can be a great and affirming experience. But if you're not ready, it can feel like a disaster.

Dr. Sandra Loiterstein, a clinical psychologist who often works with LGBTQ people, emphasizes this point. She explains, "It's important for teens to know that discovering your identity is a process, and everyone does so in their own time. Teens, especially, can have a tough time figuring out who they are because they are sorting through so many issues at once."

You might feel internal pressure to come out, or see out celebrities or people in your community and think, "I *should* be out." You can also feel pressure from other sources, such as friends or people in the LGBTQ community. Some people may say you need to come out, while others might give you completely different messages. Maybe your parents or other people say things like, "I don't understand why gay people have to put it in our faces. They should just keep it to themselves." Regardless of what others tell you, your first responsibility is to yourself.

### SERVING WITH PRIDE

During World War II, if military personnel were discovered to be LGBTQ, they were given special dishonorable discharges called "blue discharges" (because the form on which they were typed was blue). People who received blue discharges often had trouble finding employment and faced rejection in civilian life. Although LGBTQ people in the military were, until recently, forced to hide their sexual orientations and gender identities, many queer people have served their country in the armed forces, some receiving the military's highest honors.

In 2010, the Williams Institute at the UCLA School of Law estimated that 70,000 members of the US military identified as lesbian, gay, or bisexual. In 2014, the Institute estimated that 15,500 transgender Americans currently serve in the military (though that service came under challenge from the Trump presidential administration in 2017). For more information on the military's "Don't Ask, Don't Tell" policy and some LGBTQ military heroes, see pages 28–29 in chapter 1.

**Pro tip:** Looking at the history of LGBTQ people in the military and controversies surrounding their service could be a great school project. You could even interview a current or former LGBTQ service member or invite them to speak to your class or GSA.

## How's the Weather Out There? Deciding If You're Ready (and If It's Safe) to Come Out

Without a doubt, more teens than ever are coming out. Many studies, news articles, and books note the increasingly younger ages at which people are coming out. According to a 2013 survey by Pew Research Center, young people self-identify as feeling they might be lesbian, gay, bisexual, or something else other than straight at a median age of 12 years old. The median age at which people say they are certain they are LGBTQ is 17.

But some people question whether others have the ability to be certain of their orientations when they're young. "How can you possibly know at that age?" is a common question. While it's true that identity develops over an entire lifetime, you know yourself best—whatever stage of life you're in. Also, people who fit in with heteronormative culture often have no idea what *not* fitting in feels like. It's like they say—a fish doesn't know it's in water. But if you're a land animal and you're in water, you know it! You might know for sure that you're not a fish, even if you don't yet know exactly what kind of land animal you are.

Many LGBTQ young people today don't identify as one thing or another. Instead, they're comfortable existing in an open space or gray area when it comes to sexual orientation or gender identity. "Who cares about labels?" is a common attitude among teens. LGBTQ teens today typically have more straight/cis allies among their peers than in previous generations, and that can help them feel more comfortable coming out or identifying as something other than lesbian or gay, such as *mostly* lesbian or gay, omnisexual, nonbinary, genderqueer, or simply not hetero.

This fluidity in the way some people define their orientation can confuse those who are used to black-and-white notions of gay and straight or male and female. Lots of people (both outside of and within the LGBTQ community) have some catching up to do when it comes to newer terms and ideas related to sexual orientation and gender identity, and that's okay. Plus, our understanding of gender is still evolving. The longer these concepts and terms are around and the more visible and widely used they are, the more people will come to understand them. Still, coming out can be extra challenging if the person you're coming out to doesn't understand what your identity means. But there are ways to address that, as you'll see later in this chapter.

Many young people choose to come out, but that doesn't mean you have to. In fact, in some cases, coming out might not be the best decision, at least for now. Tom Sauerman, a cofounder of the Philadelphia chapter of PFLAG who counseled parents with LGBTQ children, advised young people that it might be better to wait to come out until they can be reasonably certain it won't jeopardize their safety or quality of life at home or school. This can be extremely difficult if you're feeling like you just can't be you. But your safety is a serious consideration. Also, if you're concerned about how things would be at home if you came out, it's important to be aware that teens in some states can be arrested for running away and may end up in the juvenile justice system.

### HOMELESS AND LGBTQ

According to True Colors United, which works to end homelessness among LGBTQ young people (and was cofounded by musician Cyndi Lauper), 40 percent of the 1.6 million young people who experience homelessness each year identify as LGBTQ. Considering that LGBTQ youth comprise roughly 7 percent of the overall youth population, this number is extremely high, and homelessness among LGBTQ young people is a serious issue. Learn more about True Colors United and access their guide for housing-insecure people *On Our Own: A Survival Guide for Independent LGBTQ Youth* at truecolorsunited.org. If you're thinking about running away, please first contact True Colors. Or you can contact the National Runaway Safeline at www.1800runaway.org, by calling 1-800-RUNAWAY, or by texting 66008.

## Questions to Ask Yourself Before Coming Out

Only you can decide the right time to come out, and it's important to make sure you're ready. If you're emotionally prepared to come out, you're more likely to have a positive experience than if you're not. Here are some questions to ask yourself to help determine whether you're ready:

**Am I sure I'm LGBTQ?** If you're not certain you are LGBTQ (and remember, it's okay to be questioning), you might want to wait before coming out. Most LGBTQ people come out in part because they feel the need to have others know what they're feeling and experiencing. If you're not sure whether you're LGBTQ, think about waiting. Or you can come out as queer, not straight, or not cis, rather than choosing a specific label. You might have more explaining to do in this situation, since most people have a better understanding of terms like *lesbian*, *gay*, *bisexual*, or *transgender* than broader ideas such as queer, genderqueer, or "other." But if you're up for explaining, that's perfectly fine. There's nothing wrong with telling someone you're exploring who you are. They might even end up being a good source of support for you.

**Am I comfortable with myself?** This can be a challenge. After all, you might feel what virtually every teenager feels at one time or another—that there's *nothing* comfortable about being you. This could be because of your sexual orientation or gender identity, or it could just be part of adjusting to changes in your body and your social roles. If you're comfortable with yourself and confident about your orientation or identity (whether it's a distinct label or not), the person you're coming out to is more likely to be accepting of you than if you feel upset or distressed by it.

**Why am I coming out?** Come out because you're ready. Come out to affirm yourself. Come out because you want to share with others who you are. In short, come out because *you want to*. Don't come out on a whim, to get a reaction from someone, because anyone else is pressuring you, or—perhaps worst of all—because you think it will upset your parents or guardians.

**Can I be patient with other people's reactions?** It's natural to want an immediate positive reaction from the person you're coming out to, but that probably won't always be the case. Remember how long it might have taken you to adjust to the idea that you're LGBTQ. Others may need time to adjust, too. Be mentally prepared to give them that time.

If someone gives you a negative or even just a lukewarm reaction, it's a great opportunity to practice compassion and patience. It's human nature to take time to adjust to big news, especially if that news requires a major shift in perspective. It's tempting to wish people would just get over it already, but the reality is that most people don't change the ways they think overnight (though some do). Being compassionate and patient with others is also a way of being kind to yourself. Giving others the space they need to grow rather than jumping down their throats is a much less stressful way to live. After all, if the tables were turned, wouldn't you want to be treated the same way?

## The World Around You: An Essential Checklist

Even if you feel emotionally ready, there are some external factors that could influence whether it's a good idea for you to come out:

**1. Is it safe for you to come out?** If LGBTQ people are commonly harassed or threatened where you live or go to school and there isn't much protection from abuse, it might not be safe for you to come out. According to GLSEN's *2015 National School Climate Survey*, nearly 60 percent of respondents reported feeling unsafe at school because of their sexual orientation, and 43 percent because of their gender identity or expression.

> **BEEN THERE**
>
> "Don't get me wrong. I'm proud of who I am, I just have to be proud quietly because I live in a very small (and small-minded) community. Just last year at my school, a boy who people called gay was beaten within an inch of his life. I'm a little scared to be too public about it for now." —Calista, 19

**2. What is your home environment like?** If your parents or guardians are aggressive or abusive, coming out to them could escalate the abuse. If adults at home are homophobic or transphobic, you might also decide to wait to come out until you have left home or at least have other options for living arrangements if needed. But some teens who feel safe and comfortable doing so come out to family adults. People at home can be sources of support and can help you deal with harassment from others.

In a 2009 *New York Times Magazine* cover story about gay teens, the author quotes openly gay boys' varsity soccer coach Dan Woog: "The biggest difference I've seen in the last 10 years isn't with gay kids—it's with their families. . . . Many parents just don't assume anymore that their kids will have a sad, difficult life just because they're gay."

**A NATIONWIDE CAMPAIGN**

**National Coming Out Day (www.hrc.org/explore/topic/coming-out).** Sponsored by the Human Rights Campaign, this initiative provides resources on coming out. For information on deciding whether it's the right time to come out, guidance on how to do it, and much more, visit the website or call 1-800-777-4723.

**3. Do you have a support system?** Do you have someone to turn to if the reaction to your coming out is bad? You might have a friend you've already come out to who can support you. Also, there are groups that can help. If you're concerned about how coming out might go, reaching out to one of these groups in advance is a good idea; that way you've got a fallback plan if things go badly. (TrevorSpace is one great source of support. See page 99 for more information.)

## If You Don't Have a Choice: Being Outed

Some teens don't get a choice about coming out. It's possible to be outed without your consent or intention. A parent might notice on the computer that you've gone to LGBTQ websites. A classmate might overhear a conversation you had with a friend. A school official might tell your parents that you've requested to go by a different name or to use the restroom that corresponds with your gender identity.

**BEEN THERE**

"I was only 13 when I got into a fight with my mom about a letter of mine she'd found. She had the nerve to tell me to stop acting so 'cuddly' with my girlfriends. 'It's not like you're a lesbian are you?' she shouted. Then and there I told her I was bisexual. She stormed from the room. The following day she admitted that it troubled her and that it would take a little while to get used to it, but she wasn't angry or disappointed in me." —Erin, 19

Being outed can be challenging because you have to deal with being out right away—without warning or time to plan. You might suddenly find yourself in an unsafe situation. Or family members or friends could surprise you and tell you that they support you no matter what. Chances are the reality will be somewhere in between.

## Now What? Some Tips for Outed Teens

Being outed can feel like a nightmare. Or it can come as a great relief. People don't always react as negatively as you think they might (although sometimes the opposite is true). They might even be positive and supportive.

Still, any situation you're not in control of can be scary. So what do you do if you're outed?

**1. Take a deep breath.** Being outed can be very unsettling because you weren't given a choice about it. You might feel like you weren't ready to come out. But it happened, so take a moment to think about how you want to deal with the situation. It's true that you weren't able to control being outed, but you can control how you deal with it from here.

**2. Assess the situation.** Take a look around to determine what your next move should be. Are you safe? How do you feel? How are others reacting? These questions can help you figure out whether you should try to start a conversation right now or regroup before going forward. You might want to get outside resources or help.

**3. Take action.** Based on the other person's (or other people's) reaction and your level of preparedness, you have several options for what action to take. If you feel like you can engage in a conversation, try it. By opening the lines of communication, you're taking back some degree of control over the situation, and that can be empowering. It can also help increase the odds of a positive outcome from the situation.

If the situation is too emotionally charged to engage in a constructive conversation, or if a discussion starts to get too heated, you can initiate a cooling-off period. This could be a good opportunity for you to chat with a friend, talk to an adult you trust, or reach out to an LGBTQ group for guidance and support. Some young people have an accepting aunt or uncle, grandparent, or family friend who can help smooth things over with an upset parent or guardian.

A third course of action might be more of a necessity than an option. If being outed has made you fear for your safety, either at home or elsewhere, you may need to get immediate help. It's a good idea to approach an adult for assistance, such as a trusted family member, neighbor, counselor, or school official. You could also contact an LGBTQ group that supports teens. (Many such groups are listed throughout this book.)

## Why Come Out?

People come out for a variety of reasons, and many of them are quite positive. Coming out is a way to affirm yourself. It shows others that you're happy with who you are. It can also be a way to reach out to others by sharing something very meaningful and personal with them.

Some people come out to increase the overall visibility of LGBTQ people and help advance the LGBTQ rights movement. When *Grey's Anatomy* and *Madam Secretary* actor Sara Ramirez came out as queer and bisexual in 2016, she stated she did it as a show of solidarity with LGBTQ people who were experiencing hatred and violence. (Ramirez came out in a speech she delivered to the True Colors Fund—see page 87.)

Right now, society as a whole assumes that most people are straight/cis (attitudes called heterosexism and cissexism). Many straight/cis people look at others around them and, in the absence of any obvious indication otherwise, assume everyone they see is also straight or cis. Coming out and doing things like wearing a queer-themed shirt or putting a rainbow sticker on your car are ways of challenging these assumptions.

### GOING PUBLIC

These days, lots of young celebrities choose to come out via social media. In 2016, *Hunger Games* actress Amandla Stenberg came out on *Teen Vogue*'s Snapchat channel as bisexual. In 2017, actor Keiynan Lonsdale (from TV shows and movies including *The Flash* and *Love, Simon*) came out as bisexual via Twitter. And loads of young YouTube stars, such as Jazz Jennings, have come out on their channels. There are even instructional videos about how to come out on YouTube! But while these are certainly broad and sensational ways to come out, think twice before coming out via social media. It may be more attention at once than you, as a noncelebrity, bargained for. Also, it's likely that most celebrities came out to people close to them before coming out in a highly visible forum.

### BEEN THERE

"There were 1,900 students at my school when I graduated—1,900 people who can't assume or pretend that gay people don't exist. And if you look at statistics that as many as 10 percent of people are queer, that means that when I came out there were maybe 190 queer kids who got to hear that they are not going to burn in hell, that they are not perverts, and that they can live their lives." —Anthony, 19

## Who Should I Tell First?

Many people start the coming out process by telling only one or two people, sort of like dipping your toe into a pool to test the water. Others choose to tell a lot of people all at once. Many decide to come out to a friend or sibling first because they believe they'll get a better reaction from these people than they might from a parent.

It's definitely a good idea to choose someone you think will be supportive. For some, parents or other family adults are the last people they want to tell. For others, adults at home are people they feel they can go to with anything and who they want to come out to first.

### BEEN THERE

"I have come out to my brother. He is younger than me by a year. I felt like I needed to tell someone close to me, and he was the one. It has brought us closer." —Athena, 20

There are two big reasons why it's important to take care in selecting the first person (or people) you come out to. For starters, if you have a positive first experience, you'll feel better about the prospect of coming out to other people. Having someone react positively is a boost to your self-esteem.

Also, if the first person you come out to is accepting, then you have additional support as you come out to others. You'll have someone you can talk to about how you're feeling. This person can also be someone you practice on when you're preparing to come out to others. It's very comforting to have someone you can be honest with.

**STRAIGHT ALLIES**
"My husband and I put a Human Rights Campaign sticker on our car because we have a lot of gay friends and we want them and other people to know that we support them. It's important for us that LGBTQ people know that not all straight people are against them."
—Shari, 42

## I Have Something to Tell You: Coming Out to Your Family

You've given it a lot of thought, and you feel you're ready to come out. So how do you do it, especially to (gulp) your family? While there isn't one perfect method for coming out, some ways are more likely than others to have a positive outcome.

### Be Prepared

**Do your research.** Start by testing your family members' reactions to LGBTQ people. Mention an LGBTQ character on a popular TV show. Bring up an issue like trans civil rights or queer people being allowed to adopt children and see what their reactions are. Keep in mind—these are only hints. Even if parents, siblings, or grandparents say LGBTQ people should have equal rights, that doesn't mean they'll be totally calm when they find out it's their own family member they're talking about. And the opposite could be true, too. Knowing a family member is queer might encourage them to think about what it means to be LGBTQ in a different, more positive way.

Gather resources from groups like the Human Rights Campaign, PFLAG, and GLSEN (see pages 80–81) and share them with your family. These and other LGBTQ organizations have reading lists and brochures available for both you and your family. Even if family members don't read the brochures or visit the websites right away, they might later. And while you might feel awkward about coming out to people and then handing them reading material, they're more likely to read something you give them than they are to do research on their own. It's an opportunity for you to provide them with information that's positive and accurate.

**Be patient.** Coming out to family members—especially those closest to you—is a milestone in your life. But it's a big deal for them, too. It can be tough, even heartbreaking, when someone you really care about has trouble accepting who you are. But give family members the benefit of the doubt if they don't embrace your sexual orientation or gender identity at first. Remember that you've had a lot longer to adjust to the idea and accept yourself as LGBTQ than they have. Chances are it's breaking news to them, and they may just need time to digest it.

### COMING OUT AS QUESTIONING . . . OR AS SOMETHING ELSE ENTIRELY

You might decide to come out to someone as questioning. Or maybe you want to come out as pansexual, genderqueer, or some other term you're comfortable with that is less familiar to other people. If you do, you may have some questions to answer. Saying that you identify as questioning or as one of the broader identities might be confusing for people who are only familiar with labels like straight, gay, lesbian, bisexual, or transgender. They might not understand what you mean when you come out to them.

Many people prefer to come out after they have a more concrete concept of their sexual orientation or gender identity. For others, a label such as pansexual or genderqueer *is* their identity. For those who are questioning, coming out helps them gain support from friends or family members as they go through the process of exploring their identities. Still others will keep some fluidity and choose to never label themselves as one specific orientation or gender.

However you decide to come out (*if* you decide to come out), remember to keep the lines of communication open and try to be patient with others' questions. More often than not, they're just trying to understand you better—and that's a sign that they care.

**Pick a good time.** Coming out to a parent, grandparent, or another family adult the minute they come home from work or at the big holiday dinner probably isn't a great idea. Avoid situations that are already stressful. Again, keep in mind that you've been adjusting to the idea of being queer for a while, but it might come as a complete surprise to others. Pick a time when everyone is most likely to be relaxed and comfortable.

**Hope for the best, but prepare for the worst.** Some family members might respond by kicking you out of your home. It sounds harsh, but it does happen. Have an idea of where you can go or who you can turn to if things get ugly at home.

**Practice.** Once you've decided you want to come out, practice, practice, practice. Look at yourself in the mirror or practice by talking to a poster of your favorite musician or sports figure. Or practice on a friend or someone else you've already told. It's like giving a presentation at school, only much more personal. You might think it's weird to practice, but coming out is an emotional event and it might be more difficult than you think to express yourself. If you practice what you're going to say, you'll probably sound a lot calmer and clearer when the time arrives. As you practice, try to anticipate some of the questions people might ask so you have well-thought-out responses. See the following section for some common reactions and responses you can provide.

### COMING OUT CHECKLIST

If you haven't checked off each of these, you might want to rethink your decision to come out.

- ✓ I am ready and I am comfortable with myself.
- ✓ I've asked myself why I want to come out, and I'm sure it's for positive reasons.
- ✓ I'm ready to deal with the outcome and realize that it might not be the outcome I predict or hope for.
- ✓ I'm ready to provide information and answer questions.
- ✓ I have a support system in case this doesn't go the way I'd like it to.

## Having "The Talk"

No matter how much you prepare, there's no telling what your family members' reactions will be. Nevertheless, parents and others often have common reactions and questions in response to a loved one coming out. It may help to keep the following reactions in mind as you prepare for "The Talk." State your responses as calmly and rationally as possible so you don't ignite an altercation. It can be difficult not to get worked up when you feel strongly about something, but losing your cool won't help you in the long run.

**Reaction: "How do you know?"**

***Possible response:*** "How do you know you're straight/cis? It's something I feel deep inside."

**Reaction: "It's just a phase," or, "You're too young to know."**
***Possible response:*** "I understand that you're probably surprised by this. This isn't a phase, and I think in time you'll realize that. Me being queer is new to you, but my understanding of who I am has been evolving in me for a long time."

*Another approach:* Now that you know some statistics, you can always drop some data on them by saying something like, "Actually, this is a pretty normal time for people to realize they're LGBTQ. According to Pew Research Center, most kids start to realize they're LGBTQ around age 12."

**Reaction: "Why are you doing this to me?"**
***Possible response:*** "This isn't about you. It's about me, and it's about my relationship with you. I'm telling you this because it's who I am. I respect you and want to be open with you. I want you to have a relationship with *me*, not the person you *think* I am, and that means I have to be honest with you."

**Reaction: "It's your choice to be this way."**
***Possible response:*** "No one knows exactly why people are queer, but most scientists and health professionals believe that part of it could be biology. I don't have those kinds of answers for you, but what I can tell you is that for me, this is just who I am."

**Reaction: "You're just saying that because you think it's cool."**
***Possible response:*** "Cool is about what other people think of you. It's just an opinion. This isn't about what anyone else thinks is cool or not cool. It's about who I am."

**Reaction: "But your life is going to be so hard."**
***Possible response:*** "It's true that in some ways, life can be more difficult for LGBTQ people. I know I'll have to deal with other people's prejudice and ignorance, but I can handle that. What's more difficult to deal with is prejudice in my own family, and that's why I need your support. Besides, life is challenging for everyone at one time or another. That's why we need to stick together."

**Reaction: "Why do you want to live that way?"**
***Possible response:*** "There's no 'way' LGBTQ people live. We're just like everyone else. The queer community is just as diverse in our lifestyles and opinions as the straight and cis communities. A lot of stereotypes exist about the so-called 'queer lifestyle,' but they're just that: stereotypes."

**Reaction: "I always thought you'd get married and have children."**
***Possible response:*** "Fortunately, I still *can* get married, if I find the right person and that's what my partner and I want. And if we want children, we can do that, too. Lots of parents today are same-sex or multi-gendered."

**Reaction: "It's just wrong."**
***Possible response:*** "Who I am is not wrong. I think that lying to you is wrong, and that's why I want to be open with you. I care about you and what you think is important to me, so it's painful for me to hear that you feel that way. But I also understand that this is a lot of information and you probably need some time to think about it. Please know that you can bring it up later and we can talk about it. And please understand that I'm telling you this out of love and respect for you and our relationship."

**BEEN THERE**

"My father's response was simple. He stood up, gave me a hug, and said, 'You remember I said I would always love you, right?' I said, 'Yes.' And he said, 'I meant it.'" —Scott, 19

**Reaction: "How am I supposed to deal with this? Everyone will talk about our family or think it's my fault."**
***Possible response:*** "I know it's a lot to take in, but please remember that I'm the same person you loved 15 minutes ago. I haven't changed; you just know me better now. A lot of families have been in this situation. It might help for you to talk to some of them. PFLAG is a group for families of LGBTQ people. Here is the contact information for a chapter nearby. You don't have to call or go to their website right now, but I hope you'll at least take the information and

know that there are people out there you can talk to who won't judge you or us or how you're feeling about all this."

> **BEEN THERE**
>
> "My older sister was awful when I came out to her. There were a lot of unprovoked screaming matches between the two of us for a couple of months. She eventually calmed down and is now totally accepting." —Aaliyah, 19

## Now What? After "The Talk"

Family dynamics can change a lot after someone comes out. Coming out can start arguments or, at the very least, spark a lot of questions. Will you want to bring a love interest home? Should you be allowed to have sleepovers if you've expressed same-sex attractions?

Coming out may be the end of your hiding something, but it's the beginning of reworking some of your family dynamics. The keys to dealing with these changes are patience and open communication. The questions don't have to be answered all at once. They can be addressed as you go along. Talk with your family about the issues you're facing and try to come up with solutions together. Believe it or not, you might find that coming out ends up bringing your family closer together. If your parents are struggling, one idea is for you to see a counselor together. You'll want to be sure to pick one who you're totally comfortable with and who's knowledgeable about LGBTQ and gender issues.

> **A PLACE FOR SUPPORT**
>
> **TrevorSpace (www.trevorspace.org).** TrevorSpace is a social networking site where young people ages 13 to 24 can connect with and support one another. TrevorSpace is carefully monitored by administrators designated by the Trevor Project, a national organization focused on crisis and suicide prevention for LGBTQ and intersex teens. The forum provides accurate information that is age-appropriate and teen-friendly.

It is possible that after the coming out conversation, some family members may act like you never told them. They could be hoping it will go away. They might be going through denial. Parents, for example, often struggle with shock, denial, and guilt when a child first comes out to them. They might hope that you're only going through a phase, or they might feel guilty that there was something they did that somehow caused you to be LGBTQ.

Remember that coming out is a process for all involved. Give your family time, but don't assume that no news is good news and everyone is dealing with it. It's good to check in now and then. Mention to family members that you're there and willing to talk to them if they have questions or issues they want to discuss. They might need your help coping with this change. Continue to encourage (not demand) that they get in touch with others who have LGBTQ family members. If they want to talk with you, try to keep conversations civil and productive. These discussions can get pretty heated, but if that happens, take a deep breath (or several) and try to relate to what your family might be going through. (And remember those tips for Nonviolent Communication. See pages 74–75.)

## Coming Out to Your Friends

Like a lot of young people, you might choose to come out to a friend, or many friends, before you tell adults at home. It's not surprising that a lot of teens come out to friends first. After all, they're usually the people you have the most in common with. You might feel you'll get the best reaction from them.

Just like coming out to parents, coming out to friends can lead to a variety of reactions. Some friends might be supportive, some confused, some upset, and some might have a combination of these and other feelings. Some friends might even come out to *you* in response!

**BEEN THERE**

"So far, I have only come out to one friend—my best friend—and that was only after he told me that he was bi. It was funny. We were just sitting there, and all of a sudden he says, 'I like guys. But I like girls, too.' Then I said, 'Me, too!' It was that simple, and we talk about it all the time now." —Alejandro, 19

Coming out to friends first can be great. If they're supportive, they can be there for you if you come out to your family. But just like with adults at home, consider all angles before coming out. If a friend is upset by the news, they might tell other people, which could be bad if you're trying to be selective about who knows.

As with coming out to parents and other family adults, it's a good idea to first test the waters by gauging your friend's attitudes toward LGBTQ people in general. Some friends are more mature or may have had more experience dealing with LGBTQ issues. Maybe they have other queer friends or family members.

If you decide to come out to a friend, follow the same steps you would when coming out to family members. In other words, prepare and be patient. It's important to remember that if your friend doesn't react well, it could be because they've heard negative things about LGBTQ people. Talk with them about what they think and why. Assure them that you're still the same person you've always been and you're still their friend—being queer doesn't change that.

Coming out can change your friendships. You could become closer than ever. Or your friend could be hurt that you didn't tell them before. They could worry that you changing your gender expression could also change your friendship. They might wonder if you're attracted to them or even worry that if you're queer, maybe they are, too.

## BEEN THERE

"I was lucky enough to have my closest friends be open and accepting. There were those other 'friends' who rejected me, but the ones I called my best friends kept their arms open to me. I think a lot of people act homophobic because they are scared of what people think. I think that if a friend—a truly great friend—were to find out that you are gay, they will love you for who you are." —Lily, 20

"When you come out to friends—even if you're scared and nervous—don't act like it. Tell them you're LGBTQ with confidence. If they see you are confident, they will be confident in you and your friendship." —Paulo, 19

Again, give your friend time to adjust. Make it clear that you're ready to talk whenever they are. Some friendships do end because one person comes out, but these are extreme cases. If anything, most just go through an adjustment period. Let your friend know that one of the reasons you told them is that you want to be honest with them about who you are. Tell them, too, that you're going to need their support to deal with people who aren't as accepting. Even if they're upset at first, chances are things will get better.

## Coming Out at School

Some teens feel safer or more comfortable coming out to a trusted teacher, school counselor, or administrator. Some come out as a means of reaching out for support or guidance or to get help dealing with harassment that's taking place at school. Others come out to pave the way for them to express themselves as their true genders, which may include being called by another name or using different pronouns.

Adults who aren't family members can be good advocates and can help you deal with issues you're facing. However, it's important to remember that teachers and other school officials are people just like everyone else—you can never be absolutely certain how they'll react. But because they aren't family, your coming out is less likely to trigger the more extreme emotions people at home might feel. According to GLSEN's *2015 National School Climate Survey*, a whopping 97 percent of LGBTQ students surveyed could identify at least one supportive staff member at their school. (Unfortunately, only 36 percent characterized their schools' administration as supportive of queer students.)

### BEEN THERE

"In my last year of junior high, I had this amazing personal development and relationships teacher who I think was a lesbian. She taught us about being homosexual and bisexual. I think it was in that class that I actually discovered a term for who I was."
—Iris, 19

Some schools' policies make it difficult for supportive teachers to be outspoken about their acceptance of LGBTQ people. But it's not uncommon for teachers who are supportive to let students know their stance in subtle or obvious ways (from wearing a rainbow pin to putting up a huge Pride month display in their room). If your school has a gay-straight alliance, the group probably has a faculty or staff advisor. If that teacher is approachable, they could be a good person for you to talk with when you need the advice and support of an adult. More LGBTQ teachers also are starting to be out at school, and these educators can be excellent sources of support.

School counselors are trained to talk with teens about challenges, and many of them can be very helpful. Unfortunately, some of them might also be homophobic or transphobic. School counselors are sometimes bound by confidentiality. This means they can't share what you say to them with anyone else—it has to be kept in confidence. In some cases, however, there is no confidentiality requirement. Most schools require counselors to report certain things to the administration if a student's safety is in question (especially if a student is suicidal).

Counselors can be great people to seek advice and support from. If you're worried about talking to a counselor because of confidentiality issues, check your student handbook. The school's policy toward confidentiality should appear there. If you don't have a copy of the handbook, one should be available from the administrative office or the school's website. Or you can ask the counselor directly whether they are bound by confidentiality.

As students and advocacy groups work to make schools safer, more accepting places for LGBTQ teens, teachers and staff are learning what it means to be LGBTQ and are better able to understand and support queer students.

CHAPTER 5

# Life at School

## I can't even think straight.

One of the most challenging parts of being an LGBTQ teen can be coping with life at school. You have social hierarchies and cliques, teachers piling on the homework, administrators watching your every move, and teammates who are counting on you. Meanwhile, you're going through the "normal" stages of adolescence (which may have you feeling anything *but* normal). It's typical to have times when you don't feel like you belong in your own skin. On top of all that, you're coming to terms with possibly being queer. It's a lot to manage.

## School Life for LGBTQ Teens: The Big Picture

Surveys have revealed that life at school can range from okay to pretty uncomfortable to downright dangerous for LGBTQ teens. GLSEN's *2015 National School Climate Survey*—the most comprehensive report on the experiences of lesbian, gay, bisexual, and transgender students—surveyed 10,528 students around the country between the ages of 13 and 21. Among the findings were the following:

- 85 percent of LGBTQ teens had experienced some form of harassment in the past year.
- 27 percent reported being physically harassed (such as being physically blocked from walking down the hall) because of their sexual orientation, and 20 percent because of their gender identity or expression.
- 13 percent reported being physically assaulted (for example, being punched or kicked) at school in the past year because of their sexual orientation, and 9 percent because of their gender identity or expression.
- 98 percent heard the word *gay* used in a negative way frequently or often at school. Nearly 96 percent heard homophobic remarks such as "faggot" or "dyke" at school, with nearly 59 percent saying this happened frequently or often. Nearly 96 percent of students heard negative remarks about gender expression, and nearly 86 percent heard negative remarks specifically about trans people, such as "trannie" or "he/she," at school.
- More than half (57 percent) of students who were harassed or assaulted in school did not report the incidents to school staff because they believed little or no action would be taken and that the situation could become worse if they reported it.
- Nearly 64 percent of students who reported incidents of harassment said that school staff did nothing in response or told them to ignore it.
- Nearly half (48 percent) of students reported being harassed or threatened via electronic media such as text messages, emails, instant messages, or posts on social media sites (also known as cyberbullying).
- Nearly 58 percent of students reported that they felt unsafe in school because of their sexual orientation, and more than 43 percent felt unsafe because of their gender expression.

- Students who experienced high levels of harassment because of their sexual orientation or gender identity or expression were more than three times as likely to miss school in the month preceding the survey than those who were harassed less.
- Only 10 percent of respondents attended a school that had a comprehensive safe school policy that specifically mentioned sexual orientation, gender identity, and/or gender expression.

On a more positive note, GLSEN also found that the number of sources of support for LGBTQ teens is growing, including gay-straight alliances (GSAs, also sometimes called genders and sexualities alliances). A GSA is a student-led school club that aims to create a safe, welcoming, accepting school environment for all students—regardless of their sexual orientations or gender identities. In the 2015 GLSEN survey, more than half (54 percent) of students said their school had a GSA or similar student club.

GLSEN's research shows that students in schools with a GSA reported hearing fewer homophobic remarks and experienced less harassment and assault because of their sexual orientations and gender expressions. Students at these schools were also less likely to feel unsafe because of their orientations or gender expressions, and they were more likely to tell school staff if they'd been harassed or assaulted. More information on GSAs, including suggestions for starting one in your school, can be found beginning on page 117.

The research also showed that having a safe school policy that specifically includes sexual orientation and/or gender identity and expression makes a difference. Students at these schools heard fewer homophobic remarks and were less frequently victimized because of their sexual orientations or gender expressions. In addition, staff members at these schools were more likely to intervene when they heard homophobic or transphobic remarks.

Improvements in climate were also seen in schools where staff members are knowledgeable about LGBTQ issues and the curriculum is queer inclusive. Fortunately, curriculum changes are taking place, too—slowly but surely. In 2018, California became the first state to use LGBTQ-inclusive history textbooks statewide. That same year, Massachusetts rolled out an LGBTQ-inclusive curriculum. Though its use is optional, it provides excellent resources for educators and is a great example for other states.

# Feeling Invisible . . . or *Too* Visible

Feeling invisible is something that most LGBTQ people experience at one time or another, regardless of age. It's difficult when you grow up without seeing many positive representations of people like you. You might sometimes feel like you're the only one. Living in a predominantly straight/cis society can feel very isolating at times.

## Is Anybody Else Out There?

As you walk through the cafeteria, the air is buzzing with cis girls talking about cis boys and vice versa. And then there's you, who might be interested in boys, or girls, or both, or neither, or people outside the gender binary. In situations like this, it's easy to feel like a square peg in a round hole.

Visibility can be a problem not only in the cafeteria, but also in the curriculum. Debates are taking place all across the United States about whether LGBTQ topics should be included in what you learn at school. While some schools allow and encourage teachers to integrate these subjects into the curriculum, many others do not. In some districts, teachers can even be disciplined for mentioning queerness. (At the time of this book's publication, seven states have so-called "no pro homo" laws, which prohibit teachers from discussing LGBTQ topics or people in a positive light, if at all. These states are Alabama, Arizona, Louisiana, Mississippi, Oklahoma, South Carolina, and Texas.)

If your classes don't include any mention of LGBTQ people, it can seem like you just appeared out of nowhere. It can help to remember that a lot of LGBTQ teens are out there. Many of them are going through situations and issues similar to your own. You're not abnormal, and you're definitely not alone.

**BEEN THERE**

"In high school, the fact that I was aware of my differentness made my experience difficult. Coming out created a situation that didn't allow me to shy away from my reality. By the time I graduated, I had a fairly good idea of what to expect from others and myself." —Adrian, 20

## Four Ways to Fight Feeling Invisible

Here are some positive things you can do to keep from feeling isolated:

**1. Research your LGBTQ roots.** The next time you're assigned a project for which you can choose your own topic, think about researching some of your queer predecessors. Write about poet Walt Whitman, painter Georgia O'Keeffe, composer Pyotr Ilyich Tchaikovsky, singer Bessie Smith, or professional tennis player Dr. Renée Richards. Do a science project on chromosomes that also discusses what it means to be intersex. Offer a presentation on how Title IX legislation applies to trans students. Learn about the people who came before you, their challenges, and their triumphs. It can help you appreciate what a long and rich history queer people have.

**2. Get in touch with other LGBTQ teens.** You might meet people at local LGBTQ organizations, online, or through others you know. (Chapter 6 has more information about meeting others.) It's important to talk with people who understand what you're going through and who can support you. Plus, it can be especially satisfying when you can support someone else in return.

**3. Get involved in creating change.** You might join or start a GSA at your school. You could also get involved with a local or national LGBTQ group. Being an activist is a great way to meet people with common interests, and it feels good to work for something positive.

**4. Give yourself opportunities to shine.** Take part in activities that give you a chance to feel good about yourself—maybe even show off a little. These don't have to be LGBTQ-related. If you're a great singer, try out for that solo in the spring concert. Take an art class and paint your heart out. Enter an amazing project in the science fair. Show off your speed on the track team. Dust off your guitar and start a band. Give yourself opportunities to succeed and enjoy yourself.

## I Wish I Could Just Blend In

Maybe the problem is that you feel *too* visible. If you're subjected to taunts and harassment much of the day, a little invisibility might seem like a good thing. A lot of LGBTQ teens share those feelings. Remember those statistics from the GLSEN survey at the beginning of this chapter? Young people who are LGBTQ (or are perceived to be) are frequent targets of bullying.

Even if you decide to come out voluntarily, the amount of attention it brings could be unexpected and overwhelming (although that's not always the case). You can reach out for help and find ways to make that visibility less scary by getting involved in a GSA or working in some other way to change your school environment. And you do have friends among your straight/cis peers, whether you're aware of them or not. As our society becomes more educated about what it means to be queer, more and more of our straight/cis allies are realizing that (1) we're really not so different, and (2) we need their visible support when it comes to standing up for the recognition of our civil rights.

## BEEN THERE

"All of my friends were very supportive. However, seeing the reactions of many of my classmates was extremely disheartening. Seeing that people found it entirely logical to hate me without knowing me not only hurt, but also made me lose a lot of faith in people. I wondered, 'If these misunderstandings and beliefs are so difficult for people to see through or question, what may I need to take a closer look at or question?' And that's what sparked me to really search for what I thought, not what I was told to think or what everyone else thought, politically, spiritually, socially, and personally." —Owen, 19

"Being a lesbian, or even being perceived as one, had its constraints in high school. I was always pretty guarded. My life was school and softball and work. Then I started to date someone who went to the same school and the lid blew off, but no one was saying anything. That, I think, was the worst thing for me. I was being closely watched and no one would say why. But since then, it seems that half the student population felt a need to come out. Sometimes I think I had something to do with that." —Davina, 20

# Exercising Your Rights as an LGBTQ Student

Some schools have policies that protect students from bullying and harassment based on sexual orientation and gender identity. Your school's harassment policy (it may be called a "safe schools policy") usually can be found in your student handbook. Even if your school doesn't include sexual orientation and gender identity in its policy on bullying and harassment, you still have a right as a human being to be safe at school. Administrators and teachers are legally responsible for protecting all students. And you have options for how to deal with harassment.

## Teen Heroes: Changing the Environment for Queer Students

Sometimes it's difficult to believe that one person can make a big difference, but it's possible. Many queer teens have. And what's more, you're *not* alone in the fight against discrimination and harassment. And many adults and straight/cis peers are willing to help. You *can* make a difference by standing up against prejudice and asking others to do the same.

Take a look at how some of these teens fought harassment in their schools.

**Jacob Sullivan.** You might have read about Jacob in chapter 3. In 2009, when he was 14, Jacob Sullivan and the New York Civil Liberties Union filed suit against the Mohawk Central School District. Jacob alleged that the district failed to protect him against harassment, physical abuse, and threats made against him due to his sexual orientation and nonconformity to masculine stereotypes. The US Justice Department later joined the suit, which meant that this case could set a precedent for future rulings and involve a broader interpretation of a federal law prohibiting gender discrimination. The suit was settled March 29, 2010, and as part of the agreement, Jacob's family received $50,000. Perhaps more important, the district agreed to make its schools safer for students. It enlisted the support of the Anti-Defamation League and began training staff on how to better address issues of harassment. The school district also reviewed its policies on harassment based on sex, gender identity, gender expression, and sexual orientation in an effort to create a more positive atmosphere for all students.

### NATIONAL DAY OF SILENCE

The National Day of Silence brings attention to anti-LGBTQ name-calling, bullying, and harassment in schools. Participants take a vow of silence for part or all of the school day and often hand out "speaking cards" that explain their silence and educate others about issues facing LGBTQ teens.

The National Day of Silence has become the largest student-led action promoting safer schools for all, regardless of sexual orientation, gender identity, or gender expression. The project has grown from one event and 150 participants in 1996 to more than 10,000 students in countries all over the world, including New Zealand, Russia, and Singapore, registering their participation with GLSEN each year.

The following is an example of a National Day of Silence speaking card:

*"Please understand my reasons for not speaking today. I am participating in the Day of Silence, a national youth movement protesting the silence faced by lesbian, gay, bisexual, and transgender people and their allies in schools. My deliberate silence echoes that silence, which is caused by harassment, discrimination, and prejudice. I believe that ending the silence is the first step toward fighting these injustices. Think about the voices you are not hearing today. What are you doing to end the silence?"*

For more information on National Day of Silence, including organizing kits and news updates, visit the event web page (www.glsen.org/day-silence). Another great resource for promoting LGBTQ-friendly learning environments is GLSEN's ThinkB4YouSpeak program (www.glsen.org). Visit the site to learn how you can address the use of anti-queer language (words like *fag* and *dyke*) in your school.

**Nick Garafola.** In 2009, after surviving nearly relentless taunting that culminated in a physical altercation, Nick Garafola decided something needed to be done at his school. With the help of some interested peers and an adult advisor, Nick cofounded Spectrum, his school's GSA. "We are currently working on a schoolwide beautification project, which will introduce LGBTQ-themed art into the building," Nick writes in a 2009 article. "Mostly, though, our GSA is a fun and safe place for a bunch of us like-minded students to chill out and talk about homophobia and the differences between tolerating and embracing diversity."

Nick also created a Safe Zone program at his school. "The purpose of the Safe Zone program is to give all students—gay, lesbian, heterosexual, bisexual, questioning, or transgender—someone to talk to about sexual orientation and gender." At Nick's school, a pink triangle is placed on the classroom doors of faculty members who have designated themselves as allies. These allies are taught about the issues teens face regarding sexual orientation and gender identity.

**Dylan Theno.** Dylan Theno isn't queer, but because he was perceived to be by some of his classmates, he was threatened and verbally harassed so much that he dropped out of school during his junior year. The harassment started when he was in seventh grade. Dylan brought a federal suit against the Tonganoxie School District in Kansas for failing to protect him. In 2005, he was awarded a $440,000 settlement.

**STRAIGHT/CIS ALLIES**

"I joined the GSA because many of my friends were active in it. And ever since seeing a production of *The Laramie Project* in seventh grade, I had been very aware of LGBTQ activities among my peers and wanted to be involved. Last year, I participated in the Day of Silence. I am also planning to attend the Valentine's Day dance sponsored by the Rainbow Youth Alliance." —Sabaha, 17

**Joseph Ramelli and Megan Donovan.** Joseph Ramelli and Megan Donovan, both gay, were repeatedly threatened and harassed by students at Poway High School (near San Diego, California). During their senior year, Joseph and Megan had to be homeschooled because of the harassment. The students filed a lawsuit and, in 2005, were awarded $300,000. The jury found that even though school officials were aware of the harassment, they failed to protect Joseph and Megan.

**Pat Doe.** A 15-year-old transgender student known in court documents as Pat Doe took her school to court over her right to express her gender identity by wearing girls' clothing. According to LGBTQ magazine *The Advocate*, Pat's principal had deemed it "disruptive" for a student who was male-identified at birth to wear feminine clothing. In 2000, a Massachusetts appellate court agreed with Pat, and she returned to school able to dress as she felt comfortable.

**Alana Flores.** In 1997, Alana Flores was regularly harassed at her school in Morgan Hill, California. She repeatedly received death threats written on her locker, including the words, "Die, dyke bitch," and, "We'll kill you." Alana took the threatening notes to the assistant principal, who dismissed her complaints and told her to go back to class.

In 1998, Alana and five other students sued the school district for repeatedly ignoring the reports they made about being harassed and bullied by others who thought they were gay. In 2004, the school district was ordered to pay $1.1 million in legal fees and damages. Schools in Morgan Hill also implemented a training program for teachers and administrators to try to eliminate anti-gay harassment. The case set the precedent by a federal court that schools aware of anti-gay harassment must take meaningful steps to stop it.

## LEGAL ASSISTANCE

**Lambda Legal (www.lambdalegal.org).** This national organization works for the equality of people who are LGBTQ. With offices located throughout the country, Lambda Legal may be able to help you address injustices in your school. You can reach the group by calling (212) 809-8585 or by visiting the website.

**American Civil Liberties Union (www.aclu.org).** The ACLU has supported LGBTQ civil rights with legal aid since the 1960s. Visit their website to learn about cases the group has pursued on behalf of queer students. You can also call (212) 549-2500 to report discrimination.

**Southern Poverty Law Center (www.splcenter.org).** The SPLC works to help LGBTQ people achieve full equality under the law, with a focus on states in the Deep South. Through their Teaching Tolerance project, they're working to combat bullying and foster teaching environments where all students feel safe and welcome. SPLC provides specific information to help LGBTQ young people know their rights and, in some cases, helps with legal proceedings. Visit their website or call 1-888-414-7752 for more information.

**Jamie Nabozny.** Jamie Nabozny suffered such violent abuse and harassment that he was forced to drop out of his Ashland, Wisconsin, high school. Jamie brought a lawsuit against the school district, and in 1996, a federal court ruled in his favor, stating that the school had failed to provide Jamie with a safe learning environment. The school agreed to pay nearly $1 million to settle the case. The landmark decision—that schools can be held liable for deliberately ignoring anti-gay harassment—set a precedent for similar cases and forced many schools to examine their own policies. Jamie's story is featured in the documentary *Bullied* (www.tolerance.org/bullied).

**Ashton Whitaker.** In 2016, Ashton Whitaker's family sued the Kenosha Unified School District in Wisconsin for forbidding Ashton, who is trans, from using the boys' restrooms at George Nelson Tremper High School because the gender on his birth certificate is listed as female. A district court in Wisconsin ruled that Ashton would likely face "irreparable harm" if forced to use restrooms designated as female and should therefore be allowed to use the boys' facilities. In 2017, a US appeals court affirmed the ruling, in part citing Title IX of the Education Amendments of 1972, which prohibits sex discrimination in schools and other educational institutions that receive federal funding.

**North Putnam High School.** In 2015, students at North Putnam High School in Roachdale, Indiana, tried to start a GSA, but met with resistance from the school board. Eventually, the board voted to bar the group from forming, even though clubs in the school didn't require school board approval by vote. The ACLU sued, and the school board reversed its decision, allowing the GSA to form.

According to the ACLU, since 1996, courts have awarded millions of dollars in damages to lesbian, gay, bisexual, and transgender students who filed lawsuits against schools for refusing to take adequate steps to stop anti-queer harassment.

Filing a lawsuit may not be the best solution for every situation, but it is an option. As Nick Garafola showed, you can create change without going to court. But these and similar cases across the country have resulted in some schools voluntarily protecting LGBTQ students from harassment.

## The Voice of Authority: Talking to Teachers and Administrators

Teachers, administrators, and other school officials can be some of your greatest allies, or they can be some of your biggest headaches.

For some students, even worse than bullying and harassment from other students is dealing with prejudice from school officials. According to Human Rights Watch, an international organization working for the equality of all people, many students find discrimination by teachers even more demoralizing and difficult to deal with than anything their peers say or do.

Some school officials and teachers harass teens by making anti-LGBTQ remarks. Some turn a blind eye to harassment by students or other members of the school community. Others tell LGBTQ students that the harassment is *their* fault because the students are inviting harassment by "flaunting" who they are.

However it occurs, mistreatment by school staff is unacceptable. You can take action to help make your school safer for everyone.

### Confronting Authority

Here are some ways you can confront harassment and discrimination by officials or teachers at your school:

**Action: Approach the offending official or teacher.** Tell them how their speech or behavior makes you feel. Explain that when adults ignore or participate in harassment, it sends a message to students that it's okay. Stay calm and rational as you talk to the person. This can be difficult, but it can help you make your point more effectively. (See the information on Nonviolent Communication on pages 74–75.)

**Action: Tell a parent, a guardian, or another adult.** Parents or guardians can be helpful allies in standing up to bullying, especially if the bullying is coming from other adults. Confronting an adult can be intimidating, so it's a good idea to have the support of at least one adult you trust.

**Action: Tell an administrator.** If the perpetrator of prejudice is a teacher or another staff member, report the person to an administrator such as a principal or vice principal. If the perpetrator *is* an administrator, approach the school superintendent or the school board. If you're going that high up the chain of command, it's especially helpful to have an adult backing you up—a parent, a lawyer, someone from a national LGBTQ organization, or a combination of these adults.

## On Your Side: Getting Support from School Staff

Many teachers and administrators want to protect queer students from bullying and harassment. Some might speak up when they hear anti-LGBTQ language or see physical harassment. If your school has a GSA, the group's faculty advisor could also be a good advocate for you. Enlist the help of any official who you know wants to support queer students at school.

### UNDERSTANDING THE LAW

In her book *Out Law: What LGBT Youth Should Know About Their Legal Rights*, journalist and former editor of the *Washington Blade* (Washington, D.C.'s, LGBT city paper) Lisa Keen explores legal issues relevant to LGBTQ people, including school-specific issues for young people. Though legal issues are constantly changing, this book is an excellent resource for empowering LGBTQ teens and allies. It not only discusses specific and landmark rulings, but also explains how the legal system works, including how laws are interpreted and the differences between state and federal laws.

As with coming out, when it comes to bullying, it helps to be prepared before taking action. Get informed, know what your resources are, and get yourself in a solid, positive mindset.

1. Consult with a group such as GLSEN, the American Civil Liberties Union, Lambda Legal, or the Southern Poverty Law Center to find out exactly what your legal rights are at school.
2. Research how students at other schools have had success in confronting issues with teachers or school administrators. You might be able to connect with some of these peers via email or an online social network.
3. Prepare your case with detailed notes, witnesses, and examples. Even if you're not going to court, it's helpful to think of your

situation as a case (and it may eventually become a legal case). Being organized helps others see that you're serious.

4. Be calm and rational. If you're overly emotional, authorities might try to dismiss you as overreacting.
5. Keep it simple. State your problem as briefly as you can and stick to the facts. Stay away from giving your personal opinions (unless you're asked). Instead, provide a factual account of the events.
6. Listen. There are two sides to every story. It can be tough to listen to the person doing the bullying give their version of the story, but remember that acting calmly and rationally will help demonstrate your maturity and your seriousness about confronting the problem.

It's a good idea to give school administrators a chance to address the issue before calling an attorney. In many cases, legal action can be avoided. However, if the school doesn't take action, doesn't do so in a timely manner, or is insufficient in its response, then it may be time for legal action.

For more information on dealing with bullying, including cyberbullying, see chapter 3 (page 58).

**BEEN THERE**

"I actually found out that my math teacher was a lesbian. After I graduated, we ended up becoming friends." —Jennifer, 18

## Club Life: Gay-Straight Alliances (GSAs) and Other Queer-Friendly Activities

Gay-straight alliances (sometimes called genders and sexualities alliances) are student-led groups that work to create a safe, welcoming, accepting school environment for all students.

GSAs have received a lot of coverage in the media. Some school districts have attempted to block their formation, but your right to form a GSA in your school is protected by the law. There are two laws that apply—the First Amendment (protecting freedom of speech and assembly) and the federal Equal Access Act (providing for equal treatment of all noninstructional, student-initiated clubs). All over the country, students are fighting back and standing up for their right to form GSAs.

## Common Questions and Answers About GSAs

Here are some common questions and answers about GSAs. More information is also available from GLSEN (www.glsen.org) and the GSA Network (www.gsanetwork.org).

**Q: Who gets involved in GSAs?**
**A:** GSAs welcome any student who feels that harassment and discrimination against LGBTQ people, their families, and their friends are wrong or who wants to learn more about these issues.

**Q: How many GSAs are there?**
**A:** GSAs can be found in public, private, and parochial high schools and middle schools of various sizes all over the country. According to GLSEN, there are more than 4,000 GSAs nationwide. And the *2015 National School Climate Survey* reports that just over half (54 percent) of students said their school had a GSA or similar club.

### BEEN THERE

"I cofounded the GSA at my school. My friend and I wrote the appropriate letters and had meetings with the principal. We also found a faculty advisor, figured out a place to meet, chose our meeting time, and named our group. It was an uphill battle, during which we went head-to-head with the principal several times. But we managed to do some good things, like hold events for National Coming Out Day and the National Day of Silence. The group was definitely controversial, but we helped to raise a lot of awareness."
—Arian, 19

**Q: Do people in GSAs talk about sex?**
**A:** That's not the purpose of GSAs. These groups meet just like any other school club, but the activities range from discussions of gender roles or what it means to be queer to working on projects aimed at making the school a safer space for LGBTQ students.

GLSEN supports events that many GSAs participate in. Among these are Ally Week, TransACTION!, Bisexual Awareness Week, National Coming Out Day, Intersex Awareness Day, Transgender Day of Remembrance, and National Day of Silence (go to www.glsen.org for more information).

## How to Start a GSA

If you're interested in starting a GSA at your school, here are some basic steps to get things moving:

**1. Find out and follow your school's guidelines.** You establish a GSA the same way you would any other school club. Look in your student handbook for your school's rules for starting a group. You may find guidelines or a set process you need to follow (for example, writing a club mission statement).

**2. Find a faculty advisor.** Consider teachers or staff members who you think would be supportive or who have shown support for LGBTQ issues. Your school might have guidelines about who is eligible to be a club advisor.

**3. Find other interested students.** GSAs are for both LGBTQ and straight/cis students. Straight/cis students who feel that anti-LGBTQ discrimination is wrong are often strong and vocal GSA members. Look for members all over your school. The more diverse the GSA membership is, the stronger and more effective the group can be.

**4. Talk to the administration.** Tell school officials what you're doing and try to get their support. If they're supportive, they can help the GSA gain acceptance among students, teachers, and the community. If administrators oppose the formation of the group, inform them (calmly and kindly) of your legal right to start a club.

**5. Pick a meeting place.** Select a place in the school that affords some privacy but is also easily accessible. It could be a classroom, counselor's office, or conference room.

**6. Advertise.** Let others know about the meeting through posters, flyers, a page on a social media site, word-of-mouth, the school website, and any other (appropriate) methods you can think of. Some people may tear down or put graffiti on your flyers and posters. Don't be discouraged. Have a reserve stash so you can post more.

**7. Plan an agenda.** Think about what you want to do at your first meeting and plan ahead. You can do anything from holding discussions and playing get-to-know-you games to having a guest speaker and planning a workshop. Visit the websites of organizations that support GSAs for more meeting ideas.

**THE OFFICIAL RULING**

In 2000, US District Court Judge David O. Carter made a landmark decision on GSAs. He stated in his ruling, "To the extent that the [school] board opens up its school facilities to any noncurriculum-related group, it must open its facilities to all student groups."

For more information about legal rights and GSAs, visit the websites of GLSEN (www.glsen.org), the GSA Network (www.gsanetwork.org), and the ACLU (www.aclu.org).

**8. Hold the meeting.** A good idea for the first meeting is to have members introduce themselves, discuss why the group is needed, plan your overall goals, and brainstorm projects for the year. You also might want to plan to elect group members for president, vice president, treasurer, and other club offices so that you have a leadership structure.

**9. Set ground rules.** At the first meeting, work together to create rules to ensure that discussions are safe, confidential, and respectful. Make sure group members know that everyone's views are welcome.

**10. Plan for the future.** Set goals for what you want the GSA to accomplish, not only in the next few months, but also in the long term. Be realistic about what you can do over the course of the year, but don't be afraid to think big. You might be amazed at what you can achieve.

This information is adapted from *The GLSEN Jump-Start Guide to Building and Activating Your GSA or Similar Student Club*. Check it out online at www.glsen.org.

**THE BIRTH OF THE GSA**

Did you know that the first GSA was founded by a straight/cis student? In 1988, a student at Concord Academy in Concord, Massachusetts, wanted to do something to help educate her fellow students about anti-queer bullying and harassment. She approached her history teacher Kevin Jennings (who went on to become the founder of GLSEN) and proposed the idea for the club. A short time later, Jennings became the faculty advisor for the nation's first GSA.

## Moving On: Deciding If You Need to Change Schools

Unfortunately, some queer teens end up having to change schools because officials are unwilling to address bullying and harassment. Some may ignore or even participate in the mistreatment.

### Making the Change

If you've explored all your options for bringing an end to harassment—talking with teachers, administrators, school superintendents, the school board, and people from national LGBTQ organizations—and it hasn't worked, or if you believe you're in serious danger, it might be time to change schools. Approach your parent or guardian and talk with them about why you feel it's necessary for you to make the change.

Moving to a new school won't necessarily mean an end to bullying and harassment. You might encounter problems similar to the ones you had at your previous school. It's a good idea to have your parent or guardian contact administrators at your new prospective school to find out their stance on LGBTQ harassment issues. If attitudes at your new school aren't any better (or are worse) than at your current school, it might be wise to look at other options. You could consider getting legal assistance from a national LGBTQ or civil rights organization. Homeschooling or studying for the GED at a local community college are other possibilities. A few large US cities (including New York, Los Angeles, Atlanta, and Milwaukee) even have schools—public and private—specifically for queer students.

## Staying in School

Whatever you do, continue your education. LGBTQ teens often have much higher absenteeism and dropout rates than their straight/cis peers do. According to the *2015 National School Climate Survey*, nearly 32 percent of LGBTQ students missed an entire day of school in the month before the survey because of feeling unsafe or uncomfortable at school, with 10 percent missing four or more days that month. Also, queer students who experience harassment often get lower grades than their straight/cis peers do and may disengage from school altogether. Queer teens were more likely than their straight/cis peers to report that they didn't plan to pursue any post-secondary education (or get a high school diploma or finish high school at all).

### BEEN THERE

"I dropped out of high school after six months of constant torture. Being gay, or being perceived to be gay, affected me very negatively, to the point of being suicidal, because of all the daily harassment. Now I'm being homeschooled. But I've found that being gay has opened up so many doors for me. Every once in a while I will think about what my life would have been like if I'd been straight, and, well, I don't think that I would be as happy as I am right now. I mean, why would I want to be anyone other than who I am?" —Robert, 15

An education is incredibly important, and although it might seem like a good solution at the time, dropping out of school will seriously limit your opportunities. Don't let a group of ignorant people rob you of your future. Whether you change schools, homeschool, get your GED, attend school online, or opt for early college admission, getting an education is your ticket to the life you want and deserve.

CHAPTER 6

# LGBTQ Friends

**We are family.**

If being LGBTQ is normal and queer people aren't all that different from straight/cis people, why should it matter if you have LGBTQ friends?

If you're out and have close straight/cis friends, that's great. And if your immediate or extended family members have been supportive, that's great, too. At the same time, it can help to know people who really understand what it's like to be queer. For some LGBTQ people, it isn't until they are able to spend time with other queer people that they truly feel part of a peer group.

For many teens, their most influential role models are family members. But in most cases, LGBTQ teens can't be *just* like mom or dad, a grandparent, or an aunt or uncle because odds are most of these people are straight/cis. A lot of queer teens haven't grown up with role models or friends they can truly identify with regarding certain aspects of life. Having queer friends can help LGBTQ teens feel more comfortable with their sexual orientations or gender identities.

**BEEN THERE**

"During high school, I got involved with an LGBTQ counseling/social group. I loved it. It really helped me feel more comfortable with myself. All the other kids who went there were from different schools. It was nice because it was like forming our own little community. Every week after the 'session,' which we just called 'group,' we'd go out to eat. We had so much fun." —Valencia, 19

"It's like being in your own private club. It's like having an inside joke that not everyone understands. But when you do find someone who understands, there is an immediate connection that goes beyond words and finds itself in common experiences." —Walt, 20

## Part of the Family: The Utterly Diverse, Somewhat Cohesive, Always Interesting LGBTQ Community

One of the best things about being LGBTQ is the sense of community you can feel with other queer people. In fact, one of the ways some LGBTQ people identify one another is by using the word *family*. As in, "You know Hiro, the guy in our chem class? He's family." Some people even have bumper stickers that read "Family" or "Family car."

Just like any family, though, we don't always get along. Not all LGBTQ people like or even tolerate each other. Although we're part of a larger group, we're individuals with our own personalities and histories. Being LGBTQ is a major characteristic to have in common, but it might also be the *only* thing you have in common.

At first you might feel intimidated by the LGBTQ community. You might worry about not being "queer enough" or not following the "LGBTQ rules." You'll soon discover, however, that the LGBTQ community is as diverse as people can be, and that diversity is our strength. Whether you're a drama queen, a jock, a nerd, a butch, a femme, a gender bender, a girlie girl, a manly man, a trans man, a club kid, a prep, an urban hipster, a country boy, an androgyne, a hip-hop head, a surfer dude, a hippie chick, or none of the above, there's room for you just as you are.

## IMRU2? Meeting Other LGBTQ Teens

Throughout history, queer people have come up with some pretty creative secret ways to identify each other. In the past, one gay man might have approached another man and asked, "Are you a friend of Dorothy?" If the other man answered, "yes," that meant he was also gay. This phrase, which was a reference to Dorothy in *The Wizard of Oz,* is just one example of the many ways LGBTQ people have come up with to discreetly identify one another. If you ever come across a retro T-shirt that reads "Friend of Dorothy," now you're in the know.

**GAYDAR**

Hey, what's that beeping? Did you know that the word *gaydar* is now in the dictionary? *Merriam-Webster's* dictionary defines *gaydar* as "the ability to recognize homosexuals through observation or intuition." *Gaydar* is short for "gay radar." Does gaydar really exist? Some people swear by it, but others have never heard a beep. You can decide for yourself.

### Great Places to Meet Other LGBTQ Teens

Regardless of whether you believe in gaydar (see the sidebar on page 125), here are some good places to meet other queer teens:

**Queer community centers and organizations.** LGBTQ groups sponsor programs that offer everything from social activities (like movie nights) to counseling services or homework help. These groups should be listed in your local telephone directory, or you can

## BEEN THERE

"There are a few other trans people at my school and many other people that fall across the whole spectrum, both in terms of gender and sexuality. I also connect with other LGBTQ+ people through social media like Instagram and Tumblr." —Jayson, 16

search online for "gay community center" along with your city and state. Centerlink (www.lgbtcenters.org) serves as an online directory for LGBTQ centers. The Trevor Project (www.thetrevorproject.org) also provides info on state and local organizations working with LGBTQ teens.

**LGBTQ bookstores.** Go to a reading or just show up and casually flip through some periodicals. You could bump into other young people. If there's no LGBTQ bookstore in your area, there could be a queer section in your local bookstore. In addition, many community libraries offer events and services for LGBTQ people.

### SPEAKING OF BOOKS . . . FINDING YOURSELF IN LITERATURE

Just as it's important to connect with other LGBTQ people in real life, it's also great to see yourself represented in books. Being able to read about people (real or fictional) who are like you or who have had similar experiences is important to feeling "normal." Writer and blogger Lee Wind operates an award-winning site (www.leewind.org) where he reviews and catalogs many books with LGBTQ characters and themes.

## BEEN THERE

"Even though I love my straight friends, it was a huge relief to meet other gay teens. It's nice to have people who totally understand what you're talking about, what it's like to come out, and all of that." —Elizabeth, 17

**Coffeehouses or other places where teens and students like to hang out.** This strategy for meeting other queer teens may work especially well if your town or city has a gay neighborhood. Visiting a "gayborhood" can be a great way to work yourself into your community's LGBTQ scene without having to put yourself out there too much.

**QUEER CAMP**
Did you know there are camps for LGBTQ teens and families? Lots of them, in fact. For a full list, visit www.transstudent.org/camps.

**Underage clubs.** Not all nightclubs are for those 21 or over. Many towns have underage clubs where teens can watch live music, play games, or just hang out. Going to these places can increase your chances of meeting LGBTQ people your own age.

**A NOTE ABOUT THE CLUB SCENE**
Some young people, desperate to meet or be around other LGBTQ people, sneak into queer clubs or other hangouts for people 21 or over. Sneaking into bars or clubs could spell trouble for you for a few reasons, not the least of which is that it's illegal. You also risk being in situations you're not prepared for—underage drinking, drug use, smoking—even if you're just looking for friendship. And unfortunately, some predatory adults take advantage of LGBTQ teens in the club scene. The last thing you need is a big setback in your life by getting involved in the club scene, where you could even get arrested. It's best to stick to activities and locations geared toward teens. That's also the best way to ensure you'll have opportunities to meet people your own age.

## How Do I Know If They're LGBTQ?

If you meet someone in a non-LGBTQ-centered place, it can be difficult to identify whether that person is queer. Even if your gaydar is beeping like crazy, try not to make any assumptions. Subtlety is usually the best tactic when trying to figure out if someone is LGBTQ. Regardless of how out you are, others might not take kindly to you waltzing up to them and asking, "You're queer, right?"

Here are some subtle strategies for figuring out if the person who caught your eye was actually winking or just trying to get rid of a loose eyelash:

- Start a conversation and reference something you saw on a TV show or in a movie with queer people or characters in starring roles. Maybe they'll get the hint and drop one of their own.

- If you're at a bookstore or library, bring over a copy of a queer-themed book. Tell the person you're thinking about reading it and ask if they've heard anything about it. It doesn't win the subtle award, but it will probably help get the information you're looking for.
- If you're the straightforward type, go ahead and ask. But there's no need to shout, "Hey, are you queer?" At least start a conversation first and then work it in. Think of how you might feel if someone walked up to you demanding to know your sexual orientation or gender identity. Keep in mind that if the person is straight, depending on their attitude, they might be offended by your question. Be prepared for a variety of responses (and remember, any negative responses are about the other person, not you).

## Making Connections: LGBTQ Online Communities

The internet is a great place to meet and talk with others. Whether you're an experienced surfer or you've barely gotten your feet wet, finding others online is easy.

Many websites sponsor scheduled chats, guest speakers, webinars, bulletin boards, and blogs. Some also allow you to have your own email account. You can chat online with other LGBTQ teens, post questions or conversation topics, talk to counselors, and so on.

It might take some trial and error to find what you're looking for online because there's just so much content out there. It's likely you'll end up visiting several sites before you settle on one, or a few, that you want to explore further.

**BEEN THERE**

"I've come out to people online, in large groups and in chat rooms, which is so much easier for me than in person or one-on-one."
—Fatema, 19

### The Internet: Stay Safe as You Surf

The internet has grown exponentially in terms of its content and variety of websites. Unfortunately, the risks and number of people out there using the web to victimize people—including LGBTQ teens—have also grown. Here are some things to think about when you're visiting a site:

**Who sponsors the site?** Could the site have an ulterior motive that could influence the content? One common motive is to sell you something. If you use a search engine to locate sites of interest to queer teens, it's common to find many that are actually selling subscriptions to dating and other social networking services. Some sites masquerade as help sites, but are actually sponsored by religious groups or other organizations whose missions are to "convert" LGBTQ people.

**Who's giving that advice?** Keep in mind that at some sites—especially bulletin boards—you don't know who's answering you or how valid the information is. It's a good idea to save serious questions for sites where counselors or experts provide information.

**What kind of information do they want from you?** Some sites require you to register before using them. Be wary of sites that require you to give information beyond a username and a password. *Never give out your address or your phone number.*

**Who are you talking to?** You can never be absolutely sure who you're talking to online, so be careful and make decisions about what you say accordingly. Don't give out personal information like your phone number or where you live. It can be surprisingly easy to mention personal information in conversation without thinking about it. Typing something as simple as, "My little sis, Sarah, is scared because there's a huge storm brewing here in Little Creek," tells others where you live and that you have a younger sister, as well as your sister's name. That might seem harmless, but someone with bad intentions could be looking for that type of information.

Meeting in person with someone you became acquainted with online could be extremely dangerous. Your new friend could be exactly who they say they are—or not. It's important to wait to meet someone you've met online until you can be accompanied by a family adult or another adult you trust. That doesn't mean they have to chaperone you, but hanging around nearby until you're sure things are cool is a good idea. At the very least, text a friend and tell them where you're going and who you're meeting and that you'll check back in with them at a certain time.

Be *very* wary of anyone who requests a photo online, especially if they ask for it right away, and *never* send a revealing photo. It's not safe, and it's not smart. You never know where the picture will show up, but it's a good bet that the person you send it to won't be the only one who sees it. Once it's out there, there's no getting it back. The same applies to sending sexually suggestive or explicit emails or text messages (sexting). It might seem like a fun idea at the time, but keep in mind that those messages can easily be saved and forwarded (and often are). There's even an app to take and save screenshots in Snapchat without being detected.

**SOME PLACES TO START ONLINE**

**TrevorSpace (www.trevorspace.org).** This is a social networking community for LGBTQ teens ages 13 to 24. What sets TrevorSpace apart from other social media sites is that it's monitored by adults who are part of the Trevor Project, so it's a safe space for queer teens.

**GLSEN (www.glsen.org).** This site is geared toward activism, but it's still a great place to get in touch with other teens. The organization can connect you with local chapters and GSAs, as well as other queer student groups.

When chatting online, ditch anyone who uses inappropriate, suggestive, or coercive language—you don't need to waste your time on people who make you uncomfortable, speak to you disrespectfully, or attempt to manipulate you.

## Queer Compadres: LGBTQ Friendships

As you're looking for LGBTQ friends, keep in mind that not just any queer person will do. As with all friendships, you need to be true to yourself. It's great to be friends with other LGBTQ people as long as they're people you would pick to be your friends otherwise.

Don't waste your time on people who try to talk you into doing potentially harmful things, such as using drugs and alcohol, just because they're LGBTQ. Queer people are just like anyone else—everyone is different. You'll like some, and you won't like others. But don't lower your standards just to make friends. Knowing who you are and sticking to your beliefs can ensure you won't become involved in unhealthy relationships or activities.

Thinking about all this could have you feeling like it's the first day of school all over again. Try not to worry: You'll make some good friends. Just to prove it, here are five reasons why:

1. You're true to your beliefs.
2. You're proud of who you are (or at least you're working on it).
3. You respect others' opinions.
4. You're a great listener.
5. You know that life can be challenging, but there's still a lot of room for fun.

**BEEN THERE**

"My senior year, I realized I was living for myself and no one else. I had no one to please but me. I hung out with the people I wanted to and didn't worry about people other than that. I did the things I wanted to do and spoke my mind whether or not someone else agreed with it." —Emily, 18

## Straight But Not Narrow: Other Friends

Straight/cis friendships are no less valuable than LGBTQ ones. In fact, it's good to be friends with a wide variety of people. Exposure to different viewpoints helps make you a well-rounded, considerate person.

### "That's soooo gay! Um, no offense."

It can be easy to become frustrated with some of your straight/cis friends if they make remarks that you feel are insensitive or ignorant. But try to be patient with them. Bring remarks to their attention and calmly explain why the remarks hurt your feelings or upset you. Many times you'll find that it's just a misunderstanding and your friend didn't realize how what they said sounded, they thoughtlessly said something out of habit, or they didn't think it would be offensive. We all have things we can learn from one another. Give your friend a chance. You might be the first LGBTQ person they know. (See chapter 3 for more tips on how to address phobic remarks.)

However, if you have a friend who is repeatedly offensive, or even abusive, and who doesn't care whether you're offended, you might want to rethink the friendship. LGBTQ or straight/cis, do you really want to be friends with someone who treats you or anyone else like that?

## Bridging the Gap

After you come out to a straight/cis friend, your friend might feel uncomfortable (or might be completely cool with it). Maybe they're still getting used to it and aren't exactly sure what your coming out to them means. Does it mean you're going to start dressing, acting, or talking differently? Will you still want to be friends, or will you want new LGBTQ friends instead? Does it mean you want to date them?

### BEEN THERE

"I first came out to my best friend who was honestly just confused at first, but since then he has been nothing but supportive and has done everything he can to educate himself." —Jayson, 16

These questions might come up right away, down the road, or not at all. But take time to address them if they do come up, because it will make your friendship stronger. Also, knowledge is contagious. The next time your friend hears someone demeaning LGBTQ people, they just might intervene. And that's how people and society start to change for the better.

CHAPTER 7

# Dating and Relationships

**I'm not a lesbian, but my girlfriend is.**

Depending on where you live, the dating scene for LGBTQ teens may be full of possibilities—or you may feel like a unicorn, with little to no potential for finding romance. But regardless of whether you're in an urban, a suburban, or even a rural area, options do exist. Maybe your town doesn't hold events like queer proms, but LGBTQ teens still find ways to get together and have fun. As you become more comfortable with your sexuality, you might even start dating a little . . . or maybe a lot. The important thing to remember is that whether you're experienced with dating, just beginning to date, or only starting to think about it, *you* decide how to run your love life.

## Soul Searching: Figuring Out If You're Ready to Date

When you're a teen, there can be a lot of pressure to date. But not everyone is ready. It all depends on where you are mentally and emotionally, and no two people are the same in that regard. If you're still trying to figure out who you are, it can be difficult to try to start a relationship with someone else. (And you may find this is the same all your life; lots of adults are still trying to figure out all kinds of things.) Still, for all teens—queer and straight/cis—dating can be a normal and healthy part of developing positive personal relationships with others.

**BEEN THERE**

"To be honest, I haven't really dated anyone. I've only ever kissed one girl, and I don't even speak to her now. I have found a few people through LGBTQ websites and such, but mostly people to talk to. A few have become my friends." —Katy, 19

### Trying to Fit In

Dating can be a lot of fun, but it can also feel like torture if you don't feel free to date the people you're really interested in. Many queer people end up in straight relationships or dating situations because they feel it's expected of them. Some may be attempting to fit in or trying to change their feelings of being queer.

It's common for LGBTQ teens to try to fit in. Some gay teens date people of another gender in an attempt to hide their sexual orientations or in the hopes that it will "make" them heterosexual. Some even engage in heterosexual sex to try to deny their true identities. And some who are asexual (sometimes called "ace" for short) may try to force themselves to engage in activities they're really not interested in as a means of trying to feel "normal" (though there are lots of people who identify as ace—see page 138 for more information).

If you find yourself in a situation where you're doing something that doesn't feel right, ask yourself if you're dating contrary to your wants and needs because you feel like you have to. If it's making you unhappy, you don't have to do it. If, on the other hand, these dates are more about friends hanging out and you feel good about them, that's okay. Maybe it's all just a part of your own exploration, which is great. The key is to be true to yourself and honest with the person you're spending time with.

## Dating to Figure Things Out

If you're questioning, dating might be a positive way for you to explore your sexual orientation or gender identity. You can meet new people, have fun, and figure out some things. But while dating can help you answer some questions, sex won't. Engaging in sexual activity for the purpose of figuring out who you are is a bad idea because it can lead to even more confusion, or worse, and it's not necessary. Being LGBTQ is about a lot more than who you sleep with. It's about your personal identity, so you don't need to engage in sexual activity with someone else to understand your sexual orientation or gender identity.

**THE NO-HOLDS-BARRED BARE NAKED TRUTH**

You don't have to have sex to figure out your sexuality, sexual orientation, or gender identity. Period. Exclamation point.

And you don't even have to date. If you're really feeling conflicted about your identity, the thought of dating might not appeal to you right now. The important thing is to listen to yourself. Don't do anything you're not ready for, because if you push yourself, things will just become more stressful. Remember, everything will sort itself out if you give it (and yourself) a chance.

## Am I Ready? Dating Checklist

This checklist can help you figure out if you're ready to date. So, before you check out the dating scene, be sure to check off each of these items:

- ✓ I'm confident in myself.
- ✓ I don't feel like I need someone else's approval, and I don't feel the need to please others to the detriment of myself.
- ✓ I'm confident I can say no if someone pressures me to do something I don't want to do or am not sure about.
- ✓ I can be respectful of others' feelings and beliefs and won't try to force them to do something they're not comfortable with.
- ✓ If things don't work out with one person, I understand that there will be other opportunities.

# Who Gets the Check? LGBTQ Dating Basics

Most of us get our ideas about romance from movies and TV, and there isn't an abundance of shows depicting Lance sweeping Hector off his feet and living happily ever after, of LaTisha and Gabrielle waltzing off into the sunset, or of Jaime and Chris navigating Jaime's transition while staying together (although there are a lot more than there used to be). When queer relationships are shown, sometimes they're amplified versions of unhealthy relationship patterns. The relative scarcity of positive LGBTQ dating role models can make some teens nervous about the idea of dating.

## Queer Dating Q&A

It's natural to have a lot of questions and some confusion as you enter the queer dating scene. Most likely, a lot of what you've learned is probably modeled after heterosexual binary (boy-girl) dating. So what happens if it's boy-boy, girl-girl, or totally outside the gender binary? Here are some common questions and answers:

**Q: What's an LGBTQ relationship supposed to be like? How do I know what to do if we're both boys or both girls or one or both of us is nonbinary?**

**A:** What's any relationship supposed to be like? Starting to date is a confusing time for everyone, but it can feel even more confusing if you're LGBTQ. A lot of our behavior is based on long-held ideas about the binary construct and about female and male roles in relationships. Being LGBTQ is a great opportunity to throw those stereotypes out the window and just be yourselves. Let the personalities of you and the other person dictate what the relationship is like. As long as you're true to yourself and the relationship is healthy, you're off to a great start.

**BEEN THERE**

"The best thing about my boyfriend is that I don't feel like I have to worry what he'll think about anything. We're just cool with each other, and that's the most amazing feeling—when someone likes you just how you are." —Troy, 17

**Q: How do I figure out who should pay?**

**A:** More and more people are going Dutch—each person pays for their share. Many teens don't have a lot of pocket money to start with, so it helps if you split the tab. If only one person is going to pay, it's usually the person who initiated the date. But who says dates have to cost a lot of money (or any)? See the next answer for some cheap or free options.

**Q: Where is a good place to go on a date?**

**A:** The standards are dinner, a movie, or someplace like a coffee shop, mall, or arcade where you can hang out. Nothing wrong with those—they're classics. LGBTQ-friendly places like social events at queer community centers and underage clubs are great, too, because depending on your community, it may feel easier to be yourself. Really, when it comes to what to do on a date, you're limited only by your creativity. Museums, a picnic in the park, an open mic night, or a hike are also great cheap or free options. (If you're doing something like going for a hike, bike ride, or similar outdoor activity, make sure you choose a well-traveled path and that someone else knows where you're going to be. Safety first!)

**Q: Is it true that LGBTQ people are more promiscuous? Should I expect physical contact on the date?**

**A:** Myth alert! That's not true. Queer people are, by nature, no more promiscuous than their straight/cis counterparts. And you certainly shouldn't feel like you have to engage in sexual activity to find out if you're LGBTQ, to prove something to someone (even yourself), to make another person happy, or for any other reason. Just like anyone else, you should take the time you need to be sure you're absolutely, positively ready and that the other person is the one you're ready to share that part of yourself with.

**Q: If I don't know a lot of LGBTQ people, will I just have to settle for dating whoever is around?**

**A:** Absolutely not. One of the downsides of being LGBTQ in middle or high school is that you probably have fewer dating options than some of your straight/cis friends. Nevertheless, you don't have to settle. If someone doesn't particularly interest you, you don't have to date them just because they're one of the only LGBTQ people you know.

### BEING ASEXUAL

Asexuality is defined as a lack of or low level of sexual interest in others. Those who identify as asexual are still fully capable of loving, affectionate, romantic relationships. (Those who identify as aromantic tend not to experience romantic feelings toward others.) Asexuality (sometimes referred to as "ace") is a valid, legitimate identity just like any other orientation. According to researcher Anthony Bogaert, roughly 1 percent of people are asexual.

Unfortunately, some asexual people meet with ignorance from others who speak as if being asexual represents some form of sexual immaturity or stunted development, or imply (or outright say) that someone who is asexual "just hasn't met the right person yet" or is somehow afraid of sexual activity. Asexual people, just like everyone else, can engage in deeply meaningful and satisfying relationships. Asexual partnerships are well known throughout history. In the 19th and early 20th centuries, the term *Boston marriage* was used primarily in New England to describe two women who had a household together and were involved in a long-term, committed partnership, but did not have a sexual relationship. Asexual partnerships can be engaged in by people of the same or differing genders and any orientation.

For more information on asexuality, check out the Trevor Project's page on asexuality at www.thetrevorproject.org. There are also several organizations for people who identify as asexual, such as the Asexual Visibility and Education Network (www.asexuality.org).

## What's My Type?

Among the most common misconceptions about LGBTQ people is that we always pair off according to type—butch with femme. Thankfully, these ideas are changing, especially among young people. Words like *butch* (people having a traditionally masculine gender expression) and *femme* (people having a traditionally feminine gender expression) don't even begin to take into account the full spectrum of LGBTQ people; many don't consider themselves to be one or the other. Also, attraction just is, whether you're LGBTQ or straight/cis. Even if your taste leans one way or the other, who you end up with may very well surprise you.

The concepts of butch and femme have been around a long time. In the past, they were often used as a visible means of declaring an interest in the same sex. The roles of butch and femme continue to influence some LGBTQ relationships, and there's nothing wrong with that. But they definitely don't have to.

These stereotypes also color the perception many straight/cis people have about LGBTQ relationships. Many of the ideas are based on the concept that there has to be an identified "male" and "female" in every relationship, and regardless of the sex or gender of those involved, each must take one of these roles. The truth is, so many people have been operating with these traditions for so long that they started to think of them as laws of nature. But they're not.

### CELESTIAL ENERGY

Sex educator and anthropologist Mala Madrone encourages use of the terms *solar* and *lunar*, rather than or in addition to terms like *male* and *female* or *butch* and *femme*, as broader, more freeing, genderless descriptors that refer to people's energies in relationships rather than their genders. While we all have some balance of solar and lunar energies within us (like yin and yang energies in Eastern traditions), we tend to seek partners (romantic and otherwise) who complement us as the sun and moon complement each other.

Some people choose this kind of dynamic in their relationships. But you also have a choice—you can be in a relationship with anyone, regardless of what labels you take for yourselves and even if you don't take any labels at all.

### BEEN THERE

"The dynamics of queer relationships aren't talked about very often. Ideas of butch and femme within relationships are things that are stereotyped about the queer community, but rarely addressed in a plain way. At least in my experience of being bisexual, it can be really confusing to feel like there are specific male/female roles in a different-sex relationship and then not to have that framework, or familiarity, in same-sex relationships."
—Gwen, 18

## The LGBTQ Dating Scene: A Word of Caution

Meeting other queer teens can be difficult, but it also might not be as hard as you think. If you decide that it's time to date, be sure that you're safe in how and where you meet people. Some young people, distressed about being LGBTQ or just desperate to meet someone else who is, hook up with the first person who pays them attention.

Just like any dating situation, sometimes people don't have your best interests at heart. Although it's the exception rather than the rule, sometimes older and more experienced LGBTQ people take advantage of those who are younger or less experienced. These older individuals might offer teens sympathy and compassion while luring them into sexual situations. Sometimes these people try to convince teens that having sex will make them feel better or help them figure out who they are. It can be comforting and flattering to have someone listen and pay attention to you—maybe they're the first queer person who's shown an interest in you or even the first person you've come out to. But take time to think about whether that person is thinking about you or about their own interests and agenda.

# Being "Out" on a Date

It's great to hold hands with your sweetie or give them a little kiss while you're walking down the street. Unfortunately, public displays of affection (PDA) aren't something that queer people can always take for granted. It's important, especially as a young person, to be aware of where you are and who else is around.

It's one thing for your hand-holding to cause Grandma's jaw to drop in surprise. It's another for it to attract the attention of people who might want to hurt you. That's not to say you can never give your honey a smooch or put your arm around them in public. Just be smart about where you are and who's around. If PDA could cause a safety issue, you may want to give it a second thought. It's a lot better if the date is memorable because it went well than because someone got hurt.

## Assessing the Situation

Homophobic and transphobic people aren't lurking in every shadow, but they are out there—and some of them are dangerous. Unless you're on extremely familiar or otherwise safe turf, like an LGBTQ establishment or event, before leaning in for a peck, do a quick check of your surroundings:

- Are a lot of people close by?
- What's the feeling you get from them by looking at them? What are your instincts telling you?
- Are people minding their own business, or do they seem a bit too interested in yours?
- Are you in a place that's open or easily accessible, or are you in a confined space where it would be tough to leave quickly?

Keep in mind that the degree to which you're open about your identity will always be up to you. It's a major bummer that LGBTQ people have to be concerned about a kiss in this day and age. But your safety is the most important thing. Hopefully, before too long, society will discover other things to worry about and a little queer PDA won't cause a second glance.

**SHOWING A LITTLE AFFECTION**

It can be nice to show affection. It's normal and healthy to want to express your feelings for your sweetie. But it's just bad manners to explore your partner's tonsils with your tongue in public. Queer or straight/cis, *no one* wants to see that.

## Knowing Looks and Open Stares

Even if you're not overtly displaying affection, people might know by looking at you and your date that you're out together. It might draw some attention. For example, maybe the person at the table next to yours nearly dropped their fork when you reached over and touched your date's hand. Assuming you're in a safe situation, it's up to you to decide whether you're comfortable with that.

Maybe you couldn't care less and say, "Let them stare until their eyes dry out." But if you're uncomfortable, this might be one of those times to remind yourself that there is absolutely, positively nothing wrong with being LGBTQ. It's natural to feel self-conscious when you start dating. In fact, queer or straight/cis, young or old, most people feel self-conscious on first dates. Don't worry—it will get better. The longer you're out, the more comfortable with yourself you'll be.

And don't assume people are looking because they're shocked or upset. Maybe they think you make a cute couple, maybe they feel it's refreshing to see a couple who doesn't fit the binary mold, or perhaps the person who almost dropped their fork became lost in thought wishing their daughter could find such a nice girl. You never know.

## Singing the Breakup Blues

Sadly, not all love stories end happily. All romantic relationships can run into problems, and those between LGBTQ people are no different. Dealing with a breakup can be rough. Sometimes it can be tougher for queer teens because you might have limited options for people to talk with about the breakup.

If you're going through a breakup, it's important to do things to take care of yourself. Here are some tips for getting through what can be a difficult time:

**1. Don't act like it didn't happen.** Breakups hurt—that's why the word starts with *break*. It's okay and natural to be upset.

**2. Let it out.** It's important not to bottle up your feelings. Write a top 10 list in your journal of why you're upset. Put on your headphones and sing along at the top of your lungs to the most depressing or empowering songs you can find. Go for a run and tackle the toughest hill in the neighborhood. Express your feelings and release strong emotions in healthy ways.

**3. Talk someone's ear off.** Sharing your thoughts with a good friend can help you decompress. Don't forget your friends online, too. Reach out for some cyber support. Maybe even make a video for your YouTube channel starting a conversation about everyone's best tips for dealing with a breakup. It's easy to want to isolate yourself when you're down, but connecting with others can really help.

**4. Take care of yourself.** The worse you feel, the more important it is to show yourself some TLC. Try to eat well, stay hydrated, get some physical activity, and get enough sleep. Maybe pamper yourself with a bubble bath and a good book, or try yoga and meditation—whatever helps you relax and process the intense emotions you're experiencing. It's tempting to curl up with a gallon of soda and a tub of fries and binge-watch TV, but this is just going to leave you feeling worse in the long run. (In fact, science has shown that naturally occurring antidepressant chemicals like serotonin have a lot to do with the health of your gut, so what you eat can make a big impact on what's eating you.)

**5. Take it one day at a time.** You won't get over a breakup in a day, or even two. But time does help, and you *will* start to feel better. You might even be ready to stop sticking pins into that little doll named after your ex. Seriously, though, breakups are part of life. They're hard, but they provide learning experiences and help shape who you are. When you're ready, reflect on what you can learn from the experience.

In addition to the usual breakup complications, LGBTQ teens sometimes have another issue to face—people who know about the breakup might be pretty insensitive. Unfortunately, some people don't think queer relationships are as meaningful and valid as straight/cis relationships. When you go through a breakup, they may not understand why you're so upset.

These people might say uninformed things, like encouraging you to give being straight/cis "another chance." Dealing with issues like that can be especially annoying and painful when you're trying to mend a broken heart.

**Here are possible responses to some insensitive comments:**

| *Clueless Remark:* | *Possible Response:* |
|---|---|
| "It didn't work because you're not queer in the first place." | "It didn't work because we weren't right for each other. I'm having a tough time dealing with this and I could use your support." |
| "Good—you can go back to dating girls now." | "If you and Dad split up, would you start dating women?" |
| "It's not like it was a real relationship anyway." | "It hurts when you belittle how I feel. Whether you approved of the relationship isn't the issue. This isn't about you; it's about me." |

# Abusive Relationships: Recognizing Them and Getting Help

Dating violence can involve physical harm and sexual assault, such as nonconsensual sexual activity and rape. It can also include psychological or emotional abuse—including controlling behaviors or jealousy—and cyber abuse (sending you nasty texts or making disparaging posts about you on social media, for example).

All teens can be victims and/or perpetrators of dating violence, regardless of their sexual orientations or gender identities, and some research shows LGBTQ teens may be more at risk. According to a 2013 study conducted by the Urban Institute that examined data from 5,647 teens from 10 schools in New Jersey, New York, and Pennsylvania (in areas ranging from rural to urban), queer teens showed significantly higher rates of all types of dating abuses—including as victims and as perpetrators—compared to heterosexual teens. Specific data included:

- 43 percent reported physical dating violence (versus 29 percent of heterosexual teens).
- 59 percent reported psychological dating abuse (versus 46 percent of heterosexual young people).
- 37 percent reported cyber abuse (versus 26 percent of heterosexual young people).
- 23 percent reported sexual coercion (versus 12 percent of heterosexual teens).

Additionally, higher percentages of LGBTQ young people reported perpetrating these abuses. In all categories, trans young people reported the highest rates of abuse, with nearly 89 percent reporting some kind of physical dating violence.

Why are the rates of abuse among LGBTQ teens so high? Does that mean there's something wrong with LGBTQ relationships? Not at all. The researchers who conducted the study speculated that the higher rates were in part likely due to the fact that LGBTQ young people in general are exposed to more risk factors that predispose them to abuse, such as depression and suicidal thoughts, maltreatment and abuse by family, challenges with peer or social acceptance, poor school performance, and substance abuse.

Dating violence for LGBTQ young people is very similar to abuse and violence in straight/cis teen relationships, but queer teens may face additional challenges, such as dealing with homophobia or transphobia and ignorance about LGBTQ relationships. Abusive partners also might threaten to out the person being abused. Queer teens may also be reluctant to report abuse due to fears over coming out. And abuse between male partners may be overlooked because a conflict between men is sometimes viewed as a "fair fight" (as opposed to a cis male harming a cis female). This is simply not true. Abuse of any kind is *never* acceptable.

LGBTQ teens who experience abuse might struggle with ideas of what relationships should be like because relatively few positive queer role models are available. This can make abuse harder to recognize because victims don't expect it or see it addressed in LGBTQ relationships. No matter who you're dating, you have the right to be treated with respect by your partner. There is no excuse for abusive behavior of any kind, period.

**BEEN THERE**

"The healthiest relationships are based on mutual respect. They are partnerships that give you energy and bring intimacy into your life without harming your other relationships." —Jeremy, 20

Here are some facts about dating violence and relationship abuse:

- You never deserve to be abused. No one does.
- The abuse is not your fault. It's the fault of the abuser, no matter how much that person might blame you. ("You shouldn't have said that. You know I have a temper.")
- Abuse can take many different forms. It can be physical, emotional, sexual, psychological, verbal, social (like trying to turn friends against you), and even technological (such as posting harassing comments about you on social media).
- Abuse usually happens in cycles. There might be a lot of kissing and making up afterward, but eventually the abuse starts all over again.
- Abusers often try to isolate their partners from family, friends, and teammates. The person being abused often feels scared and alone.
- Abuse is about control and power, *not* love.

Dating violence and relationship abuse are serious problems for queer and straight/cis teens alike. The good news is that many domestic violence resources are available today for LGBTQ people. If you're in an abusive relationship and need help getting out, many organizations can provide assistance.

## Kinds of Dating Violence and Relationship Abuse

Many types of abuse happen in relationships. It's good to know what they are so you can recognize them if they occur.

**Emotional abuse.** Emotional abuse can be harder to recognize than other forms of abuse, because it is often less obvious. It can include name-calling, insults, your partner putting you and your interests down, jealousy and possessiveness, jokes about you that aren't funny, and attempts to control who you see, what you do, what you wear, and even what you eat. These remarks can be subtle, so it may take some time to recognize them. If in doubt, go with your gut.

### ABUSIVE RELATIONSHIPS: GETTING HELP

**LGBT National Help Center (1-800-246-7743).** The Center offers an LGBT National Youth Talk Line, which provides support and resources for LGBTQ young people. Phone hours are limited, though. (You can check them at www.glbthotline.org/talkline.html.) You can also email help@LGBThotline.org.

**National Domestic Violence Hotline (1-800-799-7233).** If you're in an abusive relationship or concerned a friend or family member needs help, you can call or visit the website (www.thehotline.org) for chat support 24-7, along with referrals to local services.

**The National Sexual Assault Hotline (1-800-656-4673).** RAINN (the Rape, Abuse & Incest National Network) offers a 24-hour hotline and online chat, along with extensive resources and assistance for sexual assault. Call or go to their website (www.rainn.org). RAINN also can connect you with state or local domestic violence coalitions and rape or sexual violence crisis centers.

A partner might tell you that you're fat or stupid or that no one else would ever want you. If you complain about this treatment, they might tell you it's not a big deal or you're too sensitive. Maybe your partner is extremely jealous and always demands to know where you are and who you're with. Or maybe they control you with the fear of what they will do if they lose their temper (like breaking things, humiliating you in public, or hurting you). Perhaps they make extreme demands on your time (even when you have important school or family commitments) and flirt, pout, and eventually lose their temper if they don't get their way. Maybe they tell you in subtle or obvious ways that you could never find someone better than them. Whatever the method, it's all abuse. Emotional abuse can take a lot of different forms, but it all has the same result—it makes you feel bad about yourself. Emotional abuse can also set the stage for other types of abuse.

## BEEN THERE

"I was in a relationship for a few years and I actually thought it was a good one. I mean, we loved each other—what else do you need? Periodically, though, she'd tell me stuff like that I was difficult or that other people didn't really like me that much. If I told her I was hurt by what she said, she'd tell me, 'You're just too sensitive.' I eventually broke up with her, and it wasn't until I was out of the relationship for a while and had a new, healthy one that I realized just how unhealthy that other relationship was. I think because she never hit me and she was so fun a lot of the time, I just overlooked the other stuff. But it took me a long time to repair the damage to my self-esteem that relationship had done." —Carmen, 19

**Physical abuse.** Physical abuse often is the first thing that comes to mind when people think about abusive relationships. Such abuse can include hitting, slapping, shoving, grabbing, kicking, hair-pulling, biting, pinching, and throwing things. Physical abuse often is accompanied by threats of greater violence if you do or say the wrong thing.

**Sexual abuse.** Physical abuse can also be sexual in nature. Sexual abuse can include being forced or coerced into doing sexual activities you don't want to do or aren't ready for. The abusive partner might use emotional blackmail like, "If you really love me . . ." to pressure you into sexual activity.

It's important to remember that even if you have a sexual relationship with your partner, you always have the right to say no to physical or sexual contact of any kind. It doesn't matter how long the two of you have been dating. It's your body. Even if you've been sexual with your partner before, you still have the right to say no now. If your partner doesn't respect that and tries to force or coerce you, that's abuse.

## An Abusive Relationship Self-Test

It can be hard to recognize abuse when you're close to someone. Here are some questions to help you take a closer look at your situation. If you answer "yes" to any of these questions, you could be in an abusive relationship:

- Does your partner call you names, insult you, or make you feel bad about yourself?
- Does your partner often demand to know where you've been (or are going) and who you talk to, call, email, or text, or does your partner look at the messages on your phone without your permission?
- Does your partner try to control who you connect with online?
- Does your partner humiliate you, including in public or at school?
- Does your partner make all the decisions in the relationship or get ugly when you disagree with what they want?
- Do you make decisions about what you'll do or who you'll talk to based on how you think your partner will react?
- Does your partner try to control what you wear or what you eat? Do they make negative comments about your appearance?
- Does your partner share pictures of you or your private messages with their friends or others?
- Are you ever afraid of your partner?
- Does your partner ever blame you for their behavior, telling you that it's your fault they hit you, scared you, or lost their temper?

- Do you find yourself making excuses to others for your partner's behavior, especially how they treat you?
- Does your partner try to keep you from spending time with your family or friends?
- Is your partner inconsiderate of your feelings? Do they tell you that you're blowing things out of proportion or that you're overreacting when you try to discuss their behavior?
- Is your partner jealous of your time? Do they insist on being with you constantly?
- Does your partner ever force or coerce you into engaging in intimate physical contact?
- Has your partner ever physically assaulted you, regardless of whether they caused a bruise or other injury?
- Has your partner ever verbally assaulted or threatened you?
- Has your partner posted harassing things on social media, sent you nasty texts, posted critical things on your social media, or shared private pictures of you?
- Has your partner ever destroyed any of your possessions or done something else to punish you?
- Has your partner ever threatened to hurt you or themselves if you leave the relationship?

If one or more of these sounds familiar, you might be in an abusive relationship.

## Stopping Abuse

Abuse is never acceptable. It is your right to leave an abusive (or any) relationship immediately. If you identify abuse (or patterns that could lead to it) in your relationship and want to address it with your partner, here is some guidance that could help:

1. *Tell your partner how their words or actions make you feel.* Emphasize that it's your right to feel safe and supported in relationships.
2. *If they are apologetic and seem genuinely remorseful, it's up to you whether you want to give them another chance.* But be careful. Abusive relationships often have cycles. The abusive person is apologetic for what they've done and swears they will never do it again. Things are good for a while, but then the old pattern

of abuse can start again. It's a good idea to suggest that your partner seek help (such as counseling) to address their abusive patterns.

3. *If the abuse starts again, it's time to get out.* Everyone makes mistakes, but especially if your partner refuses to seek and actively engage in help, it's time to go. It may be painful to leave, but you are priority number one.

## WHAT IF IT'S YOU?

What if you're worried that *you* are the one treating your partner disrespectfully or abusively? According to a 2013 Urban Institute study, just over 36 percent of LGBTQ young people admitted to having perpetrated some kind of abuse in a relationship.

Recognizing you may be an abuser is a very important step. Consider these questions: Is this the type of person you want to be? Is this the kind of relationship you want to have, instead of one built on mutual respect and trust? There can be a lot of reasons why you're treating your partner abusively. Maybe this is the kind of relationship your parents or other family members have. Maybe you're under a tremendous amount of stress and don't have healthy ways to deal with it, are experiencing serious depression, or have experienced abuse yourself. You might need support for emotional issues you're dealing with. It's never too late to get help. You, too, can call any of the resources listed in this chapter or talk to a trusted adult. Do it not only for your partner, but for yourself. You are just as deserving of love and happiness as anyone else.

If you decide to get out of the relationship entirely, you have options. You can call national hotlines (such as the ones listed on page 146) or identify local resources by looking in a phone directory or searching online. Domestic violence organizations, rape crisis centers, and LGBTQ resource centers are all good places to start.

It can be difficult to reach out to people you know, but trusted adults can also provide support. Adults at home, older siblings, gay-straight alliance sponsors, or school officials are all possibilities. If you're not out to anyone, talking with someone in your life might not be an option. Instead, you can talk to someone anonymously at a local or national organization.

## You Deserve R-E-S-P-E-C-T

Soul singer Aretha Franklin had it right. *Respect* is the word to remember in relationships. Keep these tips in mind to be sure your relationships are healthy:

**R**eact to your partner's negative behavior by talking to them or getting out of the relationship.

**E**xpress your ideas and thoughts. If your partner tries to make you think or act a certain way, the relationship is bad news.

**S**pend your time with people who are supportive and positive. If this doesn't include your partner, leave them behind. (You can encourage them to get help, but it's not your responsibility to see that they do it or to otherwise take care of them.)

**P**ledge to yourself that you value your own well-being too much to tolerate an abusive relationship.

**E**xpect to have a partner who respects you and who you respect.

**C**hoose for yourself. Don't let your partner dictate who you talk to, what you eat, how you dress, or any of your other personal choices.

**T**alk to someone if you are in an abusive relationship. Tell this person you need help putting a stop to the abuse. It's a sign of strength to ask for help.

CHAPTER 8

# Sex and Sexuality

**Love is a many gendered thing.**

If you're thinking about relationships and dating, you're probably also thinking a bit (or maybe a lot) about sexual activity (alone or with another person). Like relationships, sexuality can be a confusing and complicated issue, but it can also be a beautiful and meaningful part of your life.

You're at a time in your life when you're trying to figure out a lot of things, and the idea of sexual intimacy could be complicating that. How do you know what you're ready for or if you're even ready for a physical relationship at all? It's a good idea to think about what questions you have and what you feel comfortable with *before* you end up in a situation where you're confronted with decisions about physical intimacy. This chapter is designed to help you do that.

Especially for LGBTQ teens, reliable information about intimate relationships and sex can be tough to find. You might feel that what you're hearing about sex from your friends, family members, adults at school, or religious leaders doesn't apply to you. If just about everyone around you assumes you're straight/cis, and if they have limited understanding about sexuality and gender, getting the information you need and want about sex can seem impossible.

There's a persistent message among young people that sex and sexual activity are no big deal. Nothing could be further from the truth. Making healthy decisions about sexual activity is tremendously important. When are you ready? What boundaries do you want to set for yourself with regard to physical intimacy? How well do you need to know someone or how much do you need to care for them before you're ready to be intimate? What are you comfortable doing? What do you think sex is and what does it mean to you? Do you know how to stay safe sexually? What does "safer sex" even mean? Are you able to talk to someone you're dating about what your boundaries are for keeping yourself healthy, physically and emotionally?

### START IN THE MIRROR

We tend to look at sex and sexual activity as something that's about other people and how we interact with them, but healthy sexuality begins with just one person—you. Most teens (and let's be honest, adults, too) struggle with self-esteem at some point. If you don't have a healthy sense of love and respect for yourself, you're not going to get it from another person. It can be easy to think that physical contact will bring comfort, but if you don't feel good about yourself, having sex isn't going to change that. It can be super challenging, especially if you're dealing with some degree of shame around your sexuality (which is normal), to feel love for yourself. But self-love is what makes it possible for you to have healthy and happy intimacy with another person. Check out chapter 9 for tips on caring for and affirming yourself.

That's a lot to think about, and trying to process all these questions can feel overwhelming. But they're important questions to answer *before* you start to engage in sexual activity. Try not to feel discouraged—accurate information is your best friend, and it *is* out there. What you know or learn about yourself, about what you believe, and about sex and sexuality will help guide you through your questions and help you make decisions that are right for you.

Beliefs—what you think is right and wrong and what is important to you—guide you in making decisions about your boundaries and behavior. Typically, your beliefs are shaped by a variety of sources, including the influences of your family, culture, and religion or spirituality. However, adolescence is an important time for establishing your independence and determining which of the beliefs you grew up with you'll keep and which you'll discard or reshape.

If you feel safe being open with them, family members, spiritual leaders, or other adults in your life could be helpful as you decide what feels right for you. However, if you come from a religious, cultural, or family belief system that strongly disapproves of queer people, figuring out what you believe can be more complicated. You may feel like you don't have role models, or you may experience shame over your sexual orientation or gender identity. If that's the case, it can help to talk about your thoughts and feelings with a counselor or health and sexuality educator who is knowledgeable about LGBTQ issues. Or maybe there's another objective person you can trust who will listen without judgment and provide unbiased feedback. Places like LGBTQ organizations and community centers (physical or virtual) can be great resources for support.

Then there's the technical stuff. How can you make decisions about what type of activity you're ready for if you don't know what the options are? Most schools give limited information about sex and sexuality and offer only the basics about how our bodies work. Very few students get any education on issues related to LGBTQ sexuality. According to a 2015 survey by the Public Religion Research Institute, only 12 percent of millennials (generally described as those born between the early 1980s and late 1990s) said that their sex education classes in school included information about same-sex relationships.

When information about sex is presented at school or at home, the usual assumption is that your partner will be cisgender and of the opposite sex. Most parents don't think to raise the issue of LGBTQ sexuality when they're talking about sex (if they talk about sex and sexual activity at all). They might focus on discussing (or lecturing on) anatomy, pregnancy, abstinence, or sexually transmitted infections (STIs). Those are important topics, but there's a lot more to know. Also, if your parents are straight/cis, their understanding of queer physical relationships is likely to be limited or nonexistent. And some parents, regardless of whether their kids are LGBTQ or straight/cis, never have "the talk," leaving teens to get information about sex—accurate or inaccurate—from sources such as peers or the internet.

When schools teach topics about human sexuality, they often avoid discussing queer sexuality or gloss over the topic. According to the *2015 National School Climate Survey* published by GLSEN, only 5.7 percent of students said that positive LGBTQ-related information was included in their health classes.

This lack of information can be extremely detrimental to LGBTQ teens. According to data from a 2015 survey on youth risk behaviors conducted by the Centers for Disease Control and Prevention (CDC), queer young people are at a significantly higher risk than their straight peers of being physically forced to have sex and of experiencing sexual dating violence. In some school districts, as many as 36 percent of queer teens reported having been forced to have sex.

### A NOTE ON DATA

Data on sexual and risk behaviors among LGBTQ young people can be confusing in large part because it usually depends on how people self-label. For example, a survey could ask teens whether they identify as lesbian, gay, bisexual, or trans, and the results could show that, say, 7 percent of respondents checked "yes" to one of those. However, if the same group was asked whether they identify as exclusively heterosexual (just changing the wording around), half of respondents might indicate "no." Does that mean that 7 percent of those teens or 50 percent of those teens are queer? It's open to interpretation. Also, are the cited numbers medians or averages or highs and lows? News reports and blogs tend to summarize data using blanket language, so if you want to know what data *really* says, it's important to look at the original source.

**Pro tip:** Showing the ways statistics can be skewed, misrepresented, or misunderstood could make a great project for a math class.

Why is this the case? There's no simple answer, but many scientists believe that these higher rates are partly due to the overall higher rates of risk factors among LGBTQ young people—such as depression, suicidal tendencies, and rejection by family members—that correlate to sexual and dating violence. So it's not that there's something inherent in LGBTQ people that makes them more prone to be abused, but rather that certain societal factors likely play a role. It all adds up to the need for more information and support for LGBTQ teens.

The fact that most schools don't mention queer sexuality in their curricula might leave you feeling invisible and uninformed. This chapter is designed to help remedy that by providing some basic information about sex and sexuality. However, there are many resources out there that provide more extensive and detailed information. Several of them are listed in this chapter.

## Making Sound Decisions About Sex

Becoming more aware of your sexuality is a major part of adolescence, whether you're queer or straight/cis. Adolescence often involves a huge increase in thinking about sex and what it means for you and wanting to experiment with and engage in sexual activity. This isn't the case for everyone. For some people who identify as asexual, the teen years are when they begin to see that they're far less interested in sexual activity than their peers are (see page 138 for more information about asexuality).

Deciding to be sexually active is a big choice and a major milestone for lots of reasons. It involves new physical experiences, intense emotions, and new responsibilities, such as learning how to keep yourself safe and healthy and being able to communicate clearly with a partner.

You might decide not to have sex right now. Or you might decide to experiment with some activities, but draw the line at others. In some ways, you might feel ready for physical intimacy, while in others, you might not. You may not even be sure how to define sex or what it entails for you.

You might have a lot of curiosity and a mix of facts and misinformation buzzing around in your mind. It all can feel extremely confusing and can leave you with a lot of questions. Here are some common ones:

**Q: I have sexual urges. Does that mean I'm ready?**

**A:** As you become more sexually aware, you're also changing emotionally. You could be having physical urges—which is completely normal—but you might also feel confused, worried, anxious, or unsure about acting on those urges, which is also totally normal.

There isn't a magic age when someone becomes ready to engage in sexual activity. The factors that contribute to being emotionally and physically ready are highly personal.

**Q: Can I be sort of ready?**

**A:** The short answer is "Sure!" You may be ready for some degree of sexual intimacy or sexual activity, but feel like there's a point that's too far for now. And that's a great and important thing to be aware of. Thankfully, sexual activity doesn't have to be an all-or-nothing proposition. From holding hands and snuggling to making out and beyond, many activities can be healthy expressions of affection and be both physically and emotionally pleasurable. You could be ready for some of them, but not others. *And if you're doing something or someone asks you to do something that makes you feel uncomfortable, listen to that feeling.* It's an indicator that you're moving beyond what you're ready for.

### WHAT *READY* MEANS

Being ready for certain types of sexual activity is not a direct sign of maturity. And on the flip side, *not* feeling ready for certain things (or anything at all) doesn't mean you're immature. On the contrary—knowing yourself well enough to identify what you are and aren't ready for, and being able to express that to a partner, is a huge flashing neon sign of maturity. Understanding this can relieve you from feeling like you have to engage in sexual activity to prove something to yourself or others.

Learning how to set boundaries is part of the process of maturing into someone who's comfortable being affectionate or sharing sexual intimacy with someone else. Part of setting boundaries is being able to communicate with your partner even when the topic feels embarrassing or difficult. Think about what you want and what's important to you. Talk with your partner about your feelings, and ask what your partner feels ready for.

Also, gradually exploring is often underrated. The thrill of taking it a little bit at a time can be fun and it can be a significant bonding experience between partners. And it's usually safer and more comfortable than jumping right in and going all the way (whatever that means for you).

**Q: Isn't pretty much everyone having sex?**

**A:** It's true that there are many teens who engage in sexual activity. There are also many teens who choose to wait and who set boundaries about their sexual activities that for now exclude certain sexual acts. Plus, "doing it" and feeling like you made the right decision about that can be two different things.

According to a report from the CDC, in 2015, a nationwide average of 41.2 percent of high school students reported having had sexual intercourse (and that was down from 47.8 percent in 2007). So although it might seem like everyone is having sex, lots of your peers aren't. If you decide you're not ready or you're not interested, you'll have *a lot* of company.

Researchers have also found that some teens who tell their peers they've had sex are stretching the truth. With all the pressure to have sex, it's understandable that some teens feel the need to lie about their experiences. Some tell stories to get attention, to feel more mature, or just to get people to quit asking if they're having sex! Knowing that they could be lying gives you another reason not to base your decisions on what your friends might or might not be doing.

Another reason to think for yourself and put your own health and safety (physical and emotional) first when making decisions about sexual activity is that according to CDC data, among your peers who *are* sexually active, many are engaging in risky behavior. Specifically, 43 percent did not use a condom (which in addition to preventing pregnancy, also helps prevent STIs), 14 percent did not use any method to prevent pregnancy, and 21 percent had drunk alcohol or used drugs the last time they had sex. Any of these decisions could contribute to some very complicated consequences.

### WHEN THE PRESSURE IS ON

It can be hard to say no to sexual activity when someone's pressuring you, but pushing someone isn't cool (whether you're the pusher or the one being pushed). Here are some possible responses if you find yourself under pressure:

| Pressure: | Response: |
| --- | --- |
| "You should try it. It's great." | "I'm sure it *will* be great . . . when I'm ready. I don't want to do something I think I'll regret. And if you really care about me, you won't put pressure on me." |
| "Don't be such a prude. Everyone's doing it." | "A lot of people might say they're doing it, but not all of them are telling the truth. And I'm my own person. I don't care what other people are doing." |
| "Sex is no big deal." | "If sex is no big deal, why do you care so much about whether I'm having it?" Or, "What I do with my body is definitely a big deal." |
| "Maybe you're just not mature enough to have sex." | "I'm mature enough to make responsible decisions about things that are important to me. I'm mature enough to stick to those decisions. And I'm also mature enough not to pressure people into doing something they've decided isn't right for them." |

If your friends really are having sex, you might feel left out or like they're growing up and you're not. That's totally normal. Keep reminding yourself that what might be right for them isn't necessarily right for you. Only you can decide what you're ready for. Besides, if your friends are worth keeping, they won't pressure you to do anything you're not okay with.

**Q: Sex is only right when you're in love, right?**

**A:** For some, sex is an expression of love between two people. Others view it as a source of physical pleasure that doesn't have to be accompanied by love. Even so, most people agree that the most fulfilling sexual experiences are those that happen with someone you care about and that demonstrate respect from the parties involved. Still, being in love doesn't mean you have to have sex.

## WAYS TO SAY NO TO A SIGNIFICANT OTHER

Saying no to a partner who wants to be sexual can be extremely difficult. But you don't owe it to anyone to have sex, no matter how long you've been together.

Here are some tips for responding to pressure from a significant other:

| | |
|---|---|
| "If you love me, you'll have sex with me." | "Sex and love are two different things. If *you* love *me*, you'll let me choose when I'm ready. Besides, if you push me into making a decision I'm not comfortable with, it could ruin our relationship. Is having sex worth that risk to you?" |
| "You say you love me, so prove it." | "I prove to you that I love you every day by respecting your thoughts and decisions. Why don't you prove *you* love *me* by doing the same?" |
| "We're the same sex, so it's not like you can get pregnant." | "Maybe not, but having sex means a lot to me. If I decide to have sex with you, then I'm deciding to share something personal and intimate. Acting like sex is no big deal tells me that you don't respect how important it is to me. I'm not comfortable with that." |
| "C'mon. I know you're not a virgin." | "Just because I've had sex before doesn't mean I want to have it now. And it doesn't mean that I'll do it with just anyone. I respect myself, and I give serious thought to who I'm intimate with." |

## BEEN THERE

"Don't let sex be the reason you are with the person you're with. Being sexually active is nothing compared with the emotional and mental connection that is important in the relationship."
—Raina, 20

**Q: But I'm in a relationship . . .**

**A:** You can love someone (a whole lot, in fact), yet still not feel ready to have sex or not be interested in sexual activity at all. It doesn't mean you don't care about that person. It means you don't want or aren't ready to move to that level of physical intimacy.

For lots of people, some of the absolute best things about being in a relationship are the firsts—the first time your eyes meet and you smile at each other, the first time you hold hands, the first time you kiss, and if everything feels right, the first time you engage in sexual activity. But the thing that makes those firsts so special and memorable is that they happen only once in a relationship, and they're most enjoyable when you're both ready.

### ALONE TIME

Not all sexual experiences need to involve another person. Masturbation is a normal and healthy part of sexual development. Experimenting sexually with yourself is also a healthy, safe way to learn what's comfortable and pleasurable for you emotionally and physically.

**Q: What if I don't want to keep having sex?**

**A:** Maybe you've already started having sex. If you're having sex and you're not feeling good about it, remember that *you can stop* or dial back your level of sexual activity. Just because you've done something doesn't mean you have to keep doing it.

Have an open discussion with your partner. If they really care about you, they'll understand and will be supportive. Bringing it up might feel a little scary or embarrassing, but if you don't feel like you can talk to your partner about sex, it's a signal that you've gotten into something too soon or with the wrong person.

**Q: What about consent? How do I know my partner is into it?**

**A:** With increasing awareness about issues around sexual assault has come more awareness of the idea of consent. If you're going to engage in sexual activity, you want to know that both you and your partner are fully onboard. But what constitutes consent? A good guideline is to think of consent as an enthusiastic yes. If you talk to your partner about a certain activity ("Do you want to try [activity]?") and you don't get an enthusiastic yes, it's best to pass. Keep talking (not to coerce or pressure them, but to better understand how they're feeling and what they're thinking), suggest something else, or ask what (if anything) they *would* like to do. One thing's for sure—consent for sexual activity is a space where you do not want any gray areas, so it's extra important to have clear, open communication. If you're not sure, it's best to either take things back to a space where there is an enthusiastic yes or pass altogether. And keep in mind that being under the influence of drugs or alcohol can color both of your perceptions of consent.

**BEEN THERE**

"I've never been sexually active. I plan to wait." —Julio, 19

## Are You Self-Aware?

Maybe the questions and situations you've been reading about are familiar, or perhaps you're asking yourself other questions. Perhaps you're just starting to think about these issues, or you may already be sexually active. Either way, the more you know about yourself, the healthier your decisions will be about your boundaries, activities, and partners.

Here are some helpful questions to ask yourself and think about while you're deciding if you're ready to be (or if you want to continue being) sexually active:

- Am I comfortable with myself and my body?
- Do I respect myself and have a strong sense of my own self-worth?
- Am I comfortable talking about sex and my boundaries with my partner?
- Do I feel comfortable saying no when I need to?
- Do I understand that I don't need to have sex to be loved? Do I understand that just because I love someone, I don't need to have sex to prove it?

- Do I know what STIs are and how they're transmitted? Do I know about and am I able to talk to my partner about safer sex? Am I confident enough to insist on using protection for any sexual activity?
- Do I understand that I can say no at any point, even if I've told someone I will have sex and even if I've said yes before? Do I understand how to confirm my partner's consent, and can I respect their choice if they do not give consent?
- Do I know that if I have sex, I don't have to keep having it?

## Five Myths (and Truths) About Queer Sex

Thinking about sex and sexuality can make anyone (not just teens) nervous and confused. This can be especially true for young people who are LGBTQ, in part because there is so much misinformation about queer sex and sexuality. Don't let your decisions about sex be influenced by myths and stereotypes.

Here are some of the more common myths about LGBTQ sexuality:

**Myth #1: Having sex is the best way to help me figure out if I'm LGBTQ.** Many people are faced with questions like, "How do I know for sure?" when they're coming out. Many people believe that being LGBTQ is about who you have sex with. Some might even tell you that if you've never engaged in sexual activity, you can't be certain of your sexual orientation or gender identity.

**Truth #1:** Being queer is about who you are as a person; it's part of your identity. It's also about who you are *emotionally* attracted to. Having sex won't prove or disprove anything that you didn't already know or suspect, so being sexually active is not the answer. And having sex could have some negative impacts if you're not ready to deal with the emotions it stirs up, or if you aren't comfortable communicating your boundaries or talking about safer sex.

**BEEN THERE**

"Don't straight people know they're heterosexual before they've had sex?" —Therese, 19

**Myth #2: LGBTQ people are promiscuous.** Some people have the idea that being LGBTQ is only about sex, and therefore having sex is the primary focus of queer people (especially those who identify as male).
**Truth #2:** The fact is, LGBTQ people aren't any more promiscuous or sexually adventurous by nature or in practice than straight/cis people are. Being LGBTQ doesn't mean you have to engage in sexual activity at all. Having sex is a personal decision, regardless of whether you're queer or straight.

### TRANS- AND NONBINARY-SPECIFIC INFO

While the information in this chapter applies to all queer young people, there are some additional issues surrounding sexual relationships for trans and nonbinary people, such as dealing with potential conflicts between anatomy and gender identity. The website Gendered Intelligence offers a *Trans Youth Sexual Health Booklet*, which provides an overview of sexual health information and considerations specific to trans and nonbinary people. Check it out at genderedintelligence.co.uk in the "Resources for Young People" section, and see chapter 2 in this book for more information about and for those with trans and nonbinary identities.

**Myth #3: Oral sex and other activities that don't involve intercourse don't count as sex.** Many people consider oral sex and other activities outside intercourse to be very intimate sexual activities, while others attach less importance to them. Some people feel that these activities lead up to intercourse. Others consider them to be sex, period—for these people, oral sex and other activities that don't involve intercourse are primary sexual activities.
**Truth #3:** Here are some truths to consider about oral sex specifically. There's no denying that oral sex is significant sexual contact. You definitely can get or give many STIs through oral sex. Plus, oral sex involves very intimate physical contact, and you're making a choice to share something very personal with someone else. As a matter of self-respect, you'll want to spend some time considering who, if anyone right now, is worthy of that level of intimacy with you.

It's important to communicate clearly about this issue with your partner. If oral sex is a big deal for you, but your partner doesn't feel the same, it can cause a problem. You could end up feeling like your partner doesn't appreciate the value of physical intimacy and how important sharing that is to you. Determining what you're ready for includes making important decisions about the full range of sexual activities, not just intercourse.

**Myth #4: Male-identified partners engage in anal sex and female-identified partners engage in oral sex.** This is one of the most pervasive sexual myths about LGBTQ people—that these are the primary activities of male-identified and female-identified same-sex partners. The myth comes from old stereotypes and from people who don't know or understand what it means to be queer, so their ideas about queer sexuality tend to be limited.
**Truth #4:** As with straight/cis people, there is a whole range of sexual activities that LGBTQ people engage in. Some male-identified partners rarely or never have anal sex (and some male-female and female-female couples do), and some female-identified partners rarely or never have oral sex. There's a huge range of sexual activity that is not at all exclusive to partners based on their anatomies or gender identities.

## PROBLEMS WITH PORN

Ever-increasing access to the internet has brought an increased availability of pornography. Porn can be problematic if you're basing your ideas of sexual behavior on what you see on the screen. Keep in mind that, by design, porn (geared to both LGBTQ and straight/cis people) tends to show sexual acts of an exaggerated nature and is intended to push boundaries for shock value. Many teens (and adults) report feeling "porn pressure"—pressure to engage in sexual activities that they aren't interested in or don't feel comfortable with or to have unsafe sex because of the influence of porn. Engaging in activities or pressuring someone else to do so just because you or they see the activities depicted elsewhere isn't wise, respectful, or part of a healthy sexual relationship.

### BEEN THERE

"Sex is not the end-all, be-all. Having sex does not make or break one's identity. Enjoy what you do because you want to be doing it, not because you think it's what you should be doing." —Joseph, 20

**Myth #5: People who are LGBTQ spread HIV/AIDS.** This is another old stereotype that stems from the fact that in the early 1980s, when the HIV and AIDS epidemic was first starting in the United States, gay and bisexual men were severely impacted. Many people grew to associate gay and bisexual men, and queer people in general, with AIDS, even though all different kinds of people were becoming sick.

**Truth #5:** *Everyone* has to be aware of HIV/AIDS and how it is transmitted, whether LGBTQ or straight/cis. Contrary to what some people believe, gay and bisexual cis men are not solely responsible for the spread of HIV/AIDS. It is a worldwide pandemic that affects people of all ages, races, genders, and orientations.

*It's not who you are, but what you do that puts you at risk for contracting HIV/AIDS.* And you can get HIV/AIDS from only one exposure. If you make healthy choices and practice safer sex (more on that later), you can decrease your risk of HIV exposure.

## The Big Picture: STIs and Pregnancy

Some other issues to consider when making decisions about intimate relationships are STIs and pregnancy. Yes, pregnancy. You may think being queer makes pregnancy less likely or even impossible, but according to a 2015 article published in the *American Journal of Public Health*, pregnancy rates are actually *higher* among LGB young people who have had sex with an opposite-sex partner (as opposed to those who have engaged only in same-sex sexual activity) than among heterosexual-identified teens. (For more about this, see page 168.)

And if you're thinking about becoming or already are sexually active, you definitely need to think about STIs, whether you're LGBTQ or straight/cis. STIs are infections passed from one person to another primarily through vaginal, oral, or anal intercourse, although intimate contact without intercourse can definitely transmit several STIs. STIs are serious business. Unfortunately, one sexual encounter (with or without protection) has the potential to result in long-term consequences.

## Just the Facts About STIs

**1. STIs are common among teens.** According to 2015–2016 data from the Centers for Disease Control and Prevention (CDC), young people ages 15 to 24 acquire half of all new STIs, and one in four sexually active anatomical females has an STI. In 2015, combined rates for chlamydia, gonorrhea, and syphilis reached the highest number ever reported, with the majority of these cases being among young people.

It's important to understand that people with STIs don't always have obvious symptoms. It's not uncommon for someone to have (and be transmitting) an STI without realizing it.

### BEEN THERE

"I have always practiced safer sex because it is so essential for my health. It's important to know where to go for condoms and testing." —Priscilla, 20

**2. HIV/AIDS still has no cure.** There are many other STIs besides HIV/AIDS, but HIV infection among teens is a serious issue. According to the CDC, young people ages 13 to 24 account for approximately one in every four new HIV infections in the United States.

While it's true that many infected people are enjoying a better quality of life than ever before due to advances in drug therapies, living with HIV/AIDS is *not* easy. Even if researchers are one day successful in developing a cure for HIV/AIDS or a vaccine to prevent it, it will likely be many years before either is available. In the meantime, HIV/AIDS transmission is a very real risk. New therapies for HIV/AIDS may give some people a misplaced feeling of security—they think they don't have to practice safer sex. It's tempting to give in to the moment, but that's a very risky gamble.

**3. Women who have sex with women transmit STIs, too.** Anatomical women who have sex exclusively with other anatomical women (cis lesbians) have historically had lower rates overall of STIs than other groups have (both heterosexual and queer).

However, herpes, HPV (genital wart virus), and bacterial vaginosis are transmitted fairly easily between anatomical women during sex, so it's important to be aware and practice safer sex. And while STIs like HIV, hepatitis B, gonorrhea, and chlamydia are less likely to be transmitted, transmission is still possible.

**GETTING TESTED**

How can you find out if you have an STI? The only way is to get tested. If you're worried about your parents finding out, you can privately ask your family healthcare provider if they will agree to test you without sharing the information with your parents. Or you can visit a clinic such as a Planned Parenthood (see page 169) for confidential testing. If you're thinking of engaging in sexual activity, you and your partner can even get tested together before you take the next step.

## Pregnancy

Some teens, terrified by the idea they might be queer, have sexual relationships with people of the opposite physical sex to prove to themselves and others that they're straight. Others engage in heterosexual sex to find a social group they think of as being more "normal" than the queer community. They might believe that life would be somehow easier if they were straight.

Make no mistake, if you're an anatomical female with functional female reproductive organs who has vaginal intercourse with an anatomical male who has functional male reproductive organs, you can get pregnant. Having a different sexual orientation or gender identity won't prevent a pregnancy. And if you're an anatomical male, even if you are gay, trans, or nonbinary, you can get an anatomical female pregnant.

**MORE INFORMATION ABOUT SEX, STIs, AND BEING SAFE**

**Scarleteen (www.scarleteen.com).** Scarleteen provides positive, accurate, nonjudgmental information for young people about sex, including articles, advice, and interactive media. The site was founded by Heather Corinna, author of *S.E.X.: The All-You-Need-to-Know Sexuality Guide to Get You Through Your Teens and Twenties*.

**Sex, Etc. (sexetc.org).** Sex, Etc., is published by Answer, an organization promoting comprehensive sexuality education for young people. The site provides extensive information on sexuality and sexual health, forums for teens to share their experiences, an extensive glossary of sex-related terms, and more.

**Go Ask Alice! (www.goaskalice.columbia.edu).** Go Ask Alice! is a health Q&A website operated by the Alice! Health Program at Columbia University. The site includes factual information about sexuality, sexual health, and relationships. Post questions, read posts from others, and get answers from experts.

**I Wanna Know (www.iwannaknow.org).** Sponsored by the American Social Health Association, this site provides teens with accurate, nonjudgmental information about STIs and sexual health. It includes information about specific STIs, how to prevent them, protection (including contraception), and how to get tested.

**Lesbian, Gay, Bisexual, and Transgender Health (www.cdc.gov/lgbthealth).** Operated by the Centers for Disease Control and Prevention (CDC), this site has extensive information on sexuality and health issues for LGBTQ people, including info specifically for young people.

**Advocates for Youth (www.advocatesforyouth.org).** Advocates for Youth has a Youth Activist Network that empowers teens to make healthy decisions about sexual activity. Visit the website for information about sexuality or to get involved in advocacy efforts.

**CDC National STD Hotline (1-800-232-4636).** A service of the CDC's National Center for HIV/AIDS, Viral Hepatitis, STD, and TB Prevention, the National STD Hotline provides anonymous, confidential information on STIs and how to prevent them. It also provides referrals to clinical and other services. It operates 24 hours a day, seven days a week.

**Health Professionals Advancing LGBTQ Equality (www.glma.org).** If you don't feel like you can talk to your doctor, this organization can help you find a queer-friendly physician near you. Visit the website and click on "Find a Provider," or call (202) 600-8037.

**Planned Parenthood (www.plannedparenthood.org).** Planned Parenthood offers an entire program of LGBTQ services, including education, referrals, counseling, and confidential STI testing. It's also a great resource if you or your partner becomes pregnant. To find a local center, visit the website or call 1-800-230-7526.

## Safe Sex vs. Safer Sex

What's the difference? The first is a myth. Other than masturbation, there is no such thing as totally safe sex. However, if you choose to be sexually active, practicing *safer sex* can significantly reduce the chances of pregnancy or of transmitting an STI. (Plus, practicing safer sex is a great way to let your partner know you care about them.)

Here are some basic facts you need to know about safer sex:

**Fact: Bodily fluids such as semen, vaginal fluids, and blood are the primary means through which STIs pass from one person to another.** It's not always necessary to exchange bodily fluids to become infected, but they are a primary means of infection for many STIs (and the only means through which HIV can be transmitted).

**Fact: Latex barriers provide the most effective protection against infection.** Whether it's in the form of a condom, a dental dam, or gloves, latex is your best friend when it comes to safer sex. You can buy latex barriers at most pharmacies, convenience stores, and discount retailers. Some restrooms are even equipped with condom dispensers. Also, many public health clinics (including Planned Parenthoods) and HIV/AIDS organizations, as well as some LGBTQ community centers, give out free condoms. Some also give out dental dams.

A few other useful things to know about latex:

- Latex condoms are the best choice for safer sex. Some "natural" condoms are made from lambskin, which infections like HIV can pass through. Latex, when used properly, stops infections. If you're allergic to latex, see page 172 for information on polyurethane barriers.
- Dental dams are square pieces of latex designed to cover the vulva, vagina, or anus during oral sex. Dental dams protect the mouth from exposure to bodily fluids that could contain bacteria or viruses.
- Dental dams can be harder to find than condoms. One alternative is to fashion a dental dam out of a condom by unrolling it, cutting off the closed end, and cutting it along the long end. This only works with an unlubricated condom that is not treated with

a spermicide. Plastic wrap can also be used as a substitute for a dental dam, but it must be the kind that isn't perforated. Plastic wrap with tiny holes in it is useless when it comes to preventing STI transmission.

**Fact: Latex is essential not only for vaginal or anal sex, but also for oral sex and mutual masturbation.** Infections can be passed during activities that include touching if a partner's hands or fingers have cuts, scratches, or other open abrasions or sores. You might not always see tiny abrasions, so it's best to use a latex glove or finger cots—latex coverings for individual fingers. These forms of protection are easily found at most drugstores near first aid products or insulin test kits.

### "PRICE CHECK ON CONDOMS!"

Nervous about going to the drugstore to buy protection? Part of gauging whether you're ready to engage in sexual behavior is assessing whether you're mature enough to practice safer sex. Keep in mind that it's easier (and less expensive) to visit the pharmacy for protection than it is to have to fill a prescription to treat an STI (though having an STI doesn't make you bad and isn't a shameful thing). If you're really nervous, think about asking a friend to go with you.

**Fact: You must be careful with latex—it only works as long as it's undamaged.** Heat and oil-based lubricants can damage latex. Unless you're going to use them right away, keeping latex barriers such as condoms in a wallet exposes them to prolonged heat, which can damage them. Also, don't use condoms or other latex barriers with oily substances such as baby oil, petroleum jelly, shortening (for example, Crisco), cooking oils, animal fats (including butter), or massage oils. Oils and petroleum-based products destroy latex.

The best bet for a lubricant is one that's water-based, which you can find in most pharmacies and grocery stores. Some LGBTQ bookstores sell lubricants as well, as do all pleasure shops. Silicone-based lubricants will also work. (The packaging should indicate whether the lubricant is oil-, water-, or silicone-based).

**Fact: Polyurethane and polyisoprene barriers can prevent transmission of HIV.** Polyurethane and polyisoprene condoms, gloves, and dental dams—when properly used—can protect against HIV infection and the transmission of other STIs. The condoms also can be used to prevent pregnancy. However, according to the FDA and *Consumer Reports*, these kinds of condoms may be more prone to breaking. These options are usually recommended only for people who are sensitive to latex or have a latex allergy.

**Fact: Anal sex is a high-risk behavior and needs extra protection.** It's one of the highest-risk behaviors for transmitting STIs, regardless of the gender identities of the partners. The inside of the rectum is a very porous membrane that can transmit infection, including HIV contained in blood or semen, directly into the bloodstream. Unprotected anal sex has recently become popular among some people who have the misconception that HIV is no longer a concern. This is a myth. Anal sex is an *extremely* high-risk behavior for the transmission of HIV and other STIs.

## Barriers to Safer Sex: Lack of Communication

The keys to safer sex are openness and mutual respect, and the best time to bring up safer sex with your partner is while you're both fully clothed. Talking about issues that might make you shy or nervous is much easier when you're not in the heat of the moment. Thinking and talking about safer sex ahead of time means you're giving yourself the opportunity to be prepared when the time comes.

### BEEN THERE

"I had never been intimate with anyone before I was with my most recent girlfriend. But before we started to get sexually active, I had her show me her recent test results for STIs." —Vanessa, 19

It's not always easy to talk about safer sex, but it's important. Even if you're not ready for sex, it's a good idea to talk to your partner now so that when you *are* ready, you'll both be on the same page.

## ARGUMENTS AGAINST SAFER SEX AND HOW YOU CAN HANDLE THEM

Sometimes partners aren't supportive of your stance on safer sex. Here are some common arguments against safer sex and the opposite point of view:

| Argument | The Other Side |
|---|---|
| "I'm allergic to latex." | It's true that some people are allergic to latex. However, due to wonderful scientific advances, condoms, dental dams, and gloves are available in polyurethane and polyisoprene as well. A latex allergy is no excuse for not practicing safer sex. (For more about latex allergies, see page 172.) |
| "Safer sex is too complicated. It's better to just go with the flow." | If safer sex seems like a pain, how complicated is getting an infection or becoming pregnant because you didn't feel like taking the time to use protection? Also, safer sex can be *sexy*. After all, it shows how much you care about each other. |
| "It doesn't feel as good with a condom, dental dam, or glove." | What really doesn't feel good is when partners don't consider each other's health and well-being. Show you care about yourself and your partner by practicing safer sex. |
| "It's embarrassing to talk with a partner about using protection." | Talking about safer sex can be uncomfortable, at least at first. But look at it this way—if you're going to be sexually intimate with someone, you should at least feel comfortable and respectful enough to get past a little embarrassment. Take a deep breath and insist that you use protection. |

| Argument | The Other Side |
|---|---|
| "My partner says they're free of STIs, and I trust them." | It's great that you trust your partner, but that doesn't make you safe. Your partner might truly believe they're free of infection, just as you might believe the same about yourself. But many STIs don't have obvious symptoms, so it's important to be tested, then tested again a few months later. Out of concern and respect for yourself and your partner, play it safer. |
| "My partner and I are both virgins, so we don't need protection." | Even if you're both virgins (and people's definitions of *virgin* can vary), practices like anal sex can be risky because of the chance of infection due to possible exposure to fecal bacteria. Also, if you're engaging in heterosexual sex, you can get pregnant even if it's your first time. Make sure your sexual experiences are healthy, both emotionally and physically. |
| "Talking about safer sex spoils the mood." | Talking about safer sex shows your partner that you care about both of you. So talk to your partner about safer sex *before* you do anything, while your clothes are still on. |

## Barriers to Safer Sex: Drinking and Drugs

One of the biggest barriers to keeping yourself safe is drinking or doing drugs. Even with the best intentions, you can find yourself in the middle of activities or situations you would have avoided if you had been sober.

According to the National Institute on Drug Abuse, among young adults ages 15 to 24 who are sexually active:

- 22 percent reported drinking or using drugs the last time they had sex.
- More than one-third reported that alcohol or drug use has influenced a decision to do something sexual.
- 38 percent reported having had unplanned anal or vaginal intercourse while using substances.

If your judgment is impaired, chances could be greater that you'll have unsafe sex or make other decisions about sex that you may not have made if you'd been sober.

Drugs + sex = risky behavior. The best decisions are ones that you make when you're 100 percent sober.

Take time to explore your sexuality and sexual identity before expressing yourself physically with another person. If you're already engaging in sexual activity, check in with yourself. Reflect on whether these activities are causing you stress or are bringing something positive to your life and your relationship. Sexual activity can be extremely positive and fulfilling if you approach it in a healthy way, and that starts with self-awareness and a willingness to do what's best for you and your potential partners.

CHAPTER 9

# Staying Healthy

**Queer by nature.**
**Absolutely fabulous by choice.**

For queer and questioning teens, adolescence can be an amazing and thought-provoking time. It can also come with its fair share of stress. In addition to normal adolescent changes, you might also be figuring out if you're LGBTQ, choosing whether or not to come out, and deciding how you feel about relationships and sex. With so much on your mind, it can be easy to put taking care of yourself on the back burner. But your physical and mental health are important and need attention, just like other parts of your life.

Researchers from the American Psychological Association have noted that LGBTQ teens run a greater risk of taking part in potentially unhealthy or dangerous behaviors because of difficulties in navigating the teen years, such as worrying about coming out or facing potential (or actual) rejection from family and friends. But they also noted that LGBTQ teens often have sophisticated ways of handling pressures and that they tend to use a broader range of coping resources than their heterosexual peers do. LGBTQ teens may also be more likely to develop greater interpersonal problem-solving skills because of having to deal with these types of stressors. (Think about the skills you could develop by giving a presentation to the school board about gay-straight alliances or by volunteering for a national LGBTQ organization.)

These latter findings are good news, because as a queer teen, you could face more difficult or complex challenges than your straight peers do. This makes it even more important to pay attention to your health so you have the emotional and physical resources to deal with whatever life throws at you.

## Chilling Out: Dealing with Stress as an LGBTQ Teen

Anger, frustration, sadness—it's natural for young people to experience these feelings. According to the Centers for Disease Control and Prevention (CDC) surveillance summary "Youth Risk Behavior Surveillance—United States, 2015," nearly 30 percent of high schoolers across the United States reported feeling so sad or hopeless almost every day for two or more weeks in a row that it prevented them from doing some of their usual activities. Nationwide, nearly 15 percent of students in grades 9 through 12 had made a plan for how to commit suicide.

These are alarming statistics. And it's believed the numbers are higher among LGBTQ students. According to the CDC, 29 percent of LGB high school students had attempted suicide at least once in the previous year, compared with 6 percent of heterosexual teens. Data on trans and nonbinary teens is harder to come by, but estimates are that as many as 41 percent of young people who are trans or gender nonconforming attempt suicide. In a 2015 nationwide report on trans adults, a staggering 92 percent reported having made a suicide attempt before the age of 25.

Rates of depression and suicide tend to be higher among queer young people because they may be struggling with issues related to sexual orientation and gender identity, as well as with societal and peer pressures. It's not that being queer is inherently stressful, but that society's mixed reactions and levels of acceptance (read: homophobia and transphobia) can make it really tough at times. This makes it especially important for you to have a game plan for how to cope when you aren't feeling your best.

> **BEEN THERE**
>
> "When I'm feeling down I sing or write. I try to do something creative; anything that will get my mind off of whatever is going on at that particular moment." —Eric, 15

## Six Great Ways to Beat the Blues

It's okay to sometimes feel frustrated or unhappy with the way things are. But letting others' ignorant attitudes affect your mood over the long term won't make life easier. Help yourself feel better by finding positive ways to deal with difficult emotions. After all, you don't want to miss out on wonderful things because you're stressed or depressed.

There are a lot of great, healthy ways to deal with stress on an everyday basis. Here are six basic things you can try:

**1. Let it out!** Find a way to express your feelings through talking, writing, dancing, acting, singing, rapping, performance poetry, or drawing. You could also make a feel-good playlist and blast it on repeat (check out Brandi Carlile's "The Joke" and Christina Aguilera's "Beautiful" for starters). There's a whole range of great ways you can let it out. You can do this privately (write in a journal—see page 181—or dance in your room) or publicly (act in a school play or perform at an open mic night). The more good ways you release stress, the better you can feel. You might even discover a talent you never knew you had. So laugh, be silly, and do something fun or meaningful!

> **BEEN THERE**
>
> "When I'm stressed, I immerse myself in literature. I try to find reflections of myself in the outside world." —Francis, 20

**2. Go deep inside.** Practices such as yoga, meditation, and mindfulness enable you to find a peaceful place inside yourself and can be effective tools for stress relief. Mindful yoga is also a great way to get in touch with and develop a positive connection to your body, which is great for anyone, but can be especially helpful for people experiencing stress and frustration over having physical bodies that don't mirror their genders. Restorative yoga (characterized by less movement) is exceptional for helping the nervous system shift out of fight-flight-freeze mode (sympathetic) into a rest-and-digest (parasympathetic) state—that restful state is where relaxation and healing happen.

## THE SCIENCE OF STRESS

Stress isn't all bad. Technically, stress is the body's response to change. Some stress—like landing the lead in a musical—is positive stress (or *eustress*). Negative stress (or *distress*) results from difficult situations, like when your housing situation is unstable or you're being harassed at school. Eustress can make you feel hopeful, positive, and energized. Distress can leave you feeling anxious, sad, or out of control. When distress is prolonged, it can have serious negative effects on your body.

Stress influences automatic responses in your nervous system called the parasympathetic (relaxation) response and the sympathetic (fight-flight-freeze) response. When you are relaxed, your body heals and restores itself, you're able to digest and absorb nutrients, and your muscles and heart rate relax—that's the parasympathetic response. Distress, however, triggers the opposite response—your body releases adrenaline, your heart rate increases, and internal healing processes nearly halt. If a close call, such as a narrowly avoided car accident, has ever left you with your heart in your throat and hands shaking, you've experienced the sympathetic fight-flight-freeze response.

While some distress is normal, prolonged periods of it can result in serious physical problems. In the sympathetic state, your body starts to release a steroid hormone called cortisol. Too much cortisol has negative effects on your body, including decreases in immune function, bone density, muscle tissue, and even brain function. It can also cause an increase in storage of abdominal fat.

**3. Exercise.** When you exercise, your brain releases chemicals called endorphins that help increase positive feelings and decrease feelings of pain or stress. Exercise is anything that gets you moving, including walking, shooting hoops, or playing a movement-oriented video game.

Exercise of all kinds can help you relieve stress—it's a matter of finding physical activities you enjoy. Try out for a team at school or join an intramural team in the community. (Some communities have LGBTQ sports teams, although they might be restricted to older teens or adults.) Or plan a game of your own. Get friends together to play volleyball, flag football, or whatever sport you enjoy. Classes in dance, yoga, or martial arts might all be options as well. If you prefer to go solo, try biking, skateboarding, inline skating, running, hiking, weight training, dancing, swimming, or doing parkour (free running that includes jumping, flipping, and other acrobatic moves). Any kind of exercise can help you feel better emotionally and physically. So get those endorphins pumping and do something good for your body.

### MINDFULNESS FOR TEENS

Mindfulness (which simply means being present in each moment) not only relieves stress, it also helps build resilience. One great online resource for learning more about mindfulness is Dr. Dzung Vo's website www.mindfulnessforteens.com. Dr. Vo is a pediatrician specializing in adolescent medicine and his site includes a variety of mindfulness meditations for teens. There are also recommendations for free meditation apps, such as Insight Timer, that you can download on a computer, tablet, or smartphone.

**4. Eat well.** A balanced diet with a lot of nutrients keeps your body healthy and happy. Eating junk can increase feelings of tiredness and sadness. Especially now, when your body is maturing, it's important to eat a balanced diet. (Check out nutritionfacts.org—an unbiased, science-based health info site—for more information.)

That doesn't mean you have to give up your favorite treats. The key is to eat those things in moderation. You can have french fries now and then, just don't make them a staple of your diet. Good food gives your body and mind fuel to be strong and resilient. Drink plenty of water to keep your cells happy and your systems running at their best. And eat lots of greens! More and more data is coming out that shows that a healthy gut contributes to better mental health, and leafy greens (which contain lots of fiber and other essential nutrients) are the best fuel for your gut biome—the healthy bacteria in your belly. (Again, see nutritionfacts.org for more info.)

**5. Take healthy risks.** Jump into life. One of the best things about being alive is trying new things. Sometimes those new things are scary, like trying out for that jazz band solo or asking someone out on a date. Sometimes they're fun, like joining the speech and debate team, traveling somewhere you've never been, or discovering you're a master gardener. When you try new things, you can broaden your horizons while learning about yourself in the process. These experiences help focus your attention on positive things, rather than dwelling on life's challenges.

**6. Get involved.** Get involved in the LGBTQ community, whether it's by participating in an online forum or meeting other queer teens in real life. (Chapter 6 has information on how to do that.) Being involved can help you realize that you're not alone and that you don't have to feel isolated. It can be comforting to know there are a whole lot of us around from all walks of life. Volunteering for your favorite cause or getting politically active are also great ways to meet people—both queer and straight/cis—who share your interests.

**BEEN THERE**

"When I'm stressed, I call my LGBTQ friends or go online and read about other people in my position. Knowing that I'm not alone in how I feel makes me feel better. Also, I keep a journal. Writing always makes me feel better, no matter what's bothering me."
—Heidi, 19

## Jump Into Journaling

Keeping a journal is a great way to reflect on your life, work through feelings, and blow off steam. There are lots of different ways to keep a journal. You can write letters to real or imagined people about how you feel (which you don't have to actually mail), sketch, write poetry, or just describe your day or feelings. Whatever form your journal takes, it's probably best to keep it hidden so you can feel free to really express yourself in it. If your journal is on a computer, password-protecting the document is a good idea.

Whether you're already a pro at journaling or just getting started, here is a strategy for writing when you feel stressed. It helps you let go of intense feelings and feel better about yourself at the same time. (You can also sign up for my free newsletter for folks of all ages at kellymadrone.com. You'll get loads of tips and meditations about writing, speaking, and communicating and about living a positive, engaged life.)

1. In your journal (whether it's a notebook or on your computer), write down exactly what is making you stressed. Tell the person who made that nasty comment just what you think of it. Tell that senator you can't believe he sponsored that anti-queer bill. Whatever you're feeling, let it out.
2. Count the number of negative statements you made, like, "I can't believe he . . ." or, "I am so sick of . . ."
3. Use a clean sheet of paper in your notebook or start a new page in your document. Make a numbered list for the negative statements. For example, if you wrote three negative things, number the list from one to three. Next to each number, write something positive about yourself or something you're grateful for. This can be a good way to put things in perspective and get some emotional balance.

   Here's an example of what this journal entry might look like:
   I am sick of having to deal with the ignorance of some of my so-called "peers."[1] Today, Isaiah made this really nasty comment about gay guys. And it was really loud, too. But Mrs. Jimenez didn't do anything about it. I can't stand her.[2] I told Aly about it during lunch, and they agree that Isaiah is a total jerk.[3]
   1. I'm a good friend.
   2. I'm sensitive to others' feelings.
   3. I'm grateful for my awesome cat, Cody.

No matter how you choose to write in your journal, just remember three key words: *Let it out!* Bottling up feelings can build up stress and anxiety, which can take a mental and physical toll. It's important to let out feelings so you can move past them.

## When Stress Turns Into Depression

Most young people have feelings of sadness or hopelessness from time to time, but queer teens, and especially trans teens, often experience them more frequently than their straight/cis peers do. Nothing about being LGBTQ means you're destined to be unhappy, but take the usual stresses of being a teen and combine them with confronting homophobia or transphobia (in peers or yourself), and you have a mixture that can take a toll on your self-esteem. Even if you're not facing harassment, you might not always feel like you fit in with the world around you. This can be true even if you generally feel good about yourself. LGBTQ teens need to be aware of the warning signs for depression (see page 185) and get help if they need it.

**BEEN THERE**

"So many innocent teenagers end their own lives because of the ignorance out in the world. I mean, if high school is like this, what is the rest of the world like?" —Amar, 15

### Ideas That Can Get You Down

Unfortunately, LGBTQ people often are not treated equally in our society. Homophobia and transphobia may take the form of overt harassment. Prejudice can also appear in more subtle forms. It's important to recognize when this kind of negativity starts to take a toll on you. Here are some common thoughts that can lead to depression and some words of reassurance that can help you remember that you are awesome just the way you are:

**I am the only LGBTQ person in the entire world.** Feeling like you're alone can really bring you down. It can help to remember that commonly accepted statistics suggest that roughly one out of every ten people is LGBTQ, and many, many more than that do not identify as exclusively heterosexual. With billions of people in this world, that's a whole lot of queer folks.

## BEEN THERE

"I had my youth group to go to every Tuesday night when I was in high school. I had three adults to talk to if I ever needed something from them, and I had the whole group. We would discuss our problems and get advice from each other on what we could do to help our situations." —Ivana, 19

**There is something wrong with being LGBTQ.** Maybe because you've heard that it's wrong to be LGBTQ for so long, part of you believes it. Many teens worry that it's bad to be queer. But being LGBTQ is completely natural. A lot of medical and mental health groups say the same thing. Here are just a few:

- American Academy of Pediatrics
- American Counseling Association
- American Psychiatric Association
- National Association of School Psychologists
- National Association of Social Workers

These groups collectively represent about half a million health and mental health professionals. They all maintain that queerness is not a mental disorder.

**I can never have a normal life.** LGBTQ people can live the most "normal" of lives—no matter what your definition of that word might be. We can be doctors, lawyers, politicians, construction workers, artists, teachers, parents, counselors, clergy, executives, business owners, factory workers . . . anything we want to be. We can have families. We can own homes. We can get married. In our lifetimes, we experience joys and sorrows, love and heartbreak, pleasure and pain, just like anyone else.

**I'm popular and I have friends. I should be happy, but I'm not.** Even if you have great friends, get good grades, and have a great family, that doesn't necessarily mean your life is easy. When you are trying to understand your sexual orientation or gender identity, you can feel like you're alone and out of sync with the rest of the world—even if everything looks good from the outside. And while occasionally feeling blue is normal, speak with an adult at home or at school if you feel this way a lot of the time.

Most mental health experts agree that the source of some people's depression has little to do with outside factors. Instead, their depression is related to imbalances in brain chemicals that regulate mood. Some people may be more prone to depression if it runs in their families. Speak with a mental health professional to help you figure out the source of your depression.

**Everybody hates me because I'm LGBTQ.** It might feel like that at times, but the truth is a lot of people care about you. For many people, it doesn't matter whether you're queer or straight. So much has changed since the first edition of this book was published back in 2003, and as awareness of queer people and issues continues to increase, so will understanding and acceptance. For example, in 2015, record numbers (well over half) of Americans supported same-sex marriage rights—rights that are now recognized nationwide.

It's true that there is sometimes backlash. (For instance, as I was preparing this edition of the book, the Trump administration declared a ban on trans people in the military and backed a court case that would allow discrimination against LGBTQ people based on religious beliefs, and many states sought legislation that would allow healthcare providers to deny care to transgender people based on the providers' religious views.) But as Martin Luther King Jr. once said, "The arc of the moral universe is long, but it bends toward justice." If you step back and look at the long arc of civil rights, advances often are followed by setbacks. This is normal, and things will continue to progress overall in spite of the present challenges. And you can be part of that change!

## Warning Signs of Depression

It's important to be aware of what's going on with your emotions, especially if you notice that you're feeling sad or upset a lot of the time. Even though family members and friends care for you and want to be sure you're healthy, they might not notice the kinds of changes that can signal depression. Depression is a serious condition in which people experience extreme feelings of sadness or hopelessness. These moods are more severe and last longer than the typical ups and downs of adolescence and can have a big impact on how teens behave. Experiencing any of the following symptoms for more than two weeks may be a sign you are depressed:

**Emotional changes:**

- ✓ anger
- ✓ guilt
- ✓ anxiety
- ✓ emotional numbness
- ✓ hopelessness
- ✓ irritability
- ✓ indifference
- ✓ loneliness
- ✓ sadness
- ✓ bitterness
- ✓ feeling worthless or helpless
- ✓ loss of motivation

**Physical changes:**

- ✓ sleeping problems (too much or too little)
- ✓ overeating or loss of appetite (often with weight gain or weight loss)
- ✓ headaches
- ✓ indigestion, stomachaches, or nausea
- ✓ aches or pains for unknown reasons
- ✓ fatigue or lack of energy

**Changes in thought:**

- ✓ difficulty remembering or concentrating
- ✓ confusion
- ✓ believing that no one cares about you
- ✓ loss of interest in things you used to enjoy
- ✓ pessimism (negative thinking about things)
- ✓ believing that you don't deserve to be happy
- ✓ believing that you're a burden to others
- ✓ blaming yourself for anything that goes wrong
- ✓ thoughts racing through your head
- ✓ thoughts of harming yourself
- ✓ thoughts of death or suicide

**Changes in behavior:**

- ✓ aggression
- ✓ moving and talking more slowly
- ✓ poor hygiene
- ✓ using or abusing drugs (including alcohol and nicotine)
- ✓ acting out (skipping school, unsafe driving, running away, taking part in risky sexual behaviors)
- ✓ crying more than usual
- ✓ underachieving or overachieving

- ✓ spending most of your time alone and withdrawing from friends or family, or fear of being alone
- ✓ hurting yourself (such as cutting, bruising, or burning yourself)

The previous checklists were adapted from *When Nothing Matters Anymore* by Bev Cobain, an excellent resource for young people going through depression.

### GET HELP!

If you're feeling suicidal or thinking about hurting yourself, it's important to talk with someone *right away*. If you don't have a trusted adult or friend you can go to, contact one of these hotlines. They can provide immediate support and can connect you with additional resources in your area. It takes a strong person to ask for help, and we all need someone to lean on now and then. (There are other support lines and chat sites available, but those listed below all operate 24-7.)

**The Trevor Lifeline (1-866-4-U-TREVOR/1-866-488-7386).** The Trevor Lifeline is a 24-hour toll-free suicide hotline for LGBTQ teens staffed by highly trained counselors. Check out the website at www.thetrevorproject.org for information about how to help someone who is suicidal, as well as information about support groups and resources for queer teens.

**Trans Lifeline (1-877-565-8860).** This 24-7 trans-specific resource is staffed by trans people. You do not have to be suicidal to call. Operators are happy to provide a full range of support services and information.

**Boys Town National Hotline (1-800-448-3000).** This crisis hotline (for people of any gender) is available 24 hours a day. Professional counselors listen and offer advice on any issue, including depression, suicide, and identity struggles.

**National Runaway Safeline (1-800-RUNAWAY/1-800-786-2929).** This hotline for teens in crisis is staffed 24 hours a day by counselors who will listen to you and help you build a plan of action to address whatever problems you're having.

Remember, there's nothing wrong with asking for help. It doesn't mean something is wrong with you, just that something is wrong in your life right now. Being depressed can make it hard to maintain perspective. That's why it's important to get support from an outsider who can help you sort through your feelings.

### Making a Deal for Life

Make a deal with a trusted friend or family member. If you're ever feeling really low, you can call this person and they'll be there for you any time you need to talk. Likewise, promise that you'll be there for them, too. You might never end up needing to call them in the middle of the night, but it can make you feel better to know you always have someone to lean on.

> We, [insert your name] and [insert your friend's name], hereby swear that we will henceforth, from here on out and into infinity, be there for each other. We know that, at any hour of the day or night, if we really need to talk, we can call and the other will listen. Also, we swear that if we ever have thoughts of doing ourselves harm, we will call the other person for help.
>
> Signed:
>
> Person #1 ______________________________
>
> Date ____________
>
> Person #2 ______________________________
>
> Date ____________

## Thinking About Drinking: Making Decisions About Alcohol

Being a teen means making decisions about alcohol, nicotine, and other drugs. It's your body, and those choices are yours to make. You'll have to live with the outcomes, though, so it's in your best interest to make the most informed decisions possible.

Studies show that, overall, substance abuse rates are consistently higher in every category for LGBTQ teens than for their straight/cis peers. For example, according to 2015 data from the Centers for Disease Control and Prevention (CDC), among LGB students:

- 75.3 percent had consumed alcohol, versus 62.5 percent of heterosexual students.
- 52.9 percent had used marijuana, versus 37.5 percent of heterosexual students.

- 11.5 percent had used hallucinogenic drugs, versus 5.5 percent of heterosexual students.
- 10.1 percent had used ecstasy, versus 4.1 percent of heterosexual students.
- 6 percent had used heroin, versus 1.3 percent of heterosexual students.
- 8.2 percent had used methamphetamines, versus 2.1 percent of heterosexual students.
- 27.5 percent had taken a prescription drug without a doctor's permission, versus 15.5 percent of heterosexual students.
- 50.4 percent had smoked cigarettes, versus 30.5 percent of heterosexual students.

While specific data on trans teens is harder to find, a 2017 study published in the *Journal of School Health* found that transgender students were 2.5 times more likely than cis students to use cocaine or methamphetamines in their lifetimes, and twice as likely to report misuse of prescription pain medication.

Why are these numbers so high? Dr. Michael Marshal, a researcher from the University of Pittsburgh and a coauthor of a 2008 study on LGBTQ young people and substance abuse, said, "Homophobia, discrimination, and victimization are largely responsible for these substance use disparities in young gay people." Still, he noted, "It is important to remember that the vast majority of gay youth are happy and healthy, despite the stressors of living in a . . . homophobic society."

Realizing and accepting that you're LGBTQ can be incredibly stressful, especially when it's added on top of the general everyday stresses of being a teenager. The verbal and sometimes physical harassment that many queer teens deal with can increase stress levels, too. That stress can contribute to depression, which may lead to substance use. Many teens looking to escape stress and worries turn to alcohol and drugs, thinking these substances will cheer them up, mellow them out, help them fit in, or numb them to issues they're dealing with.

### BEEN THERE

"Drugs and alcohol can be a problem for many LGBTQ men and women. It makes us feel temporarily like our problems are gone and life is great. But the truth is the more you do, the worse you feel. Life just gets worse. Relationships fall apart and people get hurt."
—Ben, 18

## A Gay Old Time: The Party Scene in LGBTQ Life

Some people believe the stereotypes that all or most LGBTQ people drink, smoke, and use drugs. While the bar and club scene does have a place in LGBTQ culture, the idea that all queer people party and use drugs and alcohol is far from true.

Michele Fitzsimmons, the former outreach coordinator for the Lesbian AIDS Project, said that LGBTQ teens tend to gravitate toward queer bars and clubs because they're some of the only places teens feel comfortable expressing their sexualities. "When you're coming out, your self-esteem might be shaky," Michele says. "It's very easy to slip into a situation where [drug and alcohol use] becomes an addiction or that use puts the user at risk."

Bars and clubs aren't supposed to admit people under 21, but many teens still sneak in illegally. Unfortunately, the bar and club scene can be dangerous. People desperate for acceptance may drink to fit in or smoke to strike up a conversation. Others might take ecstasy or use synthetic marijuana to boost their confidence or feel relaxed. If you find yourself in a club tempted to try these substances or others, remember the effects they can have on you. And remember, not all LGBTQ people in clubs drink, smoke, or use drugs. It's definitely not a requirement to fit in.

Being in a bar or club requires staying alert. Many people in clubs aren't thinking clearly or using good judgment because they've been drinking or using drugs. Others may be sober but looking to harm or take advantage of people. So be smart. For example, if you want something to drink, get it yourself. Don't let someone you don't know very well bring you any kind of drink—even bottled water. No matter how nice they might seem, they could easily slip GHB (G), ketamine (Special K), Rohypnol (roofie), or another substance into it. And if you're under 21, it's illegal for you to be in a bar or club. So even if you don't use drugs or alcohol, just being in these establishments can lead to consequences that have a negative impact on your life.

## The Truth About Drinking

In the US, turning 21 is considered a huge rite of passage. Many young people look forward to being able to drink legally. Some can't wait to try alcohol. But amid all this excitement, it's easy to forget that alcohol is a drug and, as such, can cause a lot of problems. Many people—not just teens—have misconceptions about how alcohol affects the body.

Here are some common myths:

**When you're feeling stressed or depressed, having a drink will make things better.** How many times have we heard people exclaim, "I need a drink!" after a tough day? Queer teens have a lot to deal with, but alcohol won't help you forget bad feelings or problems. In fact, it can compound them. Alcohol is a depressant that slows down your brain. Drinking it can contribute to sad feelings and prevent you from thinking clearly. While it might seem like alcohol is giving you a lift, it's actually bringing you down. Alcohol use can also negatively impact the quality and duration of sleep, which can make your body less able to function properly and heal itself and can intensify feelings of depression.

**Drinking makes you look cool or mature.** For LGBTQ teens, the idea that drinking can help them fit in—whether they're at a high school party or a club for people 21 and over—can be attractive. But alcohol won't suddenly make someone popular or help them fit in. In fact, underage drinking can cause you to behave around others in ways that you later regret. It also can give people the wrong impression about you and what's important to you.

**Drinking will help you meet people.** Maybe you think having a drink or two will help you relax and be more social, but meeting people while under the influence is not the way to put your best foot forward. If you're looking for meaningful relationships and new friends, you won't come across as your best self if you're drunk or high. You could say or do embarrassing things or end up making decisions about sexual contact or about using and driving that you later regret.

### BEEN THERE

"During the nine months that I was drinking, I didn't meet one person who I knew was gay. Once I could stop drinking, I made several gay friends and, ultimately, started to date again. Although I came out to my father and to all my friends when I was 16, it was almost like coming out again once I stopped drinking. I met a lot of new people and came to terms again with who I am." —Blake, 20

## Ways to Say No to Booze

By refusing to drink, you're looking out for yourself and showing confidence in who you are. What's more, you can say no to drinking without feeling awkward, self-conscious, or like a prude. Here are some tips for turning down alcohol, even when others are pressuring you:

- Order a drink, but buy club soda and lime or something else nonalcoholic. Just holding a beverage may help you feel more comfortable.
- If someone asks you if you want a drink, say, "No, thanks," hold up your cranberry juice and say, "I've got one," or say, "I'd rather go dance."
- Be a designated driver. At some clubs, designated drivers get free nonalcoholic drinks.
- If someone brings you a drink anyway, you don't have to accept it. Again, hold up your soda or juice and say, "Thanks, but I'm good." A real friend isn't going to pressure you to drink.
- Be supportive of friends who choose not to drink.

### GETTING HELP FOR ADDICTION

**Association of Lesbian, Gay, Bisexual, and Transgender Addiction Professionals and Their Allies (www.nalgap.org).** This organization is devoted to preventing and treating addiction in the LGBTQ community. Visit the site for information on the devastating effects of drug and alcohol abuse, or to seek a referral for treatment.

**National Council on Alcoholism and Drug Dependence (www.ncadd.org).** Visit this site for information on drug and alcohol addiction, as well as resources for support. Or you can call 1-800-622-2255 for local treatment referrals.

# The Truth About Tobacco

As with other substances, queer teens are more likely than their straight/cis peers to use tobacco products. A National Youth Advocacy Coalition report released in 2010 examined smoking among LGBTQ teens. The report showed that unique stressors, such as discrimination and lack of family acceptance, contributed to higher rates of tobacco use. It also revealed that many queer young people see smoking as an important social activity. In fact, of the teens surveyed, only 28 percent reported having never smoked. The average age at which respondents began smoking was 15.

For decades, the tobacco industry—a group of companies that makes their money from getting people addicted to something that can and does kill—has used ads, product placements, and other messaging vehicles to convince us that smoking is cool and will improve the quality of our lives. Some of this advertising has been aimed directly at young and queer people.

Documents from the tobacco industry that have been made public consistently show Big Tobacco targets teens with its marketing messages. Big Tobacco also targeted queer people in the 1990s with a marketing project called Project Subculture Urban Marketing, known inside the major tobacco company R.J. Reynolds as Project SCUM. Are those the kinds of companies you want to support?

## Getting Hooked on Tobacco

If you're feeling isolated or eager to meet others, smoking can seem like a good social link or a way to approach others. Some people like to use lines like, "Got a light?" or, "Can I bum a smoke?" when they want to meet someone.

Nicotine, a powerful and addictive chemical in tobacco, can make smoking easy to start but hard to stop. It provides smokers with a rush that can feel very satisfying—many people are hooked at once. Studies show that for some it's more addictive than heroin. Nicotine cravings can be so intense that people are willing to stand outside in pouring rain or subzero weather to get their fix. If you doubt how tough it can be to quit, just think about how many advertisements you see for stop-smoking programs, gums, patches, and pills.

Queer teens sometimes turn to smoking for a release from daily stresses. These young people use smoking as a way to relax or relieve some of the depressed feelings they have. Tobacco might give them a temporary feeling of relief, but it's just that—temporary. And it comes at a steep cost—increased heart rate, decreased stamina, decreased lung capacity, and increased risk of developing cancer. That's not to mention the price of cigarettes or the unavoidable foul-smelling breath, clothes, and hair.

If you're still not convinced that smoking is bad for you, consider this: According to the World Health Organization, tobacco is responsible for roughly 7 million deaths each year worldwide. And according to the Centers for Disease Control and Prevention (CDC), roughly 90 percent of cigarette smokers in the US become addicted before age 19.

## Avoiding Drugs

Just as with alcohol and tobacco, LGBTQ teens have higher rates of drug use than their straight peers do. It's not that queer teens are fundamentally prone to substance abuse. It all comes down to stress and depression. Some LGBTQ teens desperately want to feel better, and they think using drugs will help them relax and fit in with others. In the end, drugs don't work any better than drinking or smoking. They won't improve your life or help you feel good about who you are.

### BEEN THERE

"I started doing drugs when I was nine. I tried to fit in with that crowd and hide my 'secret identity.' By the time I was 13, I was put in drug rehab. . . . My rehab counselor told me I wasn't going to be able to stop using unless I was true to myself. I went home and thought about what he said. The next day I started coming out to friends." —Sam, 15

Instead of solving problems, drugs compound them. When you're feeling depressed, drugs make you feel better at first, but then, as the effects wear off, you feel much worse. For example, drugs like ecstasy may make you feel light and happy, but the next day (and for days after), there's a huge crash. Some drugs can make you feel like you're stuck in a bottomless pit (like the infamous "K-hole" from ketamine). If you're feeling stressed, drugs that are supposed to make you happy often leave you feeling paranoid, jittery, or out of control. In general, drugs are unpredictable. You don't really know what you're getting, and you can't be sure how they're going to make you feel.

If you like to go out dancing or to raves, it's likely you'll come across drugs like meth, ecstasy, ketamine, marijuana, or GHB. These so-called "club drugs" can be just as dangerous and unpredictable as any other drugs. It can be tempting to think they'll help you forget about the teasing at school or the fight you had with your parents about your boyfriend. It doesn't work that way. Drug use always has consequences, whether or not they're immediately apparent. Not only do drugs damage your body and your judgment, they're also illegal and could get you in trouble with the law.

### EDUCATE YOURSELF

**Partnership for Drug-Free Kids (drugfree.org).** Visit this website to find out more about specific drugs and their effects.

**The Truth (www.thetruth.com).** This site shows the real health effects tobacco has on your body and the marketing practices the tobacco industry uses to promote smoking among teens.

Even if you're not using drugs yourself, someone else's drug use could get you into serious trouble. Never ride with someone you think is drunk or high. If you have a license, offer to drive them somewhere. But even if they refuse, don't get in the car with them. If you do, you're putting your life in their hands.

### "BUT IT'S JUST POT"

Sound familiar? Pot has a misleading reputation of being virtually harmless. But marijuana is a drug that impairs your thinking and judgment (not to mention your lungs). According to the National Institute on Drug Abuse, which conducts scientific studies on how drugs affect the brain, "Marijuana intoxication can cause distorted perceptions, impaired coordination, difficulty in thinking and problem-solving, and problems with learning and memory. Research has shown that marijuana's adverse impact on learning and memory can last for days or weeks after the acute effects of the drug wear off. . . . Research on the long-term effects of marijuana abuse indicates some changes in the brain similar to those seen after long-term abuse of other major drugs." Plus, marijuana is still illegal in most states. Using it can lead to some very serious consequences. Even in states that have legalized the use and sale of marijuana, driving under the influence of pot and underage use are still illegal.

The fact is, no chemically induced high comes without a hitch. For anything drugs give you, they take away something else. Some teens stay away from so-called "club drugs," but try diet pills or performance-enhancing drugs. The rule still applies even if the substance is "natural." Drug use comes with consequences, some of which are life threatening.

No matter what anyone tells you or how badly you might sometimes feel, you have the potential to make anything you want of your life. You can do amazing things. If you need help getting through a rough spot, reach out for it. It's there and it's never too late.

**BEEN THERE**

"I remember shooting up a mixture of heroin and cocaine, and what happened next really scared me to the point of not wanting to touch drugs and alcohol again. I was 20 and I was down on my knees in the middle of the night, blood pouring out of my nose, throwing up. I just remember praying that if I woke from this that I would never touch drugs again. I was very lucky during that time I was using drugs that I didn't catch anything, that I wasn't raped, or that I didn't kill anyone else or myself." —Xian, 26

## Getting Clean as a Queer Teen (and Staying That Way!)

If you're using drugs, alcohol, or tobacco, quitting could be one of the most difficult things you ever do. Even though it's challenging, getting clean will also be one of the most positive things you can do. It's a crucial step to getting yourself back on track.

No matter what forces are working against you (your dad can't accept that you're queer, you're being harassed at school, you're feeling isolated, you have no idea how you'll ever afford gender confirmation surgery), you have the power to change your life. No matter what's going on outside of you, a whole lot of strength exists inside you. You *can* get clean.

Here's some advice on how to get and stay sober:

**Recognize that you have a problem.** Is it hard or even impossible for you to function without drugs, alcohol, or tobacco? Be honest with yourself. If you don't see a problem, you can't solve it.

**Get help.** The support of your family members, friends, doctor, or counselor can be of great help when you quit using. If you don't feel you can approach a parent about your substance use, seek the support of another adult you trust. Talk with your guidance counselor, your favorite teacher, a relative, a spiritual leader, a doctor, or another caring adult. It's important that someone knows about your problem and can be there to help. This can be tough because it probably will involve you coming out to the person you talk with, but you can do it. You're worth it.

**Remember why you're trying to quit.** Getting sober won't be easy. It helps, though, to remember the benefits of overcoming addiction. You'll feel better both physically and mentally. And conquering drugs and alcohol will make you a stronger person than you probably thought you could be.

After you've stopped drinking or taking drugs, it can be hard to stay off them. Here are some things that might help you:

**Once you start a treatment program, tell your friends about your decision to stop using drugs.** Your true friends will respect and support your decision. It is possible that you'll have to find a new group of friends who are completely supportive of your efforts to stay sober. Avoid hanging around people you used to drink, smoke, or do drugs with if they continue to use. It can be easy to fall back into old habits and behaviors.

**Let your friends and family know how important their support is and ask them to be there for you when you need them.** It's important that you have someone you can call in the middle of the night if you need to talk. Even if you don't end up calling, knowing someone is there can help a lot.

**Only accept invitations to events that you know (or are at least reasonably certain) won't involve drinking or drugs.** Especially when you're first recovering, it's safer to avoid situations in which you may be tempted to use.

**Plan in advance what you'll do in situations where alcohol or drugs are around.** You'll likely be tempted to start using or drinking again, but knowing beforehand how you'll approach difficult situations can make them easier to deal with. Your plan might be as simple as "get the heck out of there." Even so, if you know in advance what you'll do, it's easier to follow through and take care of yourself when you need to.

**Always remember that having an addiction doesn't make you a bad or weak person.** If you slip up in your efforts to stay clean, get help as soon as possible. But remember how difficult what you're doing is and know that there's nothing to be ashamed of. You can get back on track. You've made a lot of positive changes in your life and one lapse doesn't change that.

**BEEN THERE**

"As I complete six years clean and sober, I have just begun finding out who I really am. Now I find myself surrounded by people whose friendship I am thankful for every day." —Xian, 26

Issues like homophobia and ignorance about gender identity are things you may have little or no control over. Focusing on things you *can* control, such as adopting positive and healthy behaviors, goes a long way toward creating a happier and more fulfilling life for yourself.

CHAPTER 10

# Religion and Culture

**You are a mosaic.**

Many different aspects make up who you are as a person. Sexuality is an important part of the whole, but religion, culture, and ethnicity also play a role in your day-to-day life. They can influence your priorities, how you see yourself, and how you relate to others. If the religious or cultural beliefs you were raised with don't support or recognize LGBTQ identities, coming to terms with your gender identity or sexual orientation might leave you feeling confused about who you are or your place in the world.

Some people have trouble accepting themselves as LGBTQ or gaining acceptance from loved ones because of religious beliefs and cultural traditions. The roots of religion and culture can run very deep, and anything that challenges those beliefs can be met with resistance and even anger. Accepting yourself and coming out is even more stressful if you feel that you have to choose between your cultural or ethnic identity and being proud of yourself as LGBTQ.

Religion and culture sometimes are difficult to separate as influences because religion can play a key role in defining the beliefs and traditions common to a culture. For example, Catholicism is often an integral part of Latino and Filipino cultures. Islam is influential in cultures around the world, from the Middle East to parts of Asia, the Pacific Rim, and the US. The Christian faith is considered by many to be a cornerstone of some communities and cultures in the United States. And many other religions and faiths are practiced around the world and in many cultures.

### THE LANGUAGE OF FAITH

In this chapter, *congregation* is used to mean a gathering of people for the purpose of religious worship or instruction. It is not used to imply a reference to a specific faith. Also, it is used interchangeably with *religious community, faith community*, and *place of worship.*

If your religion teaches that it's wrong to be LGBTQ, that belief might surface throughout the culture, not just inside the place of worship. It's not surprising that you could find yourself with conflicted emotions. On one hand, you want to come to terms with your sexuality and accept yourself. On the other hand, you've grown up as a part of a religion or culture that teaches that who you are is not okay. So now what?

## States of Being: Religious Life and Queer Life

For some families with LGBTQ loved ones, religion can be a huge challenge to reconcile. For others, it's not an issue at all, either because they don't observe a religion or their religion or faith is inclusive and openly accepting of LGBTQ people. Then there are those in the middle—queer people whose families accept them but whose religions do not.

Religion is important in many people's lives and that might be true for you, too. In the US and many other countries, it's common to grow up in a family that practices some kind of organized religion. According to Pew Research Center's *2014 Religious Landscape Study*, nearly 71 percent of Americans identify as some form of Christian (this includes Protestants, Catholics, Mormons, and Jehovah's Witnesses). Nearly 2 percent identified as Jewish, nearly 1 percent as Muslim, nearly 1 percent as Buddhist, and nearly 1 percent as Hindu. Additionally, nearly 23 percent of Americans reported that they are not affiliated with a particular religion (a group that sometimes refers to themselves as the "Nones"). This includes people who identify as atheist or agnostic.

On the surface, religion and sexuality don't seem to have much to do with each other. Being LGBTQ is about your sexual orientation or gender identity—the result of a combination of biological and emotional factors. Religion is about spiritual beliefs. So why is religion such a complicated and even painful issue for many LGBTQ people?

**A POWERFUL DOCUMENTARY**

***Out in the Silence.*** This touching documentary chronicles a gay filmmaker's journey from Washington, D.C., back to his small Pennsylvania hometown, where he explores the roots of the homophobia that divides the town. The film also focuses on C.J., an out 16-year-old who has withdrawn from the local school because of escalating harassment. This open-minded film shows a broad variety of perspectives with much of the discussion centering on religion. Go to legacy.wpsu.org/outinthesilence for more information.

## A History Lesson

Many major religions have had difficulty accepting or finding a place for their LGBTQ members for various reasons. Those reasons can be scriptural, historical, rooted in cultural traditions that have become part of religious beliefs, or a combination of these.

For example, some religions believe that a union between a cis man and a cis woman is sacred either because it is stated or they *interpret* that it is stated in scripture. A strong, positive, and loving relationship is definitely something to celebrate. However, the idea that the union between a cis man and a cis woman is sacred is often held because the couple can reproduce without the use of in-vitro fertilization or a surrogate. In fact, some religions believe that a couple should have sexual intercourse only for the purpose of reproduction—not for pleasure—and that the use of contraception is immoral. As a result of such beliefs, LGBTQ people can find themselves, their sexualities, and their relationships rejected by their religions since reproduction isn't the primary purpose of their romantic and physical relationships (regardless of how many cis binary couples in their congregations do or don't actually follow the idea of only having sex to reproduce).

### A RESEARCH PROJECT

If you want to find out more about your religion's history but aren't sure where to start, searching online or at the library could be a good jumping-off point. If you feel comfortable doing so, approach a religious leader in your community and ask for recommendations, or your congregation might have its own library. Some of these sources might be biased—consider who the author is when making your assessment—but some of them could provide solid historical information. Also, many queer-positive religious organizations (see pages 206–208) have suggested resources and reading lists.

## Encouraging Open Minds: Starting a Dialogue

Knowledge can be your best path to finding acceptance and understanding in your religious community. When people start looking at where their personal beliefs and their religion's beliefs come from, it can get them thinking. The question, "Why do we believe this?" might seem simple, but people can be afraid to explore or challenge their own belief systems. Often they're afraid that what they could discover about some of their beliefs might end up invalidating all their beliefs.

If you're struggling with your religion, find out about its history and where anti-LGBTQ beliefs might have originated. Read the original writings or scriptures to get a better idea of how others have interpreted them. An issue or idea can be taken out of context, and personal opinions can influence interpretations. And something that is supposedly expressly stated in scripture might not be unequivocal after all.

If you have a loved one who's struggling with their religion and anti-LGBTQ beliefs, talk with them about what you've learned. They might not be willing to listen, or they might sit down and really consider the information. Investigating your religion's roots and starting a dialogue are positive steps toward reconciling who you are with your religious beliefs. If you're at a loss as to how to approach family, friends, or people in your religious community, refer back to the coming out information in chapter 4 for tips on effective communication. Much of that advice is appropriate for approaching a wide variety of topics that can be difficult to discuss.

**BEEN THERE**

"My mother struggled with religious issues above all else. It was very difficult for her for a long while, but then she found a book called *Prayers for Bobby* by Leroy Aarons. That book changed the way she felt almost overnight." —Robert, 15

## Room for Change

Many religious communities are engaged in debates about their queer members. These debates might include whether or not to accept LGBTQ members, specific conditions under which LGBTQ members are allowed to be part of the congregation, and whether or not to perform same-sex marriage ceremonies. While some religions might never accept LGBTQ people, many are thinking and talking about it. That's where change begins. Even when religious leaders decide not to accept LGBTQ people, debates over the issue can help open and change individuals' minds. Many individual congregations are part of the Welcoming and Affirming movement to embrace LGBTQ congregants.

It can be discouraging to hear that a group of religious leaders has officially decided not to welcome LGBTQ people. Try not to think about this in terms of an entire denomination or congregation, because within any group, some of the people will disagree and accept queer people.

## LGBTQ Religious Leaders: Changing Views Within Religious Communities

Many religious groups have or are taking part in debates about whether leadership roles can be filled by LGBTQ people. (Some of these religions still do not allow women, whether straight/cis, gay, or bisexual, to hold leadership roles.) On July 8, 2010, leaders in the Presbyterian Church voted to allow noncelibate gay people in committed relationships to serve as clergy. Previously, all clergy, deacons, and elders had to be married or celibate.

The Episcopal Church has also made great strides in LGBTQ acceptance. It not only allows openly LGBTQ people to serve as priests, but also allows them to become bishops. The church has also issued declarations of support for same-sex marriage and for transgender congregants.

The debate in the Catholic Church over allowing openly gay priests is ongoing, though one alternative Catholic denomination—the North American Old Catholic Church—had ordained several openly gay priests before it was disbanded in 2013. However, the Catholic Church still does not allow female priests, whether they are straight/cis or LGBTQ.

### HOUSE FOR ALL SINNERS AND SAINTS

It's hard to find a more open or affirming church than House for All Sinners and Saints, an Evangelical Lutheran Church in America (ELCA) congregation in Denver, Colorado. One of the two pastors of the congregation, the Reverend Reagan Humber, is a gay man who grew up in a Southern Baptist family. Though the religion he grew up with wasn't supportive of LGBTQ people, while attending college, Humber saw his campus ministers respond with love and support to the death of Matthew Shepard by holding a peace vigil on campus. That made a lasting impression on him, and eventually he decided to attend seminary to become an Episcopal priest. Though Humber's family wasn't at first accepting of his identity as a gay man, over the years they've come to embrace him, even flying across the country to San Francisco to attend his ordination. Today, Humber ministers to a congregation known for its diversity, in a church known for welcoming all comers. The church even has name tags that ask people to note their preferred pronouns. Humber says he's learned the most from the trans people in his congregation and that he feels privileged to have been part of several of his congregants' transitions, even performing special "remembrance of baptism/name change" ceremonies. Says Humber, "It's been very healing and humbling to see the Church continuing to open up in this way."

The Jewish community has both openly gay rabbis and openly gay Orthodox rabbis. In August 2010, 150 Orthodox Jewish rabbis signed a statement of acceptance toward gays and lesbians practicing in their faith. The statement read in part, "Jews with homosexual orientations or same-sex attractions should be welcomed as full members of the synagogue and school community." As of 2013, there were at least six transgender rabbis or rabbis-in-training in the US. Perhaps the best known of these is Joy Ladin, a tenured professor at Yeshiva University's Stern College for Women, who in 2008 transitioned from male to female.

## Making Room in Religion: Reconciling Your Personal Beliefs

Religion and culture can be very personal, meaningful aspects of a person's life, and that doesn't have to change because you're queer. You might find a place for yourself in your religion or in a different spiritual tradition. Or you could follow your spiritual beliefs as an individual rather than as part of a group. Many people live by an undefined set of spiritual beliefs that combine several traditions such as Buddhism and earth-centered spiritualities. You might even connect with other like-minded individuals and create your own community online.

### BEEN THERE

"I don't consider myself as having a religious background because organized religion is not the way for me to go. I consider myself a very spiritual person without the aspect of religion. Religion doesn't affect me either way, at least not on a level I notice. I know that learning that I'm LGBTQ would affect my family very negatively. They can't see beyond the religion." —Li, 20

Here are some common questions and answers that might help you figure out what's best for you right now:

**Q: What do I do if my place of worship doesn't accept LGBTQ people?**

**A:** First, are you sure that queer people aren't welcome at your place of worship, or have you made that assumption on your own? Have you been taught that it's wrong to be LGBTQ, or do you assume your congregation isn't accepting either because nothing has been said about it or because you don't know of any other LGBTQ members?

Whatever the case, you might want to approach the leader of your congregation to explore their views on having LGBTQ members. If one or both of your parents is accepting, perhaps they could accompany you. Your religious leader might be willing to explore the issue with you, and the two of you can learn and grow together. Then, perhaps the entire congregation could move toward becoming more open and accepting.

Just as accepting yourself and coming out is a process, so is change. Give your religious leader and community a chance. Several national organizations have members who are willing to visit places of worship to talk with faith leaders or congregations about becoming more open and accepting.

## LGBTQ-POSITIVE RELIGIOUS ORGANIZATIONS

Following is a selection of LGBTQ-positive religious organizations. For a more extensive list, visit the Human Rights Campaign's "Faith Resources" page at www.hrc.org/resources/faith-resources.

**Affirmation (affirmation.org).** This organization supports LGBTQ Mormons and their families and friends. The group's website has separate sections for young people, women, and people who are transgender.

**Association of Welcoming & Affirming Baptists (www.awab.org).** An organization building the Welcoming and Affirming movement within the Baptist traditions.

**Brethren Mennonite Council for LGBT Interests (www.bmclgbt.org).** An organization aimed at cultivating an inclusive and caring church for the Mennonite and Brethren LGBTQ community and its allies.

**DignityUSA (www.dignityusa.org).** An organization supporting queer Catholics and their families and friends, DignityUSA has a website that features topic-specific online discussion groups. Also available are teen resources and links to local chapters of this group.

**The Evangelical Network (www.ten.lgbt).** An association of LGBTQ-affirming Evangelical ministries and individuals.

**Friends for LGBTQ Concerns (flgbtqc.org).** A Quaker faith community within the Religious Society of Friends that proclaims to honor, affirm, and uphold the God that is in all people.

**Gay Buddhist Fellowship (gaybuddhist.org).** An organization for LGBTQ Buddhists and their allies, families, and friends.

**Gay & Lesbian Vaishnava Association (www.galva108.org).** A religious organization offering positive information and support to LGBTQ and intersex Vaishnavas and Hindus and their allies, families, and friends.

**Hidden Voices (www.hiddenvoices.info).** This group is dedicated to Muslims of all cultural and ethnic backgrounds who are gay, lesbian, bisexual, transgender, intersex, or questioning. The website includes links to articles and other resources for LGBTQ Muslims.

**Institute for Judaism & Sexuality (ijso.huc.edu).** An organization working toward complete inclusion and welcoming of LGBTQ Jews in communities and congregations.

**Integrity (www.integrityusa.org).** Integrity is a nonprofit organization supporting queer Episcopalians and advocating for their full inclusion in the Episcopal Church. The group's website contains resources, links to local chapters, and information about how to get involved.

**Interfaith Alliance (interfaithalliance.org).** A nonpartisan, clergy-led grassroots organization, Interfaith Alliance is dedicated to protecting religious freedom and promoting common ground among religions. The group is active in lobbying for LGBTQ civil rights.

**Interweave (www.uua.org/lgbtq).** An organization working for LGBTQ Unitarian Universalists and their allies, families, and friends.

**Jewish Queer Youth (www.jqyouth.org).** This site is for LGBTQ Jews ages 17 to 30. Check it out to find links to books and other resources, stories from young queer Jews, and discussion groups.

**Keshet (www.keshetonline.org).** An organization working for the full equality and inclusion of LGBTQ Jews in Jewish life.

**Many Voices (www.manyvoices.org).** A Black church movement working for queer justice by embracing the diversity of the human family and ensuring that all are treated with love and compassion.

**Metropolitan Community Churches (www.mccchurch.org).** Metropolitan Community Churches have for decades been places where LGBTQ people can worship. The organization also has a long history of advocating for queer rights. Visit the site for online classes, discussions of Bible passages often used against LGBTQ people, and other resources.

**Muslim Alliance for Sexual and Gender Diversity (www.muslimalliance.org).** An organization working to support, empower, and connect LGBTQ Muslims.

**Q Christian Fellowship (www.qchristian.org).** This ministry serves LGBTQ Christians and those who care about them. Their site includes audio and video files of sermons, testimonies, and message boards. Also check out the documentary *Through My Eyes*, which features more than two dozen young queer Christians discussing their journeys to reconcile their faiths and sexualities.

**Soulforce (www.soulforce.org).** Soulforce is an interfaith group that applies principles of nonviolence to stopping inflammatory or false information about LGBTQ people. Resources at the organization's website include publications, videos, information on interpretations of religious texts, an online community center, and information on how to become involved in advocacy efforts.

**Q: What if my religious community won't accept me?**

**A:** Unfortunately, some religious communities and congregations won't be willing to change. But even if yours is one of them, don't assume that you will be forced to abandon your religion. You might be surprised to learn that in almost every religion, some branches or denominations accept LGBTQ people. This is because the key religious texts (for example the Bible, Torah, or Koran) can be interpreted in a variety of ways. Some interpretations are more conservative; others are more liberal and inclusive. Your particular place of worship might welcome only straight/cis people, but another congregation within your faith might be more open and accepting.

How welcoming or open a place of worship is to queer people can depend on a number of different factors: where you live, the congregation's familiarity with actual LGBTQ people, how diverse the congregation is, the individual beliefs of the community's spiritual leaders, and so on.

Some people choose to stay with their original congregation but continue to work for change. Others opt to stay in their congregation and reconcile themselves to the idea that the faith community won't change. There is no right or wrong decision. Religion is a very personal issue, and only you can decide what's best for you.

### BEEN THERE

"I'm Lutheran. Some people might not realize that there are basically two different Lutheran churches—the Evangelical Lutheran Church in America (ELCA) and the Lutheran Church, Missouri Synod (LCMS). One is very liberal, and the other is more hellfire and damnation. There is a push in the ELCA to allow LGBTQ pastors in committed relationships to be ordained. In the past, you could only be ordained if you were straight or, as an LGBTQ person, chose celibacy. There are those who grew up LCMS, like my mother, who are not so accepting." —Charlotte, 19

You might be in a situation that for now makes it difficult or impossible for you to attend a different place of worship. Maybe you're too young to drive or otherwise don't have access to transportation. Whatever the reasons, you might have to wait a while to make changes.

Remember, nothing is wrong with you. You deserve as many opportunities and as much happiness as anyone else in the world. Continue to explore your religion or spirituality and look for ways to find your place in it despite the views of your congregation or religious leader.

**Q: What if I can't find another congregation within my religion that is open and accepting?**

**A:** You might be able to find a different denomination, or branch, within your religion that holds similar beliefs and has a more accepting congregation in your area. For example, Christianity has many denominations. They all work within the same basic belief system and use the Bible as their religious text, but they might have different interpretations, views, and practices. Some denominations have a lot in common, some less. You might be able to find a congregation within a similar denomination that would be comfortable for you.

If no other denomination is similar to yours or an accepting faith community within a similar denomination isn't close to you, you might have to look at other options. You may even decide to consider joining a completely different denomination or exploring other spiritual practices and traditions.

Some spiritual communities, such as the Unitarian Universalists, welcome everyone. These communities might have within the same congregation members who are Jewish, Buddhist, Muslim, Christian, or Wiccan, or who don't subscribe to a particular religious focus at all. The worship services are conducted in such a way that all beliefs are respected. While this could be a big change from the way you're used to worshipping, you can always visit to see what you think. You might love it and decide to stay, or you might feel that it's not the right choice for you.

### RESOURCES FOR QUEER CHRISTIANS

The majority of Americans self-identify as Christian. The resources below specifically address issues of homosexuality and the Bible.

***Fish Out of Water.*** Through interviews with religious leaders, as well as interviews with LGBTQ people who've experienced religious persecution, this documentary discusses the seven Bible verses that are most frequently used to condemn LGBTQ relationships.

***What the Bible Really Says About Homosexuality* by Daniel Helminiak.** Written by a Roman Catholic priest, this book provides commentary on biblical passages. The author concludes that the Bible supplies no real basis for the condemnation of homosexuality.

***Jesus, the Bible, and Homosexuality*** **by Jack Rogers.** A professor of theology, Rogers provides a discussion of LGBTQ issues in Christianity. His primary argument is that being queer and Christian are not mutually exclusive.

***For the Bible Tells Me So.*** This documentary is about the conflict between Christian fundamentalism and homosexuality. In the film, real families discuss their experiences (www.forthebible tellsmeso.org).

**Q: None of these options works for me. What can I do?**
**A:** But wait, there's more! You actually have *even more* options. Some LGBTQ people decide that they can't, at least at this point in their lives, reconcile their sexual orientations or gender identities with organized religion. While this prospect might be scary for you if you've grown up with a strong religious background, it might help to remember that religion and spirituality are about exploration. Give yourself the opportunity to explore what is right for you. And in the end, open exploration can strengthen your faith.

You might look into other religious traditions to find one that's more accepting and feels like a better fit. You could move to a new denomination, or you could eventually end up living in a place where you find an accepting religious community in your original denomination. You might also opt to practice your religion on your own. Observing your faith or exploring your spirituality in a more personal way (outside of a formal setting) may help you clarify what you believe.

Remember, whatever decision you make now doesn't have to be permanent. You can change your mind. You might decide that you need to leave organized religion, at least for a while. In the meantime, you could maintain your religious practices or explore your spiritual beliefs as an individual. Or maybe you'll eventually decide that religion doesn't have a place in your life at all.

Your decision to leave organized religion, change religions, or practice on your own might be upsetting to your family. Talking to them about it calmly and rationally can help, especially if you explain how and why you made your decision. You could choose to add (if it's accurate) that you're not closing yourself off to your family's religion, you're just taking another path, at least for now. You might come back, or you might not.

> **BEEN THERE**
>
> "Around 14 or 15, I got deeply religious and bought myself a Bible. I began attending church regularly and went to study groups and nightly Bible classes. I suppose I was trying to make it work, since everyone assumed I would get into it if I just tried harder. But in the end, it just never worked. It wasn't for me. When I think about the specifics, it's like everything I do and the things I like are all wrong, so I'm bad. But I'm not! I'm not bad, so the problem is elsewhere. Since then, I've explored a number of different religions and spiritualities." —Orlando, 19

Some parents or guardians respect such decisions (even if they don't like them). Others do not. If you're living at home, you might be in a situation where you must still attend your family's choice of religious services. Even if you hear anti-queer messages at these services, try not to take them to heart. These messages are usually the result of fear and ignorance. Not everyone in your religion believes them and neither should you. Know that you are a good, kind person who is just as worthy of love and belonging as anyone else in your faith community.

**Q: I grew up dreaming about a wedding. Do I have to give that up?**

**A:** Though same-sex marriage is now legal on the federal level in the US, some religious communities refuse to allow or condone same-sex marriages to take place in their churches or temples or be conducted by their religious leaders.

Even when this is the case, many LGBTQ people still find ways to include their beliefs by holding their own private ceremonies or by holding ceremonies within open and accepting religious communities. Same-sex weddings don't mean that one person has to wear a tux and the other a dress, although you can definitely do that if you want. A ceremony can be whatever you and your partner want it to be. It can be a traditional wedding, take place on a beach, or be in your parents' backyard. It's up to you. If a wedding that includes some aspect of your religious tradition is what you dream of, you don't have to give up that dream just because you're queer.

**Q: I'm fine with my religion. What can I do to help others who are struggling?**
**A:** If you have been able to reconcile your religious or spiritual beliefs with your sexual orientation or gender identity, you have a tremendous opportunity to help others. This is true whether reaching this reconciliation was easy for you or the result of intense soul-searching. Many people have a tough time accepting themselves because of their religious backgrounds or beliefs. Sharing your experiences with them can provide the encouragement and help they might need on their own journeys.

You could become part of, or even form, an outreach group within your own congregation. Such groups offer those who are struggling an opportunity to talk with and hear from others who have had similar experiences. You could also look into working with an interfaith alliance that addresses issues related to LGBTQ people. These groups offer many opportunities to volunteer. Or you might join or start an online group for those who are struggling with religious issues.

**WHERE RELIGION MEETS CULTURE**

For many, religious beliefs are interwoven with culture. The Human Rights Campaign offers information specifically addressing this intersection, including resources on religion and coming out for people who are Latinx, Black, and Asian Pacific Americans. Check them out at www.hrc.org/explore/topic/religion-faith.

## Cultural Differences, Being LGBTQ, and You

Cultural traditions, like religious ones, could be a big part of your day-to-day life. Culture is composed of many things—race or ethnicity, religion, where you were born or raised, the language(s) you speak. Specifically, it might influence family traditions, holiday celebrations, how your family relates to one another, nicknames, what language you speak at home or with friends, the music you listen to, and the food you eat. Culture also can be a strong influence on expectations about gender and sex roles, such as how you're supposed to behave, dress, and talk. It could even affect expectations for dating.

Reconciling your cultural and family traditions with the need to understand and accept your sexuality or gender identity can be a complex and sometimes painful process. You could feel like you're being forced to choose one identity over the other. For example, it might feel like you aren't allowed to be queer *and* a person of color. To make matters more complicated, LGBTQ people who belong to ethnic, racial, or social minorities are sometimes viewed as having "two strikes" (or more) against them in society. These individuals could face discrimination for being queer and also for being Black, Latinx, Asian, Pacific Islander, Arab, Native American, and so on.

## BEEN THERE

"I was born in Singapore. Until recently, I had not understood cultural differences from a theological perspective. Instead, I recognized cultural differences through my own experiences as a queer woman of color. My innate understanding of cultural differences left me unable to integrate all parts of my identity in certain spaces. For example, being half Asian and half white, it is often difficult to integrate my Asian identity when in the company of only white peers. In virtually all spaces, my queer identity is not integrated or even understood." —Tammy, 20

Part of the struggle can be invisibility. You might feel like your culture doesn't have a place in it for openly LGBTQ people. Those who are queer may be forced to keep a low profile. In many cultures, family and community are central parts of life. Your identity is influenced by how you relate to these groups and the roles you play within them. You might feel isolated or invisible in the queer community if you don't see others from similar backgrounds. Role models, community, and seeing yourself reflected in the society around you are important factors in being able to accept yourself.

No matter where you're from or what your ethnic background is, there have been and are queer people in your culture. How they've been viewed and treated varies widely. Some LGBTQ people find that their racial or ethnic backgrounds make being queer, or at least being out, difficult for them.

For some, it's because many of their cultural traditions are tied to religious beliefs. For others, it's because being LGBTQ is seen as going against strongly held cultural beliefs about sex roles and gender expression. In some cultures, being queer is seen as undermining the family by not carrying on the family name or by going against family expectations. Coming out can be difficult because it's seen as embarrassing or as something that brings shame on a family because it makes public something that is considered private.

These influences can form some powerful barriers to understanding and accepting LGBTQ people. Unfortunately, many queer people of color might feel especially isolated from their communities for these and other reasons.

**FOR LGBTQ TEENS OF COLOR**

There are many websites where queer people of color can socialize and connect on common issues. Some of the religion resources on pages 206–208 could also be helpful.

**Asian & Pacific Islander Family Pride (apifamilypride.org).** This group's mission is to foster acceptance of sexual and gender diversity among Asian and Pacific Islander families. The site includes links to resources including books and videos.

**Latino Pride Center (www.latinopridecenter.org).** The Center's mission is to empower, inspire, and support LGBTQ Latinx people. It runs the Latino Youth in Action program, which provides leadership training to young people to help fight the spread of HIV.

**Trikone (www.trikone.org).** Trikone is a nonprofit organization for LGBTQ people of South Asian descent (including people from Afghanistan, Bangladesh, Bhutan, India, Maldives, Myanmar, Nepal, Pakistan, Sri Lanka, and Tibet). Its goals are to bring people of South Asian heritage together, help people affirm their South Asian identities as well as their sexual orientations and gender identities, and fight discrimination.

**Zuna Institute (www.zunainstitute.org).** Zuna Institute explores issues related to being a Black lesbian in today's society and advocates for civil rights for this community. Their website includes information and resources, advocacy opportunities, and links to many other organizations and sites for Black lesbians.

Many of the national organizations mentioned throughout this book include links and information specifically for queer teens of color. Additional groups for queer people of color are organized at the local level. An online search could help you find and join local groups.

## BEEN THERE

"Being an African American woman has made it more difficult to be LGBTQ. People make it an issue that I'm a lesbian and Black—some say I won't succeed because of those factors combined. I know who I am. My culture and its negativity just make me stronger, because there is nothing worse than being ostracized by people you can identify with on many issues except this one. I've grown to not care how they feel about it because it doesn't matter how they feel, as long as I love myself." —Patrice, 20

"I do identify with my Cherokee heritage. As does anything, it has shaped my character, but in small ways. My heritage and my sexuality were never at odds with each other." —Scott, 19

On the other hand, the traditions of some groups could have a very different—and positive—impact on how you feel about yourself as an LGBTQ person in that culture. Some Native American cultures, for example, have a history of recognizing and accepting their LGBTQ members. Navajos have a word for people who are considered neither men nor women—*nadle*. The Lakota also have words to describe males and females who lived outside of typical gender roles—*winkte* and *koskalaka*. The Omahas have a word—*mexoga*—that means either someone who is neither male nor female or a person's transformation from a man or a woman to the opposite gender. (See pages 41–42 for more on queer people in Native cultures throughout history.)

## More Cultural Factors

While religion and culture have a strong impact on personal identity, many other factors can affect how society sees you—and how you see yourself, both as an individual and as a queer person. Resolving identity issues can be difficult for LGBTQ people. It can be even more challenging for queer people who are seen as "different" in another way.

Anyone who does not fit with what society calls "norms" (but which are actually just averages or what is common) and who is also LGBTQ could be dealing with issues of identity, fitting in, and visibility on many levels. Just as there are norms in society, there are norms within the LGBTQ community that can lead you to have expectations about who's queer and what queerness supposedly looks like.

If your school has a gay-straight alliance (GSA), think for a moment about all the different people who are members. You all could have a lot in common, but there are probably plenty of differences among you, too. And those differences, whether they're in the form of divergent interests, disabilities, economic backgrounds, or other things entirely, might leave you wondering where you fit in. They could leave you confronting the norms within society and also within the LGBTQ community.

For example, maybe you're in a wheelchair. Do you think people would be surprised to see you at a GSA meeting because they'd never thought about someone having a disability *and* being queer before? You might face a similar reaction if you came out at a meeting of a disabled students group. This is just one example of what it can be like to try to figure out who you are and reconcile that with the many different communities of which you could be a part. That process of figuring things out can be complicated, and it's one that will likely continue as you mature and have different experiences. But remember, even when it's complicated, diversity is a positive thing. It enriches our lives and the lives of those around us. If you think of yourself as a mosaic, with each aspect of who you are as one more colored tile, you'll see that each color contributes to creating the intricate and beautiful picture of who you are.

### UNDERSTANDING INTERSECTIONALITY

Intersectionality is the idea of looking at the ways multiple factors interact to make us who we are. Those factors include sex, gender identity, sexual orientation, ethnicity, culture, and so on. The book *Revolutionary Voices: A Multicultural Queer Youth Anthology* highlights LGBTQ young people exploring their intersectional identities through essays, poetry, and art. *This Bridge Called My Back: Writings by Radical Women of Color* is a classic of intersectional feminism and appears on the syllabus in many queer theory classes.

**Pro tip:** Create a piece of art, a poem, or an essay on your intersectional identity for class, or perform or display it somewhere in your community.

## Being a Whole Person: Integrating All Parts of Yourself

If you're having a hard time reconciling your religion, culture, disability, and so on with being LGBTQ, you could be feeling alone, confused, or rejected. It can help to remember that there are LGBTQ members of every religion, ethnicity, and cultural group, even if you don't always see them. No matter who you are, you're not alone.

It might help to talk with other LGBTQ people with backgrounds, heritages, or experiences similar to yours. If you're struggling with issues related to culture, ethnicity, or religion, talk to someone about it. Depending on where you live, support groups might be available. If not, the internet can be a great place to touch base with people who understand what you're going through.

CHAPTER 11

# Work, College, and Beyond

**Life, liberty, and the pursuit of happiness are not "special rights."**

Many teens enter the work world during high school. For others, school comes first and work and careers are something they plan to address later. Either way, if you're LGBTQ, entering the workforce or choosing a college can present questions that your straight/cis peers don't have to consider.

## Getting Past High School

Research shows that some LGBTQ teens can fall behind their straight/cis counterparts when it comes to making career choices and decisions about what to do after high school. In a 2012 survey by the Human Rights Campaign (HRC), while 54 percent of straight/cis young people ranked issues around education (such as keeping grades up, getting into college, and paying for college) as the most difficult problems facing them, LGBTQ respondents were more likely to cite their family not being accepting of them, bullying, fear of coming out, and depression as their top concerns. According to Dr. Greta Davis, a professor of counseling at Southern Methodist University, some LGBTQ young people have to divert more mental energy to their identity development than their straight/cis peers do, so they might not have as much time or focus for career aspirations.

Additionally, some LGBTQ teens—whether due to unstable housing or lack of support at home or school—may not have access to the same resources as their straight/cis peers when it comes to planning life after high school. The idea of getting into and paying for a four-year college might seem as realistic as a giant sparkly unicorn showing up on their doorstep. Others worry that their desired career or school might not be welcoming to LGBTQ people, so they may feel like they have fewer options. For example, in a 2014 study, researchers concluded that compared to the general population, LGBTQ young people appear less likely to pursue occupations in STEM—science, technology, engineering, and mathematics—fields and more likely to pursue occupations involving arts, the humanities, or social sciences. Is this because of innate inclinations or because of perceptions about career options? Do LGBTQ students tend to get less support and encouragement in pursuing STEM subjects? More research will have to be done to paint a complete picture.

Additionally, LGBTQ teens who've experienced harassment at school may fear or assume these kinds of experiences will continue in their post-high school educational or work settings. According to the 2012 HRC study mentioned earlier, among LGBTQ young people surveyed, 63 percent said they would have to move away from their town or to another part of the country to feel accepted, compared with 31 percent of straight/cis respondents.

Of course, these situations don't apply to all LGBTQ people. But they're still important issues to be aware of. While many straight/cis students are thinking about their educations and careers, some LGBTQ teens are just trying to get through each day and may need more support from counselors, teachers, and others when it comes to focusing on the future.

Whatever your experiences, goals, worries, or dreams might be, this chapter aims to present some strategies for how to shape a post-high school life that's right for you. The reality is that when it comes to some aspects of continued education and careers, you may have more challenges than your straight/cis peers do. But the good news is that help and resources *are* out there.

**AFTER HIGH SCHOOL:
COMMON TRENDS AMONG LGBTQ TEENS**

Terra Wagner, an adjunct professor and clinical supervisor at Southern Methodist University's counseling program and clinical supervisor at the Resource Center in Dallas, Texas (which serves the local LGBTQ community), says she sees several common trends among LGBTQ young people. First, many of them hope to pursue careers in advocacy work within the LGBTQ community. In addition to fulfilling a desire to help the LGBTQ rights movement, this can also be a means of finding a safe and welcoming career environment. Wagner also says that in her experience, trans students often wish to postpone further education until after they're able to transition. (For more on gender and transitioning, see chapter 3.) Finally, Wagner notes that some LGBTQ students want to pursue their post-high school education online to avoid abuse or harassment.

## Finding an LGBTQ-Friendly Company

Some teens don't care if an employer is LGBTQ-friendly. For others, it's a very important factor. Increasingly, public and private employers are including sexual orientation and gender identity in their nondiscrimination policies.

Employers tend to be open with prospective and current employees about their human resources policies, so you should be able to find out fairly easily whether a nondiscrimination policy is in place. You can search a company's website or ask one of its representatives. An employee handbook should also contain information about the company's nondiscrimination policy. Many companies post their policies in lunch or breakrooms, print them on job applications, or hand out copies automatically with other employment-related paperwork.

The Human Rights Campaign (HRC) is another source of information for LGBTQ issues on the job. The group regularly updates a Corporate Equality Index, which rates employers based on LGBTQ friendliness. HRC also maintains a database of employers where you can search for companies that include LGBTQ people in their nondiscrimination policies, offer domestic partner/same-sex spouse benefits, or have queer employee groups. Visit HRC's website at www.hrc.org to access these features.

In HRC's 2017 Corporate Equality Index, 515 major businesses achieved a 100 percent rating for being LGBTQ-friendly. This is the biggest single-year increase in the history of the Index. At these companies, which span industries from law firms and financial institutions to healthcare, advertising, and telecommunications companies, workers are protected from employment discrimination based on sexual orientation and gender identity or expression by employers' policies in areas such as diversity, training, and benefits.

Transgender workers have made major gains since the Corporate Equality Index was first published in 2002. At that time, only 5 percent of businesses rated by HRC prohibited discrimination based on gender identity or expression. By 2017, that figure had increased to 96 percent. Additionally, 387 major businesses surveyed had adopted gender transition guidelines for their employees and teams with the goal of being more inclusive of trans people.

## Being LGBTQ in the Workplace: Your Decisions and Your Rights

People approach being LGBTQ in the workplace in many different ways. Some prefer to remain private about being queer, not addressing it unless it happens to come up. Others feel it's important to have coworkers know they are queer (and for trans people, this could be a necessity if they choose to transition at work). There's no right or wrong way to address this issue. Do what you feel comfortable doing for the specific situation you're in.

### Should I Tell a Prospective Employer I'm LGBTQ?

Queer people sometimes wonder whether they should come out to a potential employer during an interview. That's a personal decision.

Especially for teens, many believe that telling others they're LGBTQ should be on a need-to-know basis. If it somehow relates to the job (like applying for a position at an LGBTQ organization), it could be appropriate to share.

Some people who are completely out prefer to be open about who they are from the beginning to make sure their gender identities or sexual orientations won't be a problem in the workplace. But telling an employer that you're LGBTQ during an interview can create an uncomfortable situation for you both. Whether you're LGBTQ or straight/cis doesn't have anything to do with how well you can do your job, but coming out in an interview might give that impression. The focus is really on finding out whether the job is a good match for you. You can also try to figure out whether the company is LGBTQ-friendly, but you don't have to come out to do that.

Here are questions you can ask to determine whether a company is queer-friendly:

**Ask about the company's policies.** "Do you have an employment nondiscrimination policy? Who does it cover?" or, "Does your employment nondiscrimination policy cover LGBTQ people?" or, "Does your employment nondiscrimination policy cover employees who are transgender?" If you're concerned about expressing that level of detail, you could just ask to see a copy of the policy.

**Ask, "How is this workplace environment for LGBTQ employees?"** This gives a pretty obvious indication that you're LGBTQ, so it's up to you to decide if you're comfortable with that.

Some trans people choose to come out during an interview, especially if they plan on transitioning while at the job or if they live as one gender but have government-issued identity documents (which are typically checked by a human resources representative during the application process or just after hiring) indicating a different gender.

## Should I Come Out to My Coworkers?

Coming out to coworkers can be a great experience because it can result in a more open and supportive work environment where you feel free to be yourself. But remember, people you work with don't have to be your best friends. It's up to you how much personal information you want them to know.

As you spend more time in the working world, you'll come across people whose religious, political, and social beliefs are very different from yours. Sometimes these encounters can be stressful or annoying. But for some of the people you're exposed to, you might be the first person they know to be queer. You could have a positive influence on their beliefs.

For those who prefer not to come out as LGBTQ at work, that's okay. It's important to do what you're comfortable with. And that could change over time.

## What Are My Rights?

Some states have enacted laws that cover job discrimination. As for federal-level protections, in April 2017, a federal appeals court in Chicago ruled that long-standing federal civil rights laws prohibit workplaces from discriminating against LGBTQ employees, calling such targeted actions a form of sex discrimination. In 2018, the US Sixth Circuit Court of Appeals decided in the case of Aimee Stephens, who had been fired because of her status as a trans woman, that the Title IX federal law banning sex bias in the workplace also protects the rights of transgender workers. These are major steps forward, and important ones.

### BEEN THERE

"I think that the quality of life for LGBTQ people in this country is getting better, but it certainly isn't great. There are a lot of benefits and rights that LGBTQ people are not allowed to receive. Being gay didn't really affect me negatively until I started to witness the hatred and bigotry in this world. But once I started to get out and see that other gay people have made it through, I started to feel much better about being a gay person in this country."
—Bengie, 15

For decades, civil rights and LGBTQ activists lobbied to get the Employment Non-Discrimination Act (ENDA) passed. The bill had already been introduced in every Congress but one from 1994 to 2013. ENDA would have provided basic protections at the federal level against discrimination in the workplace based on sexual orientation and on gender identity or expression. It would have been illegal to fire, deny employment, or harass someone because of their actual or perceived sexual orientation or gender identity. Many major corporations endorsed the bill, but it failed to pass.

In 2015, Congress introduced the Equality Act, which would amend the Civil Rights Act of 1964 to make it illegal to discriminate against LGBTQ people in areas including employment, housing, public education, and federal funding. It did not pass, but was reintroduced to Congress in 2017 with 214 original cosponsors, which is the most congressional support that any pro-LGBTQ legislation has ever received upon its introduction. (To track the status of the Equality Act, visit www.hrc.org.)

## I Am Being Discriminated Against in My Workplace. What Should I Do?

Discrimination can take many forms. Sexual harassment, off-color remarks, and passing up someone for a promotion because the person is LGBTQ are all forms of discrimination. Queer people sometimes face workplace discrimination, but you should neither expect it nor accept it.

Here are some tips for what to do if you think you are being discriminated against by an employer:

1. **1. Stop and think.** Are you sure you're being discriminated against because you're LGBTQ? You might be. It's also possible that you're misreading the situation. So stop and assess it before taking action. Does your employer (or a specific coworker) have a history of anti-LGBTQ behavior? Could you have misunderstood something that was said? If you have a trusted coworker, ask for advice. Tell your coworker what was said to you or what you overheard and ask for an opinion. The human resources (HR) department should also be able to help (though discrimination could also come from HR).

**2. Write it down.** If you suspect (or know) you're being discriminated against because you're LGBTQ, write down the incident and include names of anyone else who might have witnessed it. If several incidents occur, keep track of them all. Keep a record of any interactions you have with your employer regarding the matter and include your employer's responses. This record will be very useful if the issue is not resolved and you decide to take further action. Most HR representatives will tell you that documenting these incidents is the first step in enabling them to investigate.

**3. Come up with a plan.** If you have an HR representative assisting you, this person will help you formulate a plan or, more likely, will have a predetermined set of actions to follow. These generally follow legal regulations and guidelines.

If you're handling the discrimination on your own because you don't have access to HR help, plan what you will say to your employer or coworker and approach the person calmly and rationally. Ask to speak with them and then sit down and explain the situation and why you feel you were discriminated against.

Then—and this step is critical—listen to the response. The person might offer an explanation that puts your concerns to rest, so give them that opportunity. They might confess to the discrimination, or they might deny it completely. Try to stay calm. You're more likely to be taken seriously if you remain professional.

**4. If the response is negative, decide your course of action.** You can go back to work and ignore it, you can quit your job, or you can try to address the issue in another way. There isn't one right way to deal with the situation, just what's right for you. You might not have the time, energy, or money (in the case of a legal response) to address the issue. You might really need the job. Or you might feel like the situation is one you just can't live with.

If your issue is with a coworker or direct supervisor, it might be time to go to that employee's boss. Again, remember to stay calm and rational. Keep your comments to facts and not opinions.

If you decide to pursue the matter, the Human Rights Campaign, Lambda Legal, the American Civil Liberties Union, and the Southern Poverty Law Center are among the groups that can counsel you about your rights according to your state's laws. These groups also can refer you to attorneys in your area, if necessary, or may take on your case themselves.

Discrimination can be demeaning and frustrating. Regardless of how you decide to deal with discrimination, be sure to remind yourself that it is a result of ignorance. It has nothing to do with you as a person.

# A Perfect Match: Finding the Right School

If you're going to college, community college, or technical or vocational school, picking the right school can be challenging. First you have to go through what every other teen bound for continued education goes through: deciding whether to pursue a two- or four-year degree; choosing between a technical school, community college, state school, or private college; picking a liberal arts program or something more specialized or choosing a trade; figuring out what you can afford; applying for scholarships or financial aid; and so on. But once you've narrowed it down, how can you be sure you'll be going into an environment that's supportive of LGBTQ people?

## Tips for Finding an LGBTQ-Friendly School

If you're interested in finding an LGBTQ-friendly college, community college, or other school, it's not as hard as you might think. Here are some ideas that can help:

**Search online.** Look for schools online by searching for "LGBTQ-friendly colleges," "LGBTQ-friendly community colleges," or "LGBTQ-friendly technical schools." Many queer websites and publications have articles about queer-friendly colleges. Some even poll their readers to find out what's what.

### A NOTE ON RESEARCH

Currently it's a bit easier to find information online about LGBTQ-friendly four-year colleges and community colleges than it is to find information about LGBTQ-friendly technical schools. But you can always pick up the phone. Call a school you're interested in and ask if they have a nondiscrimination policy, if they have any LGBTQ students, and so on. If that idea makes you nervous, you could ask a friend or trusted adult (maybe even your school counselor) to help you.

When you're doing research into issues like continuing education options and scholarships (many technical and trade schools offer scholarships and other financial aid, too), your best friend could turn out to be your school or local librarian. Lots of librarians are super sleuths who are highly trained in helping people find all kinds of information, and many of them are delighted to help.

You also can use the internet to take a closer look at the schools you're interested in. You can look up nondiscrimination policies, peruse majors and course listings, find out about student groups (including whether there are any for LGBTQ people), and learn more about whether the cities or towns where the schools are located tend to be LGBTQ-friendly or not.

## SINGLE-GENDER INSTITUTIONS OPEN TO TRANS STUDENTS

In 2017, Spelman College—a women's school that is also one of the nation's historically black colleges and universities (HBCUs)—announced that it would update its admissions process to include transgender women. Other women's colleges that accept trans women and students who are genderfluid are Agnes Scott College, Barnard College, Bryn Mawr College, Mills College, Mount Holyoke College, Scripps College, Simmons College, Smith College, and Wellesley College. All-male college St. John's University admits trans men, and in 2017 Morehouse College (another HBCU) released a statement implying that it was considering doing the same.

**Check out a "best colleges" guide.** Perhaps the most up-to-date and easily accessible resource is the online Campus Pride Index (www.campusprideindex.org). This site is operated by Campus Pride, a national nonprofit group for student leaders and campus groups that works to create more LGBTQ-friendly environments at colleges and universities. The Campus Pride Index includes reviews and ratings of traditional four-year and community colleges, ranking how LGBTQ-friendly they are. It also includes information on each school's size, degree offerings, and tuition, as well as financial aid resources specifically for LGBTQ students.

**Investigate your schools of choice.** What if you have your heart set on a school that doesn't have high marks for being LGBTQ-friendly? Just because a school hasn't earned an official queer-friendly designation doesn't mean it isn't good for LGBTQ students. Here are some ways to find out if the schools you're interested in are queer-friendly:

- **Get a copy of the school's nondiscrimination policy.** All colleges should have one. Look in the student handbook or an admissions guidebook. It might even be posted on the school's website. If you see "sexual orientation" and "gender identity" as categories protected from discrimination, that's a good sign. If those words aren't there, you might not have any recourse if you become a victim of harassment or discrimination by the college or its students.
- **Investigate the campus climate.** Does the campus have an LGBTQ student group? Is the group active? Some campuses even have queer resource or community centers. Does the school offer LGBTQ-specific health services for students? Are there gender-neutral bathrooms and housing options? Does the school offer an easy way to change gender markers on official school records?
- **Talk to students.** If an LGBTQ group or gay-straight alliance is on campus, contact the organization and talk with one or more of its members to find out how active the group is, what kinds of activities and events they're involved with, and what members think of the campus climate. Most of these groups are happy to help.
- **Check out the curriculum.** If a school includes queer studies or similar curriculum, or even a few courses such as gender anthropology or gay and lesbian history, chances are it's a pretty friendly place (at least academically). Although entire queer studies programs or majors aren't exactly commonplace, many schools have one or more classes on topics like queer theory or gender in society. Departments like English, political science, sociology, and theater also are frequently home to courses on queer topics. A lot of the class information should be available online. You can also call the school and ask to speak with someone in a particular department or in an academic administrator's office.

It helps to remember that the school that's right for you includes many factors, not the least of which is academics. If an institution doesn't have the courses you're interested in or the major you want, it's not going to be a great match for you even if it appears to be queer-friendly or has an "official" queer-friendly designation.

**“ BEEN THERE**

“I was out to my closest friends from home. As a college freshman, I was re-closeted. I didn’t have anyone to talk to and just felt lost. I finally found the on-campus Alliance and have been active ever since. This year I am the copresident—I’m out to my whole campus now.” —Cathy, 20

**Visit the schools you’re most interested in.** If you can, visit the schools you’re most interested in attending. You can learn a lot on a campus visit that guidebooks, college materials, and guidance counselors don’t cover. This might be a good time to explore the LGBTQ resource center or community center or meet people in the school’s queer group. Even if you can’t do that, simple things like eating in a dining hall, reading the flyers on campus bulletin boards, and looking through the campus newspaper (which may also be online) can tell you a lot about a school’s culture and vibe. Pay attention to how you feel being on campus. Are you comfortable, or do certain things you see or hear (or don’t see or hear) make you nervous? You can also ask current students if the surrounding area is queer-friendly. This is all information you can use when it comes time to decide where you’re going to go.

**FOOTING THE BILL**

There are more scholarship opportunities than ever for LGBTQ students! A simple online search for “LGBTQ scholarships” will return loads of resources for all kinds of educational options from community colleges to grad schools. Some scholarships are based on need, while others are related to academic achievement, your planned course of study, and so on. If you don’t have access to a computer or otherwise need help doing research, ask your school or local librarian or a school counselor.

## Fraternities and Sororities

Many LGBTQ people who go to colleges and universities are members of a sorority or fraternity. In fact, Delta Lambda Phi is a fraternity that describes itself as being “founded by gay men for all men.”

You can visit the organization's website (dlp.org) for more information. Other Greek organizations bill themselves as queer-friendly, although some of this depends on the particular campus more than the parent organization. The Lambda 10 Project is an information clearinghouse for LGBTQ Greek organizations and addresses a variety of issues related to being Greek and queer. Check it out at www.campuspride.org/lambda10.

### BEEN THERE

"Some friends and I at the University of Virginia felt that while there are a number of LGBTQ groups on campus, there weren't enough options for LGBTQ students in terms of fraternities and sororities. There are several national gay fraternities and a handful of lesbian sororities, but none had any local chapters. So we decided to start our own fraternity—Sigma Omicron Rho (SOR). To the best of my knowledge, SOR is the only gender-neutral queer fraternal collegiate organization in the country.

"We seek to provide a semi-traditional Greek experience and the camaraderie that comes with it for queer, allied, and gender nonconforming students who otherwise would not feel comfortable pledging a fraternity or sorority. We never ask any of our members to identify in any way—we are totally inclusive regardless of whether you're LGBTQ or straight. It's amazing because we truly feel that all of our members value and care for one another on a personal level. I was literally moved to tears at an event last semester when I looked around and realized that the very existence of SOR had touched people's lives in a very real way." —Meredith, 21

## Going with the Flow: Some Thoughts on Getting Older

Leaving high school is a big transition for all teens. For LGBTQ teens, it can be the gateway to a whole new world. With increased independence, you'll most likely have greater access to other LGBTQ people, especially if you move to an urban area. You may discover a completely different social world, which can be exhilarating, frightening, and a big relief. You'll finally have more control over your environment than you did when you were in high school.

You might find that all of the experiences you had up through high school—even the really difficult ones—helped make you a pretty strong and amazing person.

All this change and transition makes for an exciting time. It can be tempting to do everything you weren't able to do before, like spend most of your time socializing, dating, and going out. With the sudden increase in access to a whole new community, it can be easy to get carried away. The same instincts that helped you take care of yourself and keep it together in high school are still valuable to you.

Trust yourself to make the decisions that are best for you. Even though the scenery and the people might have changed, your instincts haven't. So explore and discover new ideas and people, and most of all, enjoy yourself and your life. You deserve it.

### BEEN THERE

"The best thing about being LGBTQ is that there is so much diversity in the community. There is so much more than being LGBTQ that makes us who we are; it's just one thing that brings us together. We know how not to be judgmental of others and we grow together. When one person in this community does something positive, it affects everyone, and that is important. We always move one step forward, together." —Yvonne, 20

# Glossary

As you read this glossary, please keep in mind that the language of the LGBTQ community is always changing (even the title of this book has changed with each edition). Words aren't always perfect or even as exact as we would like them to be, but without them, we wouldn't be able to talk about LGBTQ issues. And talking about queerness is one of the most important things we can do.

While this glossary defines commonly used terms in the LGBTQ world, there are many more that I have opted not to include here for the sake of keeping things relatively concise (and less confusing for people who are totally new to this world). If you'd like an even more extensive list, I've included additional resources at the end of this glossary.

**agender:** Someone who has a gender identity that is not male or female or who does not have a defined gender identity.

**ally:** Someone who supports LGBTQ people. Non-LGBTQ people who are members or advisors of gay-straight alliances, who march in Pride parades, and who fight for LGBTQ people's equal rights are examples of allies.

**anatomy:** The physical characteristics of the body, often used in reference to a specific sex. A typical anatomical male has a penis and testicles. A typical anatomical female has a vagina, a vulva, ovaries, a clitoris, and breasts. People whose anatomies don't match their gender identities often identify themselves as transgender. People who are intersex have a combination of anatomical characteristics (and/or sex chromosomes) and are not exclusively male or female.

**androgyne, also gender bender or gender blender:** People who are androgynous or who are gender benders or gender blenders can merge gender expression in many different ways to represent either a combination of the binary genders or neither. Someone who is androgynous often does not present themselves in appearance as either binary gender. There are also people who blend genders.

For example, "riot grrrls" might shave their heads and wear combat boots, but also wear makeup and a skirt. Being androgynous or a gender bender is not necessarily a reflection of a person's sexual orientation or gender identity.

**aromantic (aro):** A person who experiences little or no romantic attraction. People who are aro typically do not feel compelled to pursue romantic relationships, but instead are satisfied with friendships and other non-romantic relationships.

**asexual (ace):** A person who experiences little or no sexual attraction.

**bicurious:** Someone who has or has had attractions to people of more than one gender. The "curious" part also connotes that they are interested in exploring these attractions.

**bigender:** Someone who is or has experiences of two genders.

**binary:** The binary is the classic or traditional division of genders as only male and female. The binary also tends to characterize anatomical sex and gender as one and the same thing.

**bisexual:** A person who is emotionally, romantically, and sexually attracted to people of two or more genders. We used to say that bisexual people were attracted to both men and women (hence *bi*, which means "two"). So you were either gay, lesbian, or bisexual. Now, as our understanding of gender and sexual orientation continues to expand, being bisexual can also mean being attracted to more than just people who have binary male or female identities.

**biological sex, also birth sex, anatomical sex, or physical sex:** It used to be thought that biological sex was limited to male or female. Now, as with gender, our understanding of biological sex is expanding. One example of this is the fact that being intersex is not as rare as was once thought.

**butch:** A term used to describe someone who acts and dresses in stereotypically masculine ways.

**cisgender (cis):** A person whose gender identity matches the sex they were assigned at birth. Cisgender is not synonymous with straight, since people who are gay or lesbian (among other sexual orientations) can also be cisgender. People who are *not* cisgender typically identify as transgender, nonbinary, agender, bigender, genderqueer, or genderfluid.

**cissexism:** This is the idea that cis people (those whose gender identities match their sexes assigned at birth) are normal and trans people are abnormal. Cissexism is also the assumption that all people are cis unless proven or declared otherwise. Cissexism contributes to transphobia. As heterosexism is to homophobia, cissexism is to transphobia.

**closeted:** A person who is closeted (or "in the closet") does not disclose their sexual orientation or their sexual or gender identity. People may also be partially closeted—only coming out to a select few.

**coming out:** Disclosing one's sexual orientation or gender identity to others. Some people never come out, others come out to a few individuals, still others are out to everyone, and for some, the coming out process takes place more slowly.

**cross-dresser:** Cross-dressers are people who dress in the clothing of the opposite sex (in a binary system). They may do this in private or in public. Cross-dressers used to also be called transvestites, but both the terms *cross-dresser*, which assumes the gender binary of male/female, and *transvestite* are falling out of use.

**demisexual:** This term is used to describe people who do not tend to feel sexual attraction to someone unless they feel an emotional connection with the person. The term comes from the idea of being "halfway between" sexual and asexual (*demi* means "half").

**drag queens and drag kings:** We used to say that drag queens were men who dressed as women and drag kings were women who dressed as men, but these definitions now represent an outdated understanding of gender. Now we could say more inclusively that a drag queen is someone who does not identify as female, and a drag king is someone who does not identify as male, but that these people dress up as those binary genders, typically for entertainment purposes. Drag queens and kings usually present larger-than-life representations of women and men. Being a drag queen or king is not necessarily a reflection of sexual orientation or gender identity.

**ex-gay movement:** This movement attempts to convert people who are LGBTQ to being straight/cis. Members encourage queer people to undergo conversion or reparative therapy. The ex-gay movement has been discredited by major medical organizations in the US that have declared that being queer isn't a choice and cannot be changed.

**femme:** A term used to describe someone who acts and dresses in stereotypically feminine ways.

**FAAB:** Female-assigned at birth. This term is often used by trans and intersex people to communicate the sexes or genders that were assigned to them when they were born. Also used are AFAB, for assigned female at birth, and CAFAB, for coercively assigned female at birth.

**FTM, also F-T-M and F2M:** Stands for female-to-male and refers to transgender people who were assigned female identities at birth but whose gender identities are male. They may express this with their appearance (clothes, hair), and they may also opt for a physical change that can involve hormone therapy and/or surgery. See also *trans man*.

**gay:** This term is often used to describe both homosexual men and homosexual women. As it refers to men, *gay* describes men who are emotionally, romantically, and sexually attracted to other men. The word *gay* didn't come into wide use to describe homosexual people until the 1950s. Before that, it was used as a code word for same-sex sexuality.

**gay-straight alliance (GSA):** A student club for gay, lesbian, bisexual, transgender, and questioning students and their straight allies. GSAs can provide a social haven and support for queer students. They can also work for positive change on LGBTQ issues within a school or school system. GSAs are legally entitled to exist according to a federal court ruling. In some spaces, GSA stands for genders and sexualities alliance.

**gender:** While this word has been used to describe anatomy, it's really about a person's identity rather than their physical characteristics. Gender is made up of many things, including behaviors, cultural characteristics, and psychological traits.

**gender confirmation surgery, also gender affirmation surgery:** Any in a group of surgical procedures undertaken with the goal of having a person's physical presentation better match their true gender identity. Gender confirmation surgeries can include genital surgery (in which a surgeon modifies a person's genitals), surgeries on secondary sex characteristics (such as the breasts or Adam's apple), and cosmetic surgeries.

**gender dysphoria:** A term for the pain, anxiety, and confusion that can result when there is a disparity between a person's gender identity and the sex they were assigned at birth. Pressure to conform to accepted gender roles and expression and a general lack of acceptance from society when a person doesn't conform to these expectations also contribute to gender dysphoria. In the mental health community, gender dysphoria is currently considered a mental health diagnosis. However, it doesn't mean there is something "wrong" with the person.

**gender expression:** How you express your gender identity. It can include your clothes, hairstyle, body language (how you walk, your posture, your gestures, your mannerisms), and even speech patterns.

**genderfluid:** Someone whose gender identity is not fixed or static.

**gender identity:** Your internal sense of being male, female, both, or neither. A person's gender identity doesn't necessarily reflect their sex assigned at birth.

**gender identity disorder (GID):** Mental health professionals used to diagnose transgender people with GID, which allowed them to access mental and physical treatment. But many argued that a diagnosis of GID carried the stigma of mental illness. In the latest edition of the diagnostic manual used by mental health professionals, the *DSM-5*, GID has been omitted in favor of gender dysphoria, which is not considered a mental disorder.

**gender marker:** The designation of gender that appears on official records such as birth certificates, driver's licenses, and school records. A transgender person's gender marker typically will indicate their sex assigned at birth unless they legally change it. However, this change is not permitted in every state, and when it is permitted, it may involve multiple steps (and fees).

**gender nonconforming:** Embracing behaviors that do not conform with stereotypical or traditional ideas associated with one's gender assigned at birth. Cisgender people can be gender nonconforming, and transgender people can be gender conforming (conforming to stereotypical or traditional ideas of gender roles).

**genderqueer:** This term describes people whose gender identities exist outside of the traditional male/female binary. Those who identify as genderqueer may identify as male and female, neither male nor female, beyond gender, or simply "other."

**gender roles:** A set of expectations regarding roles, behaviors, and responsibilities for men and women, typically based on cultural, religious, or other societal norms.

**gender transitioning:** Gender transitioning is a complex, multistep process of starting to live in a way that accurately reflects a person's gender identity when that identity is different than the one assigned to them at birth. Transitioning primarily involves social behaviors, such as changing your name, dressing differently, altering other aspects of your appearance like hair or makeup, and changing your mannerisms, your voice, and how you move. A physical transition might include taking hormones or other substances under the supervision of a medical professional. For some, transitioning also involves surgery. Some people wishing to have gender confirmation surgery undergo a real-life experience (RLE) or real-life test (RLT) in which they live as their true genders for a period of time, usually one year, before genital reassignment surgery (GRS) is performed. The purpose of this period is to confirm that the person can function successfully as that gender in society and that they are certain they want to do so for the rest of their life. However, some medical professionals do not require the RLE. Instead, they give trans people a lot of information about transitioning and what it may mean for their lives, and then allow them to make a decision for themselves without an RLE. This model is called "informed consent."

**heterosexism:** The idea that heterosexual people are the norm and LGBTQ people are somehow abnormal. Also, heterosexism includes the assumption that people are heterosexual until shown or declared to be otherwise. Heterosexism contributes to homophobia.

**heterosexual:** People who are emotionally and physically attracted to people of the opposite sex (in the gender binary).

**homophobia:** Homophobia is when someone feels a negative emotion like fear, anger, or suspicion toward someone else for having a sexual orientation other than straight.

**homosexual:** People who are emotionally and physically attracted to people of the same sex (in the gender binary).

**hormone replacement therapy (HRT):** In HRT, sex hormones and other hormonal medications are administered to a trans or gender-variant individual for the purpose of more closely aligning the person's secondary sex characteristics with their gender identity.

**IAFAB:** Stands for intersex assigned female at birth.

**IAMAB:** Stands for intersex assigned male at birth.

**intersex:** People who are born with a reproductive, genetic, genital, or hormonal configuration (or combination of these) that does not fit classic definitions of male or female. In many cases, doctors or parents choose the child's sex. This choice may involve a series of surgeries throughout infancy and childhood to definitively assign a person one anatomical sex. The surgery doesn't always result in a physical sex assignment that matches the person's gender. Being intersex is not the same as being transgender, though some intersex people may identify as trans. The term *hermaphrodite* was once used to describe intersex people, but is now considered outdated and offensive.

**lesbian:** A woman who is emotionally, romantically, and sexually attracted to other women.

**LGBTQ:** An acronym that stands for lesbian, gay, bisexual, transgender, and questioning. Sometimes the letters *I* and *A* are added, as well, for *intersex* and *asexual*. Another common acronym is LGBT+, with the plus indicating queer identities beyond lesbian, gay, bisexual, or transgender.

**MAAB:** Male-assigned at birth. This term is often used by trans and intersex people to communicate the sex or gender that was assigned to them when they were born. Also used are AMAB, for assigned male at birth, and CAMAB, for coercively assigned male at birth.

**misgender:** To misgender someone is to apply a gender label to a person that is other than the gender as which that person identifies, or it can also mean applying a gender label to a person who does not have a gender identity. This can include not using a person's preferred pronouns.

**MTF, also M-T-F and M2F:** Stands for male-to-female and refers to people who were assigned male at birth, but who have a predominantly female gender identity. They might express this with their appearance (clothes, hair) or they may opt for a physical change that can involve the use of hormone therapy and possibly surgery.

**nonbinary (enby):** A person who has a nonbinary gender identity does not identify as male or female, or may identify as both. *Enby* is a slang term for someone who is nonbinary.

**omnisexual:** See *pansexual.*

**out:** Living openly as a queer person. When LGBTQ people tell other people that they are queer, the process is called "coming out," as in "coming out of the closet." Being "outed" is when someone accidentally or purposefully reveals another person's sexual orientation or gender identity, often before that person is ready to do so.

**pangender:** A nonbinary gender identity that encompasses multiple gender identities.

**pansexual, also omnisexual:** *Pansexual* and *omnisexual* are terms used to identify sexual orientation. Those who identify in this way may be emotionally, romantically, and sexually attracted to people of any biological sex or gender expression.

**passing:** The ability for a person to be seen as their true gender when it does not match the sex assigned to them at birth. This term can also be used to describe a queer person being assumed to be straight. LGBTQ people may wish to "pass" as straight and/or cis. For others (especially in the trans community), the idea of passing may be not at all important or even offensive.

**preferred gender pronoun (PGP):** This refers to the pronoun or set of pronouns someone prefers for themselves. For example: "Hi, I'm Kelly. My pronouns are *she* and *her*." "Hi, Kelly! I'm Alyx. My PGPs are *they* and *them*.")

**puberty blockers, also puberty suppressors:** Medications administered to prevent or slow the development of secondary sex characteristics in young people who identify as transgender or nonbinary.

**puberty suppression:** A medical process using puberty blockers to pause or delay the development of secondary sex characteristics in adolescents. Puberty suppression allows young people and their families more time to make choices about hormonal interventions and can help decrease gender dysphoria, which often escalates as trans people go through puberty.

**queer:** Refers to people who are lesbian, gay, bisexual, transgender, questioning, and many other identities other than heterosexual. Sometimes used as a slur, the term has been reclaimed by many LGBTQ people who use it as an expression of pride. Some LGBTQ people prefer to identify as queer, rather than lesbian, gay, bisexual, or transgender, because they feel it encompasses more of who they are or gives them a greater sense of unity with the entire LGBTQ community.

**questioning:** Being uncertain of one's sexual orientation or gender identity and being in a space or mindset of exploration.

**secondary sex characteristics:** External physical characteristics that appear due to hormonal stimulation such as puberty or hormone supplements. Secondary sex characteristics can include breasts, facial hair and other body hair, muscle growth, and changes in distribution of fat, among others.

**sexual behavior:** Sexual behavior only describes sexual activity, not sexual identity. For example, someone who identifies as a man may identify as gay but still engage in sexual behavior with people who identify as women. That's still considered heterosexual behavior. Or someone who identifies as a woman may not identify as a lesbian, but she may take part in sexual activity with people who identify as women. That is homosexual behavior. Noting these distinctions, public health researchers in their analyses will differentiate among gay men, lesbians, men who have sex with men (MSM), and women who have sex with women (WSW).

**sexual identity:** How a person views and identifies themselves in terms of their sexual orientation, attractions, and behavior.

**sexual orientation:** A term used to describe who someone is emotionally, romantically, and sexually attracted to. A person may be attracted to someone of the same or opposite sex (in a binary system), or have attractions without regard to the other person's sex or gender. Sexual orientation—and being queer—isn't just about who you have sex with. Because of that, there have been suggestions for a more accurate phrase, such as emotional orientation or affectional orientation. But for now, sexual orientation is the common phrase.

**skoliosexual:** Someone who is attracted to people who identify as nonbinary in terms of gender.

**straight:** Synonymous with *heterosexual.*

**transgender:** Having a gender identity or gender expression that is different from your sex assigned at birth. *Transgender* is a broad term that covers many groups, and people who are trans may identify themselves in a variety of ways. Being transgender isn't a reflection of sexual orientation. Trans people can be straight, lesbian, gay, bisexual, or something else.

**transitioning:** See *gender transitioning.*

**trans man:** A transgender person who identifies as a man. Some younger people use the terms *transboy/trans boy* or *transboi.*

**transphobia:** Transphobia is when someone feels a negative emotion like fear, anger, or suspicion toward someone else for being transgender. Transphobia can also take the form of ignorance about trans people.

**transsexual:** This term was once used interchangeably with *transgender.* Though some people self-identify as transsexual, the term has largely fallen out of use. Some consider it offensive.

**trans woman:** A transgender person who identifies as a woman. Some younger people use the term *transgirl/trans girl.*

**Two Spirit:** A term referring to Native Americans (and used by indigenous people in some other countries) whose spirits were a blend of genders. Today, some Native communities have reclaimed this term as an alternative to labels such as lesbian, gay, or transgender. In their communities, Two-Spirit people were often revered as visionaries and healers.

## Additional Terminology Resources

*The ABC's of LGBT+* by Ashley Mardell (Mango Media, 2016).

Human Rights Campaign Glossary of Terms (www.hrc.org/resources/glossary-of-terms).

The University of California, Davis, LGBTQIA Resource Center Glossary (lgbtqia.ucdavis.edu/educated/glossary.html).

# Resources

It's nearly impossible to create an exhaustive list of all the great LGBTQ resources available, and the list continues to expand. This information is intended to give you an idea of what's available and to provide you with starting points to explore a variety of topics. Additional resources, as well as more detailed explanations of many of the entries here, can be found throughout this book. The selected bibliography on pages 250–254 also includes materials that might interest you.

## Organizations

**Advocates for Youth**
(202) 419-3420
www.advocatesforyouth.org
Advocates for Youth is an organization that helps young people make informed and responsible decisions about their reproductive and sexual health. The group's website also includes information on sexuality, spirituality, relationship abuse, and queer harassment.

**American Civil Liberties Union (ACLU)**
(212) 549-2500
www.aclu.org
The ACLU works in the courts to defend civil liberties for all people. Check out the website for information on a wide range of LGBTQ issues, including safe school initiatives.

**GLAAD (Gay & Lesbian Alliance Against Defamation)**
(212) 629-3322
www.glaad.org
GLAAD works to promote fair, accurate, and inclusive representations of LGBTQ people and events in newspapers, magazines, movies, television shows, and other media.

**GLMA: Health Professionals Advancing LGBTQ Equality (GLMA)**
(202) 600-8037
www.glma.org
GLMA is an association of gay and lesbian medical professionals who provide referrals to queer-friendly physicians and health agencies. The group can help connect you with local medical providers who are respectful and supportive of LGBTQ people.

**GLSEN (Gay, Lesbian & Straight Education Network)**
(212) 727-0135
www.glsen.org
GLSEN offers information about national efforts to create queer-friendly classrooms, as well as resources you can use to help create a gay-straight alliance in your school.

**Hetrick-Martin Institute**
(212) 674-2400
www.hmi.org
The Hetrick-Martin Institute has a wide variety of programs for LGBTQ people ages 12 to 21 in the New York City area. While programs are not offered nationwide, the institute's website is a good source of information for queer young people.

**Human Rights Campaign (HRC)**
1-800-777-4723
www.hrc.org
HRC works to protect the rights of LGBTQ people. The organization's website includes information on National Coming Out Day, safe schools, workplace equality, queer-related legislation, and many other issues.

**interACT**
(707) 793-1190
interactadvocates.org
interACT works to raise visibility of intersex people and issues, empower young intersex advocates, and work for laws and policies that support intersex young people.

**Lambda Legal**
(212) 809-8585
www.lambdalegal.org
Lambda Legal works to protect the civil rights of people who are LGBTQ.

**National LGBTQ Task Force**
(202) 393-5177
www.thetaskforce.org
The National LGBTQ Task Force offers referrals to attorneys, physicians, counselors, and other professionals.

**PFLAG**
(202) 467-8180
www.pflag.org
This national organization has more than 500 affiliates across the United States. PFLAG's website features information supporting queer people and their families.

**SMYAL**
(202) 546-5940
www.smyal.org
SMYAL supports the health of young LGBTQ people. Offering outreach programs in the Washington, D.C., metro area, SMYAL also provides advocacy information at its website.

**Transgender Legal Defense & Education Fund (TLDEF)**
(646) 862-9396
www.transgenderlegal.org
TLDEF works to end discrimination against trans people and provides advocacy services, including helping low-income trans people get access to free legal name-change services.

**Trans Youth Equality Foundation (TYEF)**
(207) 478-4087
www.transyouthequality.org
TYEF provides education, advocacy, and support—including a School Action Center—for trans teens and their families.

**True Colors United**
(212) 461-4401
truecolorsunited.org
True Colors United, founded by musician Cyndi Lauper, works to end homelessness among LGBTQ young people through advocacy, education, and collaboration programs.

## Hotlines

**Boys Town National Hotline**
1-800-448-3000
www.boystown.org
The Boys Town National Hotline is available 24-7 for teens of any gender in need of help. Professional counselors staff the hotline and can provide advice on any issue, including depression, suicide, and identity struggles.

**IMAlive**
www.imalive.org
IMAlive is a chatline for people who are depressed or suicidal or who are concerned about someone who is. Teens can chat at any time of day or night with volunteers trained in crisis intervention.

**LGBT National Help Center**
1-888-843-4564
www.glbthotline.org
The Help Center offers lots of resources, including several hotlines, as well as online support spaces where LGBTQ youth can connect.

**National Runaway Safeline**
1-800-RUNAWAY (1-800-786-2929)
www.1800runaway.org
This hotline provides information for teens who have or are planning to run away from home. It also provides information and referrals for other crisis situations, including home violence, drug or alcohol abuse, and depression.

**RAINN (Rape, Abuse & Incest National Network) National Sexual Assault Hotline**
1-800-656-HOPE (1-800-656-4673)
www.rainn.org
This hotline offers crisis support and referrals for those who have been sexually assaulted. Advice and resources are also available online.

**Trans Lifeline**
1-877-565-8860
www.translifeline.org
This 24-7 trans-specific resource is staffed by trans people. You do not have to be suicidal to call. Operators are happy to provide a full range of support services and information.

**The TrevorLifeline**
1-866-488-7386
www.thetrevorproject.org
This 24-7 hotline sponsored by the Trevor Project is for LGBTQ teens who are depressed or who simply need someone to talk to (or email with).

## Websites

**Gender Spectrum**
www.genderspectrum.org
This website provides practical information (including materials in Spanish) to help teens and their families understand the concepts of gender identity and expression.

**Go Ask Alice!**
www.goaskalice.columbia.edu
While not specifically for LGBTQ teens, this website features reliable information about sexuality, relationships, and health issues.

**It Gets Better Project**
itgetsbetter.org
This website, featuring videos from queer teens and their supporters, can help you remember that plenty of accepting, open-minded people are out there.

**I Wanna Know**

www.iwannaknow.org

Sponsored by the American Social Health Association, this site provides teens with accurate, nonjudgmental information about STIs and sexual health.

**National Council on Alcoholism and Drug Dependence (NCADD)**

www.ncadd.org

This site provides treatment referrals and other useful information.

**Oasis Journals**

oasisjournals.com

This online magazine was written by and for LGBTQ teens. Though it's now closed, they have archived the site at web.archive.org/web/20150218074838/http://oasisjournals.com so you can still access past issues.

**Scarleteen**

www.scarleteen.com

Check out this website for nonjudgmental and accurate information about sex, along with message boards and referral services.

**Sex, Etc.**

sexetc.org

Sex, Etc., is published by Answer, an organization promoting comprehensive sex education for young people.

# Selected Bibliography


Allen, S. "Just How Many LGBT Americans Are There?" *The Daily Beast*, January 14, 2017, www.thedailybeast.com/just-how-many-lgbt-americans-are-there.

American Civil Liberties Union Foundation, Lesbian, Gay, Bisexual, Transgender & AIDS Project. *The Cost of Harassment: A Fact Sheet for Lesbian, Gay, Bisexual, and Transgender High School Students*. New York: American Civil Liberties Union Foundation, 2007.

American Psychological Association. *Answers to Your Questions for a Better Understanding of Sexual Orientation and Homosexuality*. Washington, DC: American Psychological Association, 2008.

American Society of Plastic Surgeons. "First Ever Data on Number of Gender Confirmation Surgeries." American Society of Plastic Surgeons, asps.multimedia-newsroom.com/index.php/2017/05/22/first-ever-data-on-number-of-gender-confirmation-surgeries.

Austin, S.B. et al. "Sexual Orientation and Tobacco Use in a Cohort Study of US Adolescent Girls and Boys." *Archives of Pediatric Adolescent Medicine* 158 (April 2004): 317–322.

Bogaert, A.F. "Asexuality: Prevalence and Associated Factors in a National Probability Sample." *Journal of Sex Research* 41, no. 3 (August 2004): 279–287.

Bornstein, K. *Gender Outlaw: On Men, Women, and the Rest of Us.* New York: Vintage Books, 2016.

Brinton, S. "I Was Tortured in Gay Conversion Therapy. And It's Still Legal in 41 States." *The New York Times*, January 24, 2018.

Centers for Disease Control and Prevention, Division of STD Prevention. *Sexually Transmitted Disease Surveillance 2015.* Atlanta, GA: US Department of Health and Human Services, 2016.

Cianciotto, J. and S. Cahill. *Youth in the Crosshairs: The Third Wave of Ex-Gay Activism*. New York: National Gay and Lesbian Task Force Policy Institute, 2006.

Cohn, D. "Census Says It Will Count Same-Sex Marriages, But with Caveats." *Fact Tank*, Pew Research Center, May 29, 2014, www.pewresearch.org/fact-tank/2014/05/29/census-says-it-will-count-same-sex-marriages-but-with-caveats.

Dank, M. et al. "Dating Violence Experiences of Lesbian, Gay, Bisexual, and Transgender Youth." *Journal of Youth and Adolescence* 43, no. 5 (May 2014): 846–857.

Denizet-Lewis, B. "Coming Out in Middle School." *The New York Times Magazine*, September 23, 2009.

De Pedro, K. et al. "Substance Use Among Transgender Students in California Public Middle and High Schools." *Journal of School Health* 87, no. 5 (May 2017): 303–309.

Dhejne, C. et al. "Long-Term Follow-Up of Transsexual Persons Undergoing Sex Reassignment Surgery: Cohort Study in Sweden." *PLoS ONE* 6, no. 2 (2011): e16885.

Duberman, M., M. Vicinus, and G. Chauncey Jr., eds. *Hidden from History: Reclaiming the Gay & Lesbian Past.* New York: Penguin Books, 1989.

Earls, M. *GLBTQ Youth.* Washington, DC: Advocates for Youth, 2005.

Ethier, K.A., L. Kann, and T. McManus. "Sexual Intercourse Among High School Students—29 States and United States Overall, 2005–2015." *Morbidity and Mortality Weekly Report (MMWR)* 66, nos. 51 & 52 (January 2018): 1393–1397.

Federal Bureau of Investigation. *Hate Crimes Statistics, 2015.* Washington, DC: US Department of Justice—Federal Bureau of Investigation, 2016.

Gates, G.J. *Lesbian, Gay, and Bisexual Men and Women in the US Military: Updated Estimates.* Los Angeles: The Williams Institute, 2010.

GLSEN. *The GLSEN Jump-Start Guide to Building and Activating Your GSA or Similar Student Club.* New York: GLSEN, 2000.

Greytak, E.A. et al. *From Teasing to Torment: School Climate Revisited, A Survey of U.S. Secondary School Students and Teachers.* New York: GLSEN, 2016.

Hass, A.P., P.L. Rodgers, and J.L. Herman. *Suicide Attempts Among Transgender and Gender Non-Conforming Adults: Findings of the National Transgender Discrimination Survey.* New York: American Foundation for Suicide Prevention and the Williams Institute, 2014.

Herman, J.L. et al. *Age of Individuals Who Identify as Transgender in the United States.* Los Angeles: The Williams Institute, 2017.

Human Rights Campaign. *Corporate Equality Index 2017: Rating Workplaces on Lesbian, Gay, Bisexual and Transgender Equality.* Washington, DC: Human Rights Campaign Foundation, 2016.

Human Rights Campaign. *Growing Up LGBT in America: HRC Youth Survey Report Key Findings.* Washington, DC: Human Rights Campaign Foundation, 2012.

Human Rights Campaign. *Transgender Americans: A Handbook for Understanding.* Washington, DC: Human Rights Campaign Foundation, 2008.

Human Rights Watch and interACT. *I Want to Be Like Nature Made Me: Medically Unnecessary Surgeries on Intersex Children in the US.* Washington, DC: Human Rights Watch, 2017.

Jackson, T. "NYCLU Sues Herkimer Co. School District for Failing to Protect Gay Youth from Harassment." *LGBT News*, August 19, 2009.

James, S.E. et al. *The Report of the 2015 U.S. Transgender Survey*. Washington, DC: National Center for Transgender Equality, 2016.

Jones, R.P. and D. Cox. *How Race and Religion Shape Millennial Attitudes on Sexuality and Reproductive Health: Findings from the 2015 Millennials, Sexuality, and Reproductive Health Survey*. Washington, DC: Public Religion Research Institute, 2015.

Kann, L. et al. "Sexual Identity, Sex of Sexual Contacts and Health-Related Behaviors Among Students in Grades 9–12—United States and Selected Sites, 2015." *MMWR Surveillance Summaries* 65, no. SS-9 (2016): 1–202.

Kann, L. et al. "Youth Risk Behavior Surveillance—United States, 2015." *MMWR Surveillance Summary*, 65, no. SS-6 (2016): 1–174.

Kosciw, J.G. et al. *The 2015 National School Climate Survey: The Experiences of Lesbian, Gay, Bisexual, Transgender, and Queer Youth in Our Nation's Schools*. New York: GLSEN, 2016.

Kranz, G.S. et al. "White Matter Microstructure in Transsexuals and Controls Investigated by Diffusion Tensor Imaging." *Journal of Neuroscience* 34, no. 46 (November 2014): 15466–15475.

Lake, C. and E. LeCouteur. *Talking About Respect: A+ Messages for Those Working to Create Safe Schools for Lesbian, Gay, Bisexual and Transgender Youth*. New York: GLSEN, 2003.

Laughlin, S. "Gen Z Goes Beyond Gender Binaries in New Innovation Group Data." *J. Walter Thompson Intelligence*, March 11, 2016, www.jwtintelligence .com/2016 /03gen-z-goes-beyond-gender-binaries-in-new-innovation-group-data.

Lindley, L.L. and K.M. Walsemann. "Sexual Orientation and Risk of Pregnancy Among New York City High-School Students." *American Journal of Public Health* 105, no. 7 (July 2015): 1379–1386.

Mallory, C., T.N.T. Brown, and K.J. Conron. *Conversion Therapy and LGBT Youth*. Los Angeles: The Williams Institute, 2018.

Marshal, M. P. et al. "Sexual Orientation and Adolescent Substance Use: A Meta-Analysis and Methodological Review." *Addiction* 103 (2008): 546–556.

National Youth Advocacy Coalition. *Coming Out About Smoking: A Report from the National LGBTQ Young Adult Tobacco Project*. Washington, DC: National Youth Advocacy Coalition, 2010.

Pew Research Center. *Religious Landscape Study*. Washington, DC: Pew Research Center, 2014. www.pewforum.org/religious -landscape-study.

Pew Research Center. *A Survey of LGBT Americans: Attitudes, Experiences and Values in Changing Times*. Washington, DC: Pew Research Center, 2013.

Poulin, C. and L. Graham. "The Association Between Substance Use, Unplanned Sexual Intercourse and Other Sexual Behaviours Among Adolescent Students." *Addiction* 96, no. 4 (April 2001): 607–621.

Roberts, T.A. and J. Klein. "Intimate Partner Abuse and High-Risk Behavior in Adolescents." *Archives of Pediatrics & Adolescent Medicine* 157, no. 4 (April 2003): 375–380.

Ryan, C. and D. Futterman. *Lesbian & Gay Youth: Care & Counseling*. New York: Columbia University Press, 1998.

Savin-Williams, R.C. *The New Gay Teenager*. Cambridge: Harvard University Press, 2006.

Shain, B.N. and the Committee on Adolescence. "Suicide and Suicide Attempts in Adolescents." *Pediatrics* 120, no. 3 (September 2007): 669–676.

THR Staff. "Lana Wachowski's HRC Visibility Award Acceptance Speech (Transcript)." *The Hollywood Reporter*, October 24, 2012, www.hollywoodreporter.com/news/lana-wachowskis-hrc-visibility-award-382177.

Troiden, R. "The Formulation of Homosexual Identities." *Journal of Homosexuality* 17, no. 1-2 (1989): 43–73.

UNAIDS. *Global Facts and Figures*. Geneva, Switzerland: Joint United Nations Programme on HIV/AIDS and World Health Organization, 2009.

US Department of Defense. *Report of the Comprehensive Review of the Issues Associated with a Repeal of "Don't Ask, Don't Tell."* Washington, DC: US Department of Defense, 2010.

Wallien, M.S. and P.T. Cohen-Kettenis. "Psychosexual Outcome of Gender-Dysphoric Children." *Journal of the American Academy of Child and Adolescent Psychiatry* 46, no. 12 (December 2008): 1413–1423.

Weinberg, G. "George Weinberg: Love Is Conspiratorial, Deviant & Magical." Interview by R. Ayyar. *GayToday.com*, November 1, 2002.

Winfield, C.L. *Gender Identity: The Ultimate Teen Guide*. Lanham, MD: Scarecrow Press, 2016.

*Youth Knowledge and Attitudes on Sexual Health: A National Survey of Adolescents and Young Adults. Special analysis prepared for Dangerous Liaisons: Substance Abuse and Sexual Behavior, a one-day conference sponsored by the National Center on Addiction and Substance Abuse (CASA) at Columbia University*. Menlo Park, CA: The Henry J. Kaiser Family Foundation and the National Institute on Drug Abuse, 2002.

# Index

## D



## E

## N



## O



## P



## Q

# About the Author

Liz Hough Photography

**Kelly Huegel Madrone** is a freelance writer, writing coach, and youth motivational speaker. She has worked for the Metropolitan Washington, D.C., chapter of PFLAG, where she helped provide support and educational services for LGBTQ people and their families. The author of two books and more than one hundred published articles, Kelly has a special passion for working with teens. She holds a degree in secondary education, is a licensed massage therapist and massage educator, has a certificate in plant-based nutrition, and is a martial arts black belt. Kelly lives in New Mexico with her partner Mala and their daughters. Kelly welcomes readers to follow her updates on LGBTQ politics and people, message her directly via Twitter @LGBTQguide, or subscribe to her newsletter at www.kellymadrone.com.